THE GOVERNORSHIP OF SPANISH FLORIDA

THE GOVERNORSHIP
OF SPANISH FLORIDA
1700-1763

JOHN JAY TEPASKE

Department of History

The Ohio State University

DUKE UNIVERSITY PRESS

Durham, North Carolina

1964

For NEOMI, SUSAN, *and* MARIANNA

This volume has received a subvention from the
Duke University Council on Hispanic Research
under a grant made by the Ford Foundation for
the promotion of international studies.

PREFACE

This work is a study of the governorship of Spanish Florida, 1700-1763. I have analyzed the governorship as a frontier institution and examined the administrative, judicial, economic, military, social, and religious problems with which the governor had to deal. The period, 1700-1763, is an arbitrary one, but one that is both significant and convenient. It is significant as a time when the clashes and bitter intercolonial rivalries of the English, French, and Spanish were the sharpest; it was also a time when frontier institutions in Florida were most clearly defined and most fully developed. The period is convenient because of the change in dynasties in Spain in 1700 and because of the loss of Florida to the English in 1763, which ended the so-called First Spanish Period (1513-1763). In addition, sixty-three years proved a long enough time in which to develop institutional patterns for this frontier province on the fringes of New Spain.

My approach is topical rather than chronological, and I have discussed separately the relationship of the governor to various aspects of life in colonial Florida. I recognize the dangers in such a method. It means analyzing the same event or personality two, three, or more times in a different context and at times forsaking the friendly protection of chronology. I am convinced, however, that the topical approach is more valuable in order to secure a clearer understanding of institutions on the Spanish imperial frontier. I hope, too, that by using this method I have transcended the realm of local history.

A work of this sort demands assistance of all kinds, and for this I am deeply grateful. A fellowship from the Institute of International Education and a Duke University Traveling Scholarship enabled me to carry on research in Spain and England in 1956-1957. In Seville I enjoyed the friendship and help of Don José de la Peña and his staff at the Archives of the Indies. They extended me every courtesy and special favors over and above those ordinarily expected. My friends and colleagues at the School of Hispanic American Studies in Seville offered encouragement and advice, especially in those early days when I was floundering in my research. In England the archivists in the Public Record Office in London assisted me in many ways. In this country I owe thanks to the staffs of the Saint Augustine Historical Society, the North

PREFACE

Carolina Department of Archives and History, and the Rollins College Library. The Duke University Graduate Research Council generously awarded a publication subsidy for my study.

I am also indebted to various individuals. I am most deeply grateful to Dr. John Tate Lanning, James B. Duke Professor of History at Duke University —for his unfailing support and timely encouragement, his infectious enthusiasm for things Hispanic, the introduction to the "bug bibliophile," and for the high standards he sets for himself and his students. Professor Charles Arnade of the University of South Florida, Professor Donald Worcester of Texas Christian University, and Professors John S. Curtiss and Robert S. Smith of Duke University pointed out many foibles in the manuscript and aided immeasurably in other ways. Mr. Terry Campbell of Ohio State University labored over the maps, and Miss Jean E. McConnell and Mrs. Colette Armstrong of the same institution typed the manuscript.

I am led finally to the indispensable statement that I alone am responsible for errors in fact and interpretation.

Ohio State University JOHN J. TEPASKE

CONTENTS

I. THE GOVERNORSHIP OF SPANISH FLORIDA   *3*

Conquest and Early Colonization of Florida   *3*
Colonial Development to 1700   *5*
Spanish Origins of the Governorship   *7*
Beginnings of the Governorship in Florida   *9*
Appointment and Terms of the Eighteenth-Century
    Governors of Florida   *10*
Appointment and Term of the Interim Governor   *14*
Backgrounds of the Governors, 1700-1763   *16*
The Inauguration Ceremony   *19*
Duties, Responsibilities, and Privileges of the Governor   *20*
The Council (Junta)   *24*
Attempts at Democratic Reform   *26*
The Governor and Colonial Patronage   *27*
The Governorship of Florida and Opportunities for
    Advancement   *32*

II. CHECKS ON THE GOVERNOR   *33*

General Checks on the Governor   *33*
Specific Checks on the Governor:
    The Visita *and the* Pesquisa   *34*
Specific Checks on the Governor:
    The Residencia   *39*
A Case Study: The Residencia *of Governor*
    Joseph de Zúñiga y Cerda   *40*
A Case Study: The Residencia *of Governor*
    Francisco del Moral Sánchez   *45*
The Residencia: *A Check on the Governor?*   *56*

III. THE GOVERNOR ADMINISTERS JUSTICE   58

    The Theory and Practice of the Administration of
       Justice in Florida   58
    The Governor Punishes Petty Offenders   61
    Formalization of the Judicial Process:
       The Ayala-Pedroso Case   64
    Governor Benavides Administers Justice:
       The Nieto-Rozo Case   68
    Governor Benavides Administers Justice:
       The Primo de Rivera Case   70
    The Governor Punishes Illicit Traders   71
    Governor Fernández de Heredia Uncovers an
       Illicit Trade Scandal   73
    The Governor Administers Justice: A Critique   76

IV. ECONOMIC PROBLEMS OF THE GOVERNOR   77

    The Subsidy   77
    Governor Zúñiga Seeks Additional Help in Spain   79
    Revision of the Subsidy System   82
    Reappearance of the Old Abuses   83
    The Governor Suggests Economic Reforms   86
    The Colony Survives through Expedients:
       Misapplication of Funds   91
    The Reform of 1740: The Royal Havana Company   97
    The Burden of Extra Expenses   103
    An Economic Awakening: The Rise of a
       Naval Stores Industry   105

V. THE GOVERNOR AND DEFENSE, 1700-1733   108

    The State of the Military and Defenses in 1700   108
    The Siege of Saint Augustine, 1702   110
    Moore's Revenge: The Massacre at Ayubale   113
    Military Policy in Florida during Queen Anne's War 116
    Refortification of Apalache   122
    Governor Benavides and Fort King George:
       The Brink of War   125
    Palmer's Raid: The End of an Era   130

VI. THE GOVERNOR AND DEFENSE, 1733-1763   *133*

 Reaction in Florida to the Founding of Georgia   *133*
 Governor Moral's Defense Diplomacy   *135*
 The Urge to War (1736-1738)   *137*
 The War of Jenkins's Ear in Florida:
  The Defensive Stage   *139*
 Montiano and the Fiasco at Bloody Marsh   *146*
 Oglethorpe's Counterattack   *152*
 The Quiet Border, 1743-1763   *154*
 Military Reorganization: The New Law of 1753   *156*
 The Governor as a Military Tactician: A Critique   *157*

VII. THE GOVERNOR AND THE CHURCH   *159*

 Organization of the Regular and Secular Clergy   *160*
 Creation of a Bishopric in Florida   *161*
 A Replacement for Resino   *164*
 Buenaventura in Florida   *167*
 The Auxiliary Bishop: A Check on the Governor?   *170*
 The Governor and the Secular Clergy   *171*
 The Governor as Arbiter of Religious Controversies   *175*
 The Governor and the Regular Clergy:
  Support for the Franciscans   *178*
 Early Signs of a Split within the Order   *181*
 The Crisis of 1735   *184*
 Remedies for the Religious Ills of Florida   *187*
 The Factional Struggle, the Governor, and
  the Colony: An Assessment   *191*

VIII. THE GOVERNOR AND INDIAN POLICY   *193*

 Governor Zúñiga and Spanish Indian Policy   *193*
 Queen Anne's War and the Florida Indians   *196*
 Resurgence of an Indian Program, 1715-1718   *197*
 New Problems, 1718-1726   *204*
 Indian Problems near Saint Augustine   *208*
 Collapse of the Spanish Indian Alliances, 1730-1739   *209*

The War of Jenkins's Ear and Spanish Indian
    Policy, 1739-1745   214
New Attempts to Woo the Indians:
    A Trading Post in Apalache   215
The Lower Creeks Return to Spanish Allegiance   218
The French and Indian War and the Florida
    Indians, 1753-1763   222
The Governor's Indian Policy: A Critique   225

ix. POSTSCRIPT: THE GOVERNORSHIP ON THE
SPANISH FRONTIER   227

Appendix I. GOVERNORS OF FLORIDA,
    1699-1764   231

Appendix II. GOVERNORS OF CUBA,
    1695-1765   232

Appendix III. VICEROYS OF NEW SPAIN,
    1701-1766   233

BIBLIOGRAPHY OF WORKS CITED   234
INDEX   239

THE GOVERNORSHIP OF SPANISH FLORIDA

Chapter I

THE GOVERNORSHIP OF
SPANISH FLORIDA

Florida[1] was far more than just the first permanent settlement within the present boundaries of the United States; it was a strategic outpost of the Spanish Empire in America and a cradle of frontier institutions. The colony was a barrier against foreign encroachments on the Gulf of Mexico, key to the riches of New Spain, and a protection for the Bahama Channel on the route of homeward-bound Spanish treasure fleets. Settlement of Florida also kept the enemies of Spain from turning the peninsula into a haven for sea dogs and pirates who sought to prey on the galleons plying the narrow Bahama waterway. After the founding of Virginia in 1607, the province stood as a Spanish bastion against English expansion into the Southeast and later blocked French pretensions to the same area. Finally, effective occupation buttressed Spanish territorial claims on Florida based on papal donation, prior discovery, and exploration.

[*Conquest and Early Colonization of Florida*]

From the time of its discovery in 1513 until its permanent settlement in 1565, Florida was more than a match for the most intrepid Spanish conqueror. To hard-bitten soldiers like Hernando de Soto and Juan Ponce de León, the province yielded little but extreme privation, incredible hardship, and violent death.[2] For almost fifty years Spanish

1. The boundaries of Spanish Florida fluctuated greatly during the colonial period. Initially Spain claimed all territory lying between the Atlantic Ocean in the east and a north-south line drawn through the mouth of the Río Grande in the west. The Gulf of Mexico and the Florida Keys constituted the southern limits of the province, while to the north the colony reached to the vaguely defined "land of the codfish," probably present-day Nova Scotia. For this sixteenth-century delineation see *Colección de documentos inéditos relativos al descubrimiento, conquista, y colonización de las posesiones españolas en América y Oceanía* (Madrid, 1864-1884), XV, 440.

2. The early explorers and conquerors who tried but failed to settle Florida were Juan Ponce de León in 1513 and 1521, Lucas Vásquez de Ayllón in 1526-1527,

conquistadores tried unsuccessfully to conquer and colonize this inhospitable land. In fact Spain actually gave up its efforts to settle Florida in September, 1561.[3]

In the spring of 1562, however, a small group of Huguenots planted a tiny settlement in Florida, an action that immediately renewed Spanish interest in the province. The Spanish monarch Philip II saw the French as heretical intruders who must be eliminated from his domain. Indian attacks, disease, and starvation—the nemeses of previous Spanish colonizers—removed the French threat without military action, but in 1564 these same tenacious Huguenots set up a second colony (Fort Caroline) at the mouth of the Saint John's River in Florida territory. This time Pedro Menéndez de Avilés, one of the ablest Spanish naval officers of his day, offered his services to Philip II. Menéndez promised to rid the province of the French menace and to occupy Florida effectively for Spain.[4]

He accomplished both tasks. Early in the fall of 1565 this Spanish admiral and a large band of soldiers and colonists founded Saint Augustine, destroyed Fort Caroline, and annihilated its defenders. Hoping to expand the area under Spanish control, Menéndez established small garrisons at San Mateo (site of Fort Caroline), San Pedro (Cumberland Island), Guale (Santa Catalina Island), Santa Elena (coastal South Carolina), Tocabaga (Tampa Bay), San Antonio (Charlotte Harbor), Santa Lucía (half-way between what is now Fort Pierce and West Palm Beach), and Tequesta (Miami). From these beginnings he envisioned a flourishing new center of Empire with an economy based firmly on agriculture, mining, and pearl fishing, but these dreams of a new utopia in the Florida wilderness were soon shattered. Attempts to grow crops and raise cattle failed, food became scarce, and disease took its toll.[5] Menéndez obtained supplies in Spain and the Indies to sustain

Pánfilo de Narváez in 1528, Hernando de Soto in 1539-1541, Father Luis Cancer in 1549, and Tristán de Luna y Arellano in 1559-1561.

3. See Woodbury Lowery, *The Spanish Settlements within the Present Limits of the United States, 1513-1561* (New York, 1901), p. 376. Lowery points out that Philip II closed Florida to further colonial endeavors in the fall of 1561.

4. The story of the Menéndez period has been well told. See Eugenio Ruidíaz y Caravia, *La Florida su conquista y colonización por Pedro Menéndez de Avilés* (Madrid, 1894); Jeannette Thurber Connor, ed. and trans., *Pedro Menéndez de Avilés, Adelantado, Governor and Captain-General of Florida, Memorial by Gonzalo Solís de Meras* (Deland, 1923); Francis Parkman, *Pioneers of France in the New World*, Part I (Boston, 1895), pp. 96-156; Woodbury Lowery, *Spanish Settlements within the Present Limits of the United States, Florida, 1562-1574* (New York, 1905), pp. 101-386.

5. Menéndez had the foresight to furnish his colonists with seeds, agricultural imple-

his colonists, at least partially; but his long absences away from the new settlement left it without a steadying influence. By 1570 most of the original migration of 1,500 had become disillusioned about their future and departed for Spain, leaving less than three hundred hearty souls to carry on in Florida.[6]

Still the colony managed to survive. Although Menéndez failed to develop another Mexico or Peru, he still managed to maintain his precarious foothold in Florida and to keep the settlement from perishing. By the time of his death in 1574 he had laid a foundation deep enough to last. His many distinguished predecessors had failed to set up a permanent settlement, but Menéndez had the tenacity and resourcefulness to keep the colony going and could mark this as a real achievement.

[Colonial Development to 1700]

After 1574 Florida did not develop significantly but remained a backward, unpopular military and mission outpost with little of the glitter and pomp that characterized life in busier imperial centers. Saint Augustine, the capital and most important city of the colony, lay on the east coast in northern Florida on the west bank of the Matanzas River directly across from Santa Anastasia Island. By 1600 a church, convent, six-bed hospital, fish market, and approximately 120 shops and houses graced the streets of the town.[7] Fort San Marcos, located on the northern edge of Saint Augustine, defended the shallow entrance to the harbor and the northern approaches to the Florida capital.[8] Residents were primarily soldiers, their wives and children, and shopkeepers catering to the needs of the military. A few administrators, friars, Indians, and Negroes partially tempered the garrison atmosphere of Saint

---

ments, and animals for breeding purposes, but the settlers soon came to depend exclusively upon outside aid, since they could not make headway in the sandy wasteland surrounding Saint Augustine or in tiny settlements established in the hinterland. At Santa Lucía conditions were so desperate that soldiers chewed shoes, leather belts, snakes, rats, and dwarf palmettoes as real delicacies. There is some evidence that they also resorted to cannibalism to stay alive. See Lowery, *Spanish Settlements, 1562-1574;* pp. 224-225, 239-240.

6. The most reliable estimates of the Florida population during the colonial period are found in John R. Dunkle, "Population Changes as an Element in the Historical Geography of St. Augustine," *Florida Historical Quarterly*, XXXVII (July, 1958), 3-22.

7. Verne E. Chatelain, *The Defenses of Spanish Florida, 1565 to 1763* (Washington, D.C., 1941), p. 57.

8. The fort had an interesting history. See Jeannette Thurber Connor, "The Nine Old Wooden Forts of St. Augustine," *Florida Historical Society Quarterly*, IV (Jan.-April, 1926), 103-111, 171-180.

Augustine, but for the most part, it was a soldiers' town.[9] Fort San Luis at Apalache near present-day Tallahassee was the principal Spanish outpost in the western part of Florida during the seventeenth century but was evacuated in the first decade of the eighteenth century. Pensacola was settled late in the seventeenth century but had closer ties with the viceroy in New Spain than with the governor in Florida.

Missionaries were active in Florida, particularly in the seventeenth century. The Jesuits were the first to carry on mission work in the province, but after many hardships they gave up their endeavors in 1570. In 1573 the Franciscans filled this vacuum and extended their influence throughout the Southeast. By 1655 over fifty brown-robed friars labored in thirty-nine villages located in present-day Florida, Georgia, Alabama, and South Carolina. At the same time the Franciscans claimed 26,000 Indian converts.[10] With their soldier protectors these missionaries strengthened Spain's territorial claims on the Southeast and stood as bulwarks against English and French expansion into Florida territory. In 1670, however, the founding of English Carolina broke the friars' hold on the Indians and set off a sharp decline in the Franciscan religious program.[11]

For their livelihood Floridians depended almost entirely upon a yearly subsidy *(situado)* of money and supplies shipped from New Spain. Until his death Pedro Menéndez de Avilés supported and maintained the settlement, but this obligation shifted to the crown in 1574 and remained a royal responsibility throughout the colonial period. Philip II originally awarded 24,000 ducats (approximately 33,000 pesos) for the wages and supplies needed by the 150 soldiers stationed in Florida. When he doubled the garrison in 1578, he increased the *situado* to 35,000 ducats (approximately 48,000 pesos).[12] This amount slowly rose to 65,000 pesos by the middle of the seventeenth century until it reached approximately 100,000 pesos in 1700.[13]

9. Without large deposits of gold and silver, rich soil, or a large sedentary Indian population, Spain found it difficult to develop Florida into more than just a military outpost. It successfully fulfilled its military function throughout the colonial period, but in other ways Florida failed to fit the usual pattern of colonial development.

10. John Tate Lanning, *The Spanish Missions of Georgia* (Chapel Hill, 1935), p. 169.

11. See Verner W. Crane, *The Southern Frontier, 1670-1732* (Durham, 1928), pp. 3-46.

12. Jeannette Thurber Connor, trans. and ed., *Colonial Records of Spanish Florida*, (Deland, 1925-1930). See I, 205-209, and II, 245.

13. See photostat of the document from the Archives of the Indies contained in the Spanish Records of the North Carolina Historical Commission, 1535-1802, Raleigh,

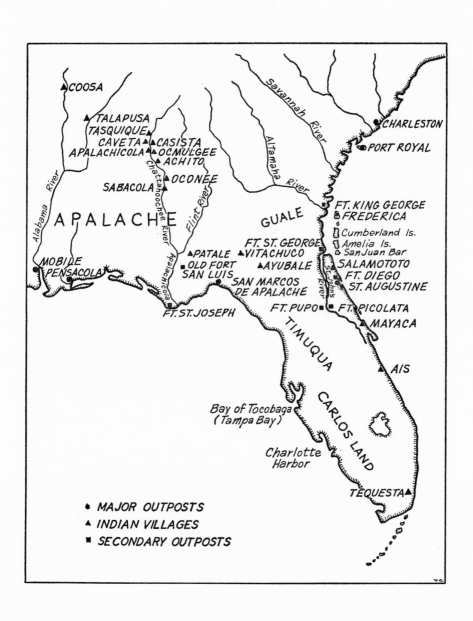

COOSA

TALAPUSA
TASQUIQUE
CAVETA   CASISTA
APALACHICOLA   OCMULGEE
ACHITO
SABACOLA   OCONEE

Savannah River

CHARLESTON

PORT ROYAL

Altamaha River

APALACHE

GUALE

FT. KING GEORGE
FREDERICA
Cumberland Is.
Amelia Is.
San Juan Bar

FT. ST. GEORGE
VITACHUCO
AYUBALE

PATALE
OLD FORT
SAN LUIS

SALAMOTOTO
FT. DIEGO
ST. AUGUSTINE

MOBILE
PENSACOLA

SAN MARCOS
DE APALACHE

FT. PUPO   FT. PICOLATA

FT. ST.JOSEPH

MAYACA

TIMUQUA

AIS

Bay of Tocobaga
(Tampa Bay)

CARLOS LAND

Charlotte
Harbor

TEQUESTA

Alabama River

Chattahoochee River

Flint River

Apalachicola

St. Johns River

• MAJOR OUTPOSTS
▲ INDIAN VILLAGES
■ SECONDARY OUTPOSTS

Attempts to make Florida self-reliant and less dependent upon the subsidy proved futile. In 1624 plans to bring Indians from Guatemala to develop a cochineal and indigo industry never materialized.[14] Efforts made to introduce farming, fruit raising, fishing, and silk culture were feeble and unproductive. Soil was poor near Saint Augustine, and unfriendly Indians often scalped ambitious innovators and destroyed their attempts to improve their existence away from the protective walls of Fort San Marcos. Christian Indians in Apalache, where soil was richer, provided a few staples like corn and beans, but production was irregular and undependable.[15] For the Floridians the subsidy remained the principal means of support throughout the colonial period.

The system used to govern the colony was not intricate. Thinly populated and unproductive, Florida was not worth large expenditures of money and personnel. It was more practical and cheaper to keep administrative machinery simple. The governor was by far the most significant provincial official. Dominating the entire colony, he dealt almost singlehandedly with the multitude of problems arising in his province. His two principal assistants, the accountant (contador) and treasurer (tesorero), had only limited powers. They kept accounts of the subsidy, made disbursements to the garrison, inspected supplies stored in the royal warehouses, and occasionally advised the governor on colonial problems. Sometimes colonial military and religious leaders joined the two treasury officials to form a temporary advisory council (junta), but otherwise no other Spanish governmental institutions took hold. Even the familiar and fundamental town council (cabildo) failed to become a part of the political machinery of the province.[16] Throughout the colonial epoch the governor remained the key to policies and politics in frontier Florida.

[Spanish Origins of the Governorship]

Like many Spanish colonial institutions the governorship had its roots in medieval Spain. Although the title "governor" was not commonly used until the time of the Catholic Kings, officials fulfilling the

---

North Carolina, 58-2-29. Carta del gobernador de la Florida (Alonso Aranguiz y Cotes) al rey, October 10, 1662.

14. Indice general de los papeles del Consejo de Indias (Madrid, 1923-1926), IV, 214.

15. Herbert E. Bolton and Mary Ross, The Debatable Land (Berkeley, 1925), p. 76.

16. During the early years of the Florida settlement, Menéndez established a cabildo as an aid in governing the colony, but after the exodus of 1570 the cabildo dissolved and was never reconstituted.

functions of governor became a part of the Spanish administrative system much earlier. In the thirteenth century the Aragonese monarch and Count of Barcelona, Jaime I (1213-1296) appointed a royal procurator *(procurador real)* for the two newly conquered provinces of Valencia and Majorca. These *procuradores,* like later viceroys and governors in both Spain and the Empire, represented the king in all administrative, judicial, financial, and military matters. They enforced royal laws and decrees, tried civil and criminal cases, appointed minor functionaries, and maintained order.[17] Later sovereigns in Aragón and Castile followed Jaime's pattern. They yielded direct personal control over territory taken from the Moors and rebellious nobles in favor of rule through appointed subordinates, who came to represent royal interests throughout Spain. These subordinates, who assumed the title vice king or viceroy, replaced the procurators and served in Aragón, Catalonia, Galicia, Majorca, Navarre, and Valencia. By the middle of the sixteenth century the viceregal system was also extended into the Spanish Empire in both Europe and America.[18]

Like the viceroyalty the governorship became an especially useful institution in the New World. From the time of the discovery of America in 1492, the governorship was a means by which the crown could control and regulate its colonial domains. Christopher Columbus was the first Spanish governor in America. By the Capitulations of Santa Fé of April 17, 1492, reinforced by two later privileges *(privilegios),* he received, among other titles, that of "governor of the Indies." When he established his permanent settlement on Española in 1494, Columbus began exercising his rights and responsibilities under this title. It was not long, however, before he lost his special privileges. In 1500 Ferdinand and Isabella, desiring to bring the Admiral and his discoveries more closely under royal control, stripped Columbus of all his titles except that of admiral and withdrew many of his political privileges. At the same time they appointed a trusted adviser, Francisco de Bobadilla, to the governorship in Española. Later they replaced Bobadilla with another loyal subject, Nicolás Ovando.[19] By putting their favorites into governorships, they could more easily promote and

17. Alfonso García Gallo, *Los orígenes de la administración territorial de las Indias* (Madrid, 1944), pp. 48-49.

18. Alfonso García Gallo, *Curso de historia del derecho español: introducción y historia de los bases de formación del derecho y de las fuentes y del derecho público* (Madrid, 1950), I, 418.

19. García Gallo, *Curso de historia del derecho español,* I, 419.

protect royal interests. As new areas of the Indies fell to Spanish arms, the king appointed such officials to rule over this newly acquired territory. Cuba, Puerto Rico, Jamaica, Nicaragua, and Panama all received royal governors immediately or soon after conquest. In Peru and New Spain, regions that produced great wealth, the monarch established a viceroyalty, but in smaller provinces the governorship became the principal governmental institution. Like the procurator of medieval Spain, the governor carried out the royal will in territory that the king or vice king could not rule personally.[20]

[Beginnings of the Governorship in Florida]

Theoretically, the first governors of Florida were those early conquerors who attempted to exploit and settle the province. They found their rights as governor embodied in their title of adelantado. This designation, peculiar to the sixteenth century, was a convenient device used by the crown to encourage the expansion of its colonial Empire. As adelantados, enterprising soldiers or colonizers received liberal semi-feudal concessions from the king. In return they agreed to bear the expense of subduing the areas in which they obtained their special privileges. A contract (asiento) defined the adelantado's specific rights and responsibilities and included the governor's title.[21]

Five would-be colonizers obtained the governorship of Florida in their grants as adelantado. Juan Ponce de León, Lucas Vásquez de Ayllón, Pánfilo de Narváez, Hernando de Soto, and Pedro Menéndez de Avilés all received the governor's title, but only Menéndez ever exercised authority as governor. The others failed to set up a lasting settlement and did not assume the governor's mantle.[22] Menéndez served vigorously for almost ten years, but at the time of his death in 1574 his proprietary rights fell to the crown. Florida thus lost its status as a semi-independent fief and became the exclusive domain of the king, who brought it more rigidly under his personal control. After 1574 the monarch appointed loyal subjects to the governorship and regulated their activities by means of royal laws and decrees.

The passing of the adelantado in Florida and throughout the rest

20. The captain generalship was another colonial office similar to the governorship. The captain general usually governed an area larger than a governorship and smaller than a viceroyalty. For his functions and place in colonial affairs, see Clarence Haring, The Spanish Empire in America (New York, 1947), pp. 77-78, 119-122, 124-127, 132.

21. Roscoe R. Hill, "The Office of Adelantado," Political Science Quarterly, XXVIII (Dec., 1913), 646-668.

22. Hill, "The Office of Adelantado," p. 656.

of the Empire during the last half of the sixteenth century marked the beginning of a new era in Spanish imperial administration. This epoch saw the crown gradually discard its liberal attitudes toward conquest and colonization in the Indies and assume for itself more and more of the special privileges and responsibilities previously granted to enterprising soldiers. Colonial administration became more strictly regimented. Royal law began to define the conduct of colonial officials more minutely. The *adelantado* became an anachronism that did not fit the rapidly developing system of centralized administrative control. Under closer surveillance and more rigid regulation, colonial officials lost their wide powers and privileges. The governor of Florida was no exception.[23]

[*Appointment and Terms of the Eighteenth-Century Governors of Florida*]

Each candidate for the governorship of Florida had to meet two requirements. He must have attained the rank of colonel and have been born in Spain. The first requirement was essential because of the purely military character of the colony, which required the disciplined hand of an experienced officer. A colonel had the necessary rank and training to handle such a difficult assignment. The second requirement, peninsular birth, ostensibly endowed the governor with administrative and moral qualifications denied pure-blooded Spaniards born in the Indies (Creoles). Spanish origin also helped to insure loyalty to the crown, a dubious quality in most colonials. Occasionally, authorities in Spain deviated from these requirements, particularly the first, and sometimes filled the governorship with soldiers below the rank of colonel whose outstanding record of loyalty and service merited the office. The requisite of Spanish birth, however, was more rigid.

A qualified candidate for the governorship usually received his appointment from the king upon recommendation of the Council of the Indies.[24] With notable exceptions the ten permanent governors of Florida between 1700 and 1763 obtained their posts in this manner. When a vacancy occurred in the governorship, the Council drew up a

23. *Recopilación de leyes de los reynos de las Indias* (Madrid, 1943), Libro 5, título 2, *passim.*

24. The Council of the Indies was the agency in Spain that deliberated on colonial affairs and problems. It was the king's chief advisory body on the colonies and had important functions in determining colonial policy. See Haring, *Spanish Empire*, pp. 102-118.

slate of three candidates *(terna)*, listing them in order of preference. The Council then submitted this trio of names to the king, who had several alternatives once he received the nominations.[25] He might choose one of the three as the new governor or reject all recommendations and call for a new *terna*. He might disregard the Council's recommendations completely and make his own choice, or he might delegate the authority of appointing a new governor to a trusted official in the Indies. Normally, it was easier for the overworked monarch to accept the Council's recommendations.

Procedure varied in making appointments to the governorship of Florida. When he sought to replace Governor Joseph de Zúñiga y Cerda in 1704, Philip V found the Council's first list of candidates unacceptable, particularly the nomination of the veteran soldier Domingo de la Canal y Soldevilla, and requested a new slate.[26] The king's choice from the revised list was the talented engineer and soldier, Andrés de Arriola, but he refused the office. The second candidate, Francisco de Córcoles y Martínez, then won the appointment and served as governor for eleven years.[27] Philip V ignored the nominations of the Council in finding a successor to Córcoles in 1716 and appointed his own favorite, Pedro de Olivera y Fullana.[28] Olivera died, however, after only three months in Saint Augustine and was replaced by Antonio de Benavides, chosen from the *terna* submitted by the Council.

In 1733 Philip deviated from all normal procedures. He put the responsibility for naming the new governor of Florida on the shoulders of the governor of Cuba, Dionisio Martínez de la Vega.[29] In this case Don Dionisio appointed Francisco del Moral Sánchez, a conscientious infantryman who had risen through the ranks in Havana to become a captain. On the surface Moral seemed a good choice, but immediately after he took office in 1734, he turned most of the colony against him with his corrupt, arbitrary rule. This resulted in his dramatic ouster in

25. AGI (Archivo General de Indias, Seville, Spain), Audiencia de Santo Domingo (hereafter Santo Domingo), Legajo 836. Consulta del Consejo de las Indias, November 22, 1714. This document is typical of the *terna* usually submitted to the king by the Council.

26. AGI, Santo Domingo, Legajo 851. Consulta de la Junta de Guerra, April 17, 1704.

27. AGI, Santo Domingo, Legajo 851. Consulta del Consejo de las Indias, March 12, 1705.

28. AGI, Santo Domingo, Legajo 851. Consulta del Consejo de las Indias, Dec. 3, 1715.

29. AGI, Santo Domingo, Legajo 851. Consulta del Consejo de las Indias, Feb. 9, 1733.

1737 and also prompted the king to return to the usual methods for choosing the governor. Hereafter the governor of Cuba picked only interim governors.[30]

The Florida governorship was not always an easy post to fill. Service in the colony, even in the prestigious governor's office, had little appeal. For many ambitious Spanish officers it seemed far wiser to seek a position in more important areas of the Empire, where they could more easily put their talents on display and be more fully appreciated by their superiors. Tucked away in Florida, even the most efficient administrator could gain little attention. For most Spanish officials service in Florida was a curse, a terrible burden to be avoided if at all possible. Two appointees even went so far as to risk the king's wrath by refusing to take the governorship.[31]

Such refusals threw Spanish officialdom into great turmoil. In Spain the king and the Council of the Indies had to repeat the laborious, time-consuming process of nomination and appointment. In Florida the incumbent governor had to sit back to await his replacement before he could assume another post, a waiting period that often lasted years. This failure to fill the governorship was often critical, for it paralyzed the movement of administrators all over the Indies. Since the crown periodically shifted its colonial officials from place to place, the inability of one individual to take a new post prevented the quick, efficient shift or realignment of administrative personnel throughout the colonies.[32]

In Florida the time spent by the incumbent governor awaiting his replacement seemed interminable. By law the governor's term was five years if he came from Spain and three years if he came from the Indies.[33] Still, all terms were at the king's discretion and subject to administrative inertia. Joseph de Zúñiga y Cerda became governor of Florida in 1699 for a three-year term. Early in 1703, after serving one year more than the required three, he secured a new post as governor of Cartagena, but it took three more years before he could assume his new

30. Both Joseph de Justís (1737) and Fulgencio García de Solís (1752-1755) were interim appointees of the governor of Cuba.

31. Andrés de Arriola in 1705 and Francisco de Bustamante in 1714 both pled ill health in order to avoid taking the governorship. AGI, Santo Domingo, Legajo 836. Consulta del Consejo de las Indias, Feb. 26, 1705. AGI, Santo Domingo, Legajo 833. Consulta del Consejo de las Indias, Nov. 22, 1714.

32. The delays in sending dispatches between Spain and the Indies also helped to lengthen the process considerably. Dilatory administrative procedures were not always completely responsible.

33. *Recopilación de las Indias*, Lib. 5, tít. 2, ley 10.

office. Procrastination in naming his successor, red tape, Andrés de Arriola's refusal to accept the governorship, and delays in sending Francisco de Córcoles y Martínez kept Zúñiga in Saint Augustine until 1706, four years longer than his allotted term.[34] He might have taken the chance of leaving before a replacement arrived, but the law specifically forbade such practice.[35] Although colonial officials often disregarded laws governing their conduct, they rigidly adhered to this rule. Ignoring it might embroil them in long, costly litigations and jeopardize their future. Zúñiga had secured the alluring governorship of Cartagena, and he meant to take that office.

Zúñiga's case was not unique. The term of Francisco de Córcoles y Martínez dragged on six years after it had formally expired. Antonio de Benavides served almost seventeen years, longer than any other eighteenth-century governor. Twice Philip V extended his term, much to the distress of the unhappy Benavides, who constantly fretted over his continuance in office.[36] He claimed that the abominable Florida climate was ruining his health and that he could not even mount his horse because of excruciating pain from old wounds, aggravated by the damp, unsalutary air.[37] But the king ignored these complaints. He found it easier to keep Benavides in the governorship than to find a capable replacement for the beleaguered administrator.

Even in cases of incompetence machinery for replacing the governor worked slowly. Word of the excesses of Governor Francisco del Moral Sánchez reached Spain soon after his appointment in 1734, yet Moral remained in office until March, 1737, almost until his term officially expired. Moral's successor, Manuel de Montiano, served a greatly extended term. Becoming governor in 1737, he did not depart until 1749, nine years more than the usual tenure in office. Florida needed an able, efficient administrator. When the king found one like Benavides or Montiano, he was content to maintain the status quo and avoid the trouble of naming a new governor.

34. AGI, Santo Domingo, Legajo 840. Carta del gobernador de la Florida al rey, June 6, 1703. Carta del gobernador de la Florida al rey, May 15, 1705.

35. *Recopilación de las Indias*, Lib. 5, tít. 2, ley 49.

36. AGI, Santo Domingo, Legajo 837. Título de gobernador y capitán general de las Provincias de la Florida para otros cinco años mas para Don Antonio de Benavides, July 21, 1722. AGI, Santo Domingo, Legajo 2541. Despacho del rey al gobernador de la Florida, May 20, 1729.

37. AGI, Santo Domingo, Legajo 851. Memorial de don Antonio de Benavides, Jan. 23, 1724. Carta del gobernador de la Florida al rey, June 16, 1725. Carta del gobernador de la Florida al rey, Sept. 24, 1726. Carta del gobernador de la Florida al rey, Aug. 15, 1731.

After 1749 the pattern changed significantly, evidence that perhaps Bourbon efficiency was now permeating colonial administration. From 1749 to 1763 the governor of Florida served little more than the three or five years required under the law. At the same time the shift of administrative personnel from one place to another was more efficient. Only once was there an appreciable delay in putting a new governor in an office. Alonso Fernández de Heredia, appointed to the governorship in 1751, took three years to get from Guatemala to Florida. When word of his appointment first reached Guatemala, he was in the jungles of Central America fighting Indians—no one knew exactly where.[38] Then, when the news finally got to him, he was uncertain about leaving Central America. The king had already ordered him to head an expedition against the English in the Río Tinto area; at the same time the captain general of Guatemala had urged him to undertake this venture and to ignore the *cédula* concerning the Florida governorship.[39] Finally, after some correspondence, the king ordered the perplexed Fernández to Saint Augustine.[40] In this case the delay worked no hardship on the temporary governor, Fulgencio García de Solís, who enjoyed his job immensely and hoped to become permanent governor.[41]

[Appointment and Term of the Interim Governor]

Five governors between 1700 and 1763 were temporary—Juan de Ayala Escobar (1716-1718), Ignacio Rodríguez Rozo (1726), Manuel Joseph de Justís (1737), Fulgencio García de Solís (1752-1755), and Alonso de Cárdenas (1761-1762). Royal decrees set an automatic succession to this post. If the governor died or left the colony temporarily, the sergeant major, second-in-command to the governor, took office until a permanent replacement arrived or the governor returned.[42] If the sergeant major were not able to fill the vacancy, the senior military

38. AGI, Santo Domingo, Legajo 2542. Carta del gobernador de Cuba al rey, May 17, 1753.

39. AGI, Santo Domingo, Legajo 2542. A royal *cédula* of July 4, 1752, ordered Fernández to go immediately to Florida, countermanding a previous order of January 18, 1752, that he stay in Central America. Fernández still procrastinated, however. Carta del gobernador de Cuba al rey, May 17, 1753.

40. AGI, Santo Domingo, Legajo 2542. Carta del gobernador de la Florida al rey, April 28, 1755.

41. AGI, Santo Domingo, Legajo 2541. Carta de los oficiales reales de la Florida al rey, June 3, 1752. Carta de los oficiales reales de la Florida al rey, September 4, 1752. Carta del gobernador interino de la Florida al Marqués de la Ensenada, Sept. 4, 1752.

42. AGI, Santo Domingo, Legajo 2581. Carta del sargento mayor de la Florida al rey, Dec. 16, 1761. He refers in this letter to the law bearing on the proper succession to the governorship.

captain in the garrison took the post.[43] The interim governor had full authority in the colony, but he did not receive the governor's salary or perquisites.

Juan de Ayala Escobar became temporary governor in 1716. He had become sergeant major in 1703, and when Governor Pedro de Olivera y Fullana died after only three months and nineteen days in office, the interim governorship fell to Ayala. Old, doddering, and unpopular with some residents of Saint Augustine, he served almost two years until a new governor arrived in 1718.[44]

During the Benavides' administration it became necessary to make an interim appointment because of the governor's illness. In 1726 Benavides suffered an attack of appendicitis and had to leave for Cuba to undergo an operation. Since Ayala, the sergeant major, was in prison in Havana, the task fell to the senior officer in Saint Augustine, Captain Ignacio Rodríguez Rozo, whose term proved very short. A skilled Cuban surgeon, "from first to last pursuing the method by which the King of France, Louis XIV, was healed," sent Benavides back to Florida within three months, relegating Rozo to his former place in the garrison.[45]

Two later interim governors took office in a different manner. Both Joseph de Justís and Fulgencio García de Solís were appointees of the governor of Cuba. Neither was in any way connected with Florida prior to assuming the temporary governorship. In March, 1737, Governor Juan Francisco de Güemes y Horcasitas, later viceroy of New Spain, appointed Justís to replace the accused Moral Sánchez. In 1752 García de Solís replaced Governor Melchor de Navarrete, who was on special orders to proceed immediately to Yucatán without waiting for his successor to arrive.[46]

Alonso de Cárdenas, the last interim governor of the first Spanish period, took office in December, 1761, under special circumstances. Like Ayala he was a sergeant major at Saint Augustine and merited the appointment because of his position in the colony; but before his death, the ruling governor, Lucas de Palacio y Valenzuela, had placed Cárdenas

43. AGI, Santo Domingo, Legajo 844. Carta del gobernador de la Florida al rey, Sept. 28, 1727. This letter contains the provisions of a royal *cédula* dated November 17, 1691, setting down this procedure.

44. AGI, Santo Domingo, Legajo 864. Carta de la comunidad de San Francisco de la Florida al rey, Nov. 28, 1716.

45. AGI, Santo Domingo, Legajo 844. Certificación del médico de la Havana que curó al gobernador hasta dejarle bueno, Nov. 28, 1726.

46. This was unusual and deviated sharply from normal procedure.

in house arrest for disobeying a gubernatorial order.[47] With Cárdenas under arrest the senior military officer had priority on the interim governorship; but instead, the acting sergeant major, the treasurer, and the governor's secretary—the three most important officials left in Florida—decided on Cárdenas. They dismissed the charge against him, released him from house arrest, and swore him in as the interim governor.[48] Not long after, in the spring of 1762, the king's permanent appointee arrived to relieve Cárdenas.

[*Backgrounds of the Governors, 1700-1763*]

Without exception the eighteenth-century governors were military men whose training and experience suited the military character of the colony. In Florida there was little need for the legal acumen of the Spanish barrister, the canonical judgments of the high clergyman, or the pompous magnificence of the Spanish nobleman. The king had other posts reserved for men of this stamp. In Saint Augustine military background and experience were the prime requisites.

All eighteenth-century governors met this requirement. Joseph de Zúñiga y Cerda (1699-1706) had a distinguished military career in both Europe and Africa during his twenty-eight years of army service prior to taking the governorship.[49] His successor, Francisco de Córcoles y Martínez (1706-1716) had an even more impressive record. He had risen through the ranks, first as a cadet, then as lieutenant, *reformado*,[50] captain, and finally as governor of Florida. He had campaigned in Catalonia, Ceuta, Milan, Palamos, and Gibraltar. He had been a prisoner of war in France and counted wounds in his right leg and left arm among his battle trophies.[51]

Those who followed were cut from the same mold. Pedro de Olivera y Fullana (1716) was governor of the Spanish town of Fraga near Lérida and major general in the army of Aragón and Estremadura.[52] Antonio de Benavides (1718-1734) rose from a second

47. AGI, Santo Domingo, Legajo 2581. Carta del gobernador de la Florida al rey, May 1, 1760. Despacho del rey al gobernador de Cuba, June 10, 1761.

48. AGI, Santo Domingo, Legajo 2543. Carta del gobernador interino de la Florida al rey, Dec. 16, 1761.

49. AGI, Santo Domingo, Legajo 840. Consulta de la Junta de Guerra, Oct. 30, 1700.

50. A military officer on detached service.

51. AGI, Santo Domingo, Legajo 833. Memorial del Capitán de Infantería Española, Don Francisco Córcoles, April 20, 1705.

52. AGI, Santo Domingo, Legajo 837. Título de gobernador y capitán general

lieutenancy in the royal guards to become commander of his own body of grenadiers. He served in Flanders and participated in 1702 in the siege of Acre, where he suffered severe wounds that bothered him later in Florida.[53] Francisco del Moral Sánchez (1734-1737) had obtained his experience in rough-and-tumble Cuba. His faithful service as captain of a Cuban infantry company and as acting sergeant major in Havana earned him the Florida governorship.[54] Manuel de Montiano (1737-1749) was one of the few governors who achieved the governorship by impressing the Council of the Indies with a list of his military achievements. Like his predecessors, he had come up through the ranks and after twenty-four years of service had finally become a captain. In North Africa Montiano fought two years near Oran, where he had disregarded serious wounds and fever to lead a company of grenadiers to important victories over the Moors. He also campaigned in Darién in Central America.[55]

Later governors followed the same pattern. Melchor de Navarrete (1749-1752) had spent forty-two years in the army before taking the governorship. He had been active in New Granada (Colombia) at Cartagena, where he had fought valiantly against the English expeditionary force led by Admiral Edward Vernon in 1740.[56] His most distinguishing characteristic, however, was his penchant for complaint. His correspondence contains a stream of letters concerning back, chest, and leg pains aggravated by the Florida climate.[57] Another hard-bitten soldier, Alonso Fernández de Heredia, was governor between 1755 and 1759. He had served against the English and Indians in Nicaragua, Honduras, Guatemala, Costa Rica, and Jamaica until he had attained the rank of brigadier.[58] Fernández earnestly believed that his wide

---

de las Provincias de San Agustín de la Florida para el Coronel Don Pedro de Olivera y Fullana, Jan. 22, 1716.

53. AGI, Santo Domingo, Legajo 851. Memorial de don Antonio de Benavides, Jan. 23, 1724.

54. AGI, Santo Domingo, Legajo 2541. Título de gobernador de San Agustín de la Florida para Don Francisco del Moral, Sept. 17, 1733.

55. AGI, Santo Domingo, Legajo 2541. Memorial de don Manuel de Montiano, Feb. 26, 1737.

56. AGI, Santo Domingo, Legajo 2541. Carta del gobernador elegido de la Florida (Navarrete) al rey, May 15, 1749.

57. AGI, Santo Domingo, Legajo 2541. Carta del gobernador de la Florida al Marqués de la Ensenada, July 30, 1750. Carta del gobernador de la Florida al Marqués de la Ensenada, Oct. 3, 1751.

58. AGI, Santo Domingo, Legajo 2542. Título de gobernador y capitán general de la Provincia y Presidio de San Agustín de la Florida, para el Brigadier Don Alonso Fernández de Heredia, Dec. 28, 1751.

experience in the Indies qualified him for a seat on the Council of the Indies, and he spent much of his time in the governorship futilely attempting to secure such an appointment.[59] Lucas Fernando de Palacio y Valenzuela (1758-1761) claimed thirty-six years of loyal service in the Spanish army. He had distinguished himself in Gibraltar, Navarre, Ceuta, Oran, and Italy.[60] Palacio was the only governor to marry during his term; but if his wedding was a time for celebration in the spring of 1761, his sudden death later in that year was a sad event for the Florida populace and his young Creole bride, Josepha Escobedo y Angulo.[61] The last governor before the British occupation was Melchor Feliú (1762-1764), who apparently completed the unbroken chain of military leaders for the colony. His principal duty, once he reached Saint Augustine, was to evacuate all Spanish residents to Cuba.[62]

Interim governors had the same wide military experience as their permanent counterparts. Juan de Ayala Escobar (1716-1718) had spent most of his life in Saint Augustine, rising from infantry footsoldier to the rank of captain and sergeant major.[63] Ignacio Rodríguez Rozo (1726) was senior infantry captain at Fort San Marcos when Governor Benavides left for Havana to seek medical care. Joseph de Justís (1737) served first as a cadet in a Sevillian regiment, then as an infantry captain in the Basque province of Guipúzcoa, and finally as sergeant major in Santiago de Cuba.[64] The record of Fulgencio García de Solís (1752-1755) included tours of duty in North Africa near Ceuta, in Italy at Milan, and in Spain at Pamplona and San Sebastián. In Cuba he won a battlefield promotion to lieutenant colonel in a fight against Admiral Edward Vernon at Guantánamo Bay.[65] Like Ayala, Alonso de Cárdenas

59. AGI, Santo Domingo, Legajo 2542. Carta del gobernador de la Florida al rey, April 7, 1756. Carta del gobernador de la Florida al rey, June 12, 1756.

60. AGI, Santo Domingo, Legajo 2542. Título del gobernador y capitán general de las Provincias de San Agustín de la Florida para el Brigadier Don Lucas Fernando Palacio, July 7, 1757.

61. The young widow was terribly distraught; her letters requesting aid and succor from the king were pathetic.

62. I have no documentary evidence on Feliú's background, but military officers assumed the governorship with such regularity that it would be surprising if Feliú did not fit into this pattern.

63. AGI, Santo Domingo, Legajo 851. Consulta de la Junta de Guerra, May 10, 1703.

64. AGI, Santo Domingo, Legajo 2541. Carta del gobernador de Cuba al rey, May 24, 1737.

65. AGI, Indiferente de Nueva España, Legajo 151. Relación de los méritos y servicios de don Fulgencio García de Solís, capitán que fué de Regimiento de Infantería

(1761-1762) was a veteran of many years' service in Florida. His reward was the sergeant major's post and the interim governorship in 1761.

[*The Inauguration Ceremony*]

Unlike the pageantry attending inaugural rites for the viceroy in Lima and Mexico City, the ceremony in Florida was short and simple. In Saint Augustine there were no parades, tournaments, bull fights, lavish banquets, poets' contests, or eulogistic speeches to celebrate the arrival of a new governor. Florida was a rude military outpost. A change in governors meant little more than a shift in commanding officers of a military garrison. Such an occasion hardly merited extreme formalities or pompous displays of love, loyalty, and affection.

The inaugural procedure followed a simple pattern. Immediately upon arrival in Saint Augustine, the new governor presented his credentials to the incumbent governor and his two treasury officials. They checked and certified the appointee's dispatch of title and other documents. They then administered the oath of office to the incoming governor, who pledged three times to obey all royal laws and statutes, to act always in the royal interest, to attend to the well being of those residing in Florida, and to provide adequate defenses for the colony. He then received the keys to Fort San Marcos and to the gates of Saint Augustine, symbol of his inauguration as governor.[66]

An inspection of the fort and the town followed this short ceremony. Accompanied by the outgoing governor, the accountant, and the treasurer, the new governor surveyed the walls and defenses of Saint Augustine and Fort San Marcos. He also inspected the arms, powder, and supply warehouses and checked the condition of the artillery. The two treasury officials provided him with certified inventories of the supplies, equipment, and money contained in the colony. He then checked this list against one prepared on his original tour of inspection. All discrepancies between the two inventories were reported to the Council of the Indies. There were also informal briefing sessions between the old and the new governor concerning conditions, problems, and personnel in Florida.[67]

---

de Portugal, y actual Sargento Mayor interino de la Plaza de Santiago de Cuba, Dec. 15, 1747.

66. AGI, Santo Domingo, Legajo 2541. Carta del gobernador de la Florida al rey, Aug. 13, 1749. This letter describes the ceremony in detail.

67. Two letters mention these informal conversations. AGI, Santo Domingo, Legajo

Occasionally the outgoing governor was not available to inaugurate his successor, but there was little change in the inaugural procedure. Temporary governors took their oath of office from the accountant, treasurer, public secretary, and a high-ranking military officer. Temporary governors inaugurated their permanent replacements by administering the oath and awarding them the keys to the fort and the town.

[Duties, Responsibilities, and Privileges of the Governor]

Spanish colonial administration did not operate under the separation-of-powers principle. In the colonies there were few, if any, officials or councils that handled executive, legislative, or judicial responsibilities exclusively. Most colonial administrators and agencies had a multitude of duties and functions. The powers of the viceroy, for example, spread into the executive, legislative, and judicial spheres; so did those of his advisory council (audiencia). In Florida the situation was no different. The governor had wide powers that spread into all phases of colonial life. His titles alone—governor, captain general, royal vice patron of the church—gave him more than just executive responsibility. As governor he received political power usually inherent in such a title—administrative authority and limited appointive power. As captain general he took command of all soldiers serving in the colony. As royal vice patron of the church he had at least partial control over religious activities. Since Florida was too poor and too meagerly populated to support a court system, the governor was also the chief colonial judicial officer. He arranged all civil and criminal trials and forwarded legal documents to the Council of the Indies in Spain when the offense warranted review or trial by this body.

The governor found his many duties and responsibilities defined in two principal sources—his initial dispatch of title and royal law. Unlike his English counterpart, the Spanish colonial governor did not receive lengthy instructions, both open and secret; he obtained only a short dispatch of title that set down his functions in a general way. Signed by the king, sealed with the royal coat of arms, and countersigned by the secretary of state (after 1717), this dispatch of title granted him the governorship for a three- or five-year term. The document ordered him to guard and defend the province of Florida against all enemies, to

---

2541. Carta del gobernador de Vera Cruz (Benavides) al rey, Nov. 3, 1734. AGI, Santo Domingo, Legajo 2542. Carta del gobernador de la Florida al rey, May 31, 1758.

observe all laws governing the conduct of his predecessor, to make an investigation of the outgoing governor's administration, and under no circumstances to forsake his post until a replacement arrived. The document also outlined his salary and perquisites in great detail.

Salary and perquisites were always a knotty problem. Until 1715 the governor's income was 2,000 ducats—1,000 ducats from the "fruits of the land" and 1,000 ducats from the annual subsidy.[68] By the wage standards of the day for civil servants, it seemed a well-paying job of almost 2,750 pesos. In practice, however, the governor realized no income from colonial enterprises, no "fruits of the land." His actual wage was, therefore, never more than the 1,000 ducats paid him from the subsidy. Sometimes, when the *situado* ship did not arrive, he received nothing. A change occurred in October, 1715, when Philip V set the governor's salary at 4,000 pesos—2,000 from the subsidy and 2,000 from profits made in the colony, but this amounted to a meager increase of only 625 pesos, hardly a significant raise for the distressed governor.[69]

Continuous complaints about low salary did little to improve the governor's financial condition. In 1724 Philip V equalized the salaries of all governors serving in Peru and New Spain (of which Florida was a part), but this failed to help the governor. The king claimed that the 4,000 pesos awarded to Benavides was an adequate wage, far above the gubernatorial average.[70] In 1738 Governor Montiano reopened the salary issue by arguing strongly that he could not support himself on 2,000 pesos. He needed more income to dignify his office. The Council of the Indies, however, refused to allow Montiano's request. No governor anywhere in Spain or the Indies received more than the 4,000 pesos awarded to the governor in Florida. His plea for an increase, stated the Council's report, had no justification.[71]

Wage provisions of the dispatch of title remained the same until 1753, when Ferdinand VI finally granted the governor an additional 1,000 pesos.[72] Since the accountant's post had been eliminated in Saint

68. AGI, Santo Domingo, Legajo 833. Consulta de Cámara de las Indias, Sept. 2, 1738.
69. AGI, Santo Domingo, Legajo 833. Consulta de Cámara de las Indias, Sept. 2, 1738.
70. AGI, Santo Domingo, Legajo 833. Consulta de Cámara de las Indias, Sept. 2, 1738.
71. AGI, Santo Domingo, Legajo 833. Consulta de Cámara de las Indias, Sept. 2, 1738.
72. AGI, Santo Domingo, Legajo 2584. Carta del contador de la Florida al Marqués de la Ensenada, Feb. 4, 1754.

Augustine, extra funds were available for an increase without putting a new strain on the royal treasury. For the most part, however, the governor considered himself poorly paid, a seemingly chronic complaint among public officials anywhere.

Salary was not the only financial consideration set down in the dispatch of title. A second important provision concerned the *media anata,* the requirement that all those taking the governorship post a bond amounting to one-half of their first year's salary and one-third of any perquisites accruing to them by virtue of their office.[73] This deposit might be used later to pay fines in case of malfeasance or misfeasance in office and became a device to insure honest administration. Theoretically officials in Spain hoped that colonial administrators would avoid any type of misconduct in office, which might result in the forfeiture of this bond. The dispatches of title issued to Zúñiga and Córcoles required a *media anata* of 1,000 ducats. From 1715 to 1753 the governor had to deposit 2,000 pesos; after 1753, 2,500. Sometimes the dispatch of title provided for payment of the *media anata* on the installment plan, but no matter what the payment plan, the *media anata* was a requirement set down in each title granted to incoming governors.[74]

In eighteenth-century Florida, however, the *media anata* was ignored. No governor paid one peso of the required bond. He either disregarded the *media anata* provision of his dispatch of title or was excused from it by the king and the Council of the Indies. Since the governorship was a profitless, undesirable post, it appears that the king and members of the Council deliberately ignored the provision. Being released from payment of the *media anata* was at least a partial recompense for the administrator assigned to serve in Florida. In 1727 the king and the Council excused payment in cases where an official exercised authority that was purely military, evidence that they recognized the burden such a requirement imposed.[75] Theoretically Florida was more than a military outpost; practically, however, the governor had primarily military functions and was more like a commanding officer than

73. AGI, Santo Domingo, Legajo 2540. Carta del gobernador de la Florida al rey, April 20, 1735.

74. AGI, Santo Domingo, Legajo 2541. Título del gobernador de San Agustín de la Florida para Francisco del Moral, Sept. 17, 1733. AGI, Santo Domingo, Legajo 833. Consulta de Cámara de las Indias, Sept. 2, 1738.

75. AGI, Santo Domingo, Legajo 2541. Consulta de Cámara de las Indias, Sept. 2, 1738. This document quotes a royal decree of Sept. 23, 1727, exempting all officials with purely military functions from payment of the *media anata*.

a political official. It was improbable, too, that the soldiers chosen for the office could even raise the required sum.[76]

Although the dispatch of title generally defined the governor's duties and responsibilities and specifically set forth his emoluments, this document had little importance. Far more significant in controlling the governor's activities was the constant flow of *cédulas* (royal orders in Council) arriving in Saint Augustine from Spain. These *cédulas* regulated the governor's every move. All colonial questions, large and small, fell within the scope of these decrees. Whether orders-in-Council granted a few pesos to a hard-pressed widow or set forth plans for a military offensive against an enemy stronghold, they were the governor's chief guide in making decisions.[77]

Cédulas issued to his predecessors also bound the governor. Before 1681 it was his duty to learn the content of the multitude of decrees contained in the former governor's files. After 1681 these laws could be found in the convenient *Recopilación de leyes de los reynos de las Indias*. This monumental work, a compilation and condensation of the *cédulas* issued since the discovery of America, contained the most important laws governing the conduct of colonial officials. It became (or should have become) the governor's handbook, setting down specific rules to follow. He was expected to furnish a notarized inventory of his wealth to the *audiencia* nearest the area in his jurisdiction.[78] He had to deposit a guarantee or bond in the treasury of the province where he exercised his authority.[79] He could not marry without license from the crown,[80] nor could he leave the colony without the king's permission.[81] He had to live in the governor's palace, never with residents or friends.[82] He could not leave until his successor arrived, nor could he depart without completing the judicial review (*residencia*) of his predecessor's administration.[83] A mass of laws also covered such

---

76. For each governor the procedure was the same. He took office without paying the *media anata*. He then wrote to the Council of the Indies requesting exemption from the requirement, pointing out that his predecessor had been excused. A *fiscal* or legal adviser of the Council of the Indies determined the precedent—exemption in the case of Florida—and usually decided in favor of the governor. The king and the Council inevitably accepted the *fiscal*'s decision on the *media anata*.

77. The governor's economic, religious, Indian, military, and social responsibilities will be discussed in later chapters.

78. *Recopilación de las Indias*, Lib. 5, tít. 2, ley 8.

79. *Recopilación de las Indias*, Lib. 5, tít. 2, ley 9.

80. *Recopilación de las Indias*, Lib. 5, tít. 2, ley 44.

81. *Recopilación de las Indias*, Lib. 5, tít. 2, ley 34.

82. *Recopilación de las Indias*, Lib. 5, tít. 2, ley 48.

83. *Recopilación de las Indias*, Lib. 5, tít. 2, ley 49; Lib. 3, tít. 2, ley 6.

areas as the subsidy, defense, Indian relations, religious affairs, adminis-tration of justice, slavery, regulation of inns and taverns, trade, and a multitude of other questions with which the governor had to deal.

The laws regulating colonial officials aimed at centralization of Spanish colonial administration. Ideally the king hoped to direct and control the actions of all colonial functionaries from the august viceroy in Mexico City to the lowliest constable in the most out-of-the-way provincial hamlet. The agency supervising colonial affairs in Spain, the Council of the Indies, was the king's vigilant overseer. From its re-ports the king drew up the laws and *cédulas* prescribing the behavior and policies of administrators all over the New World. In this way the monarch hoped to insure absolute conformity with his will and secure personal control over his domains.

Such a policy of centralization was neither practical nor possible. The king simply could not foresee the sudden crisis or emergency that often forced colonial administrators to act on their own initiative with-out explicit royal directions. Since the king and the Council were neither prophets nor seers, they could not legislate for every contingency. Distance from the colonies and slowness in communication also kept the system from operating as the monarch desired. Spain was an ocean away. Colonial officials could not wait a year or more for their supe-riors' decisions on matters demanding immediate attention. In practice colonial administrators exercised wide discretionary powers, no matter how closely their activities seemed to be regulated under the law. The governor in Saint Augustine, for example, could not wait to obtain the king's permission to purchase food illegally from Carolina traders. His starving colonists had to eat to live, and he was responsible for their welfare. If he waited until approval came from Spain, his colony would perish. Only the most sycophantic or naïve administrator ex-pected to abide completely by the letter of the law or planned to adhere strictly to the wishes of his superiors. Such a policy would have meant the complete breakdown of administration everywhere in the Indies.

[*The Council* (Junta)]

Despite his wide powers, the governor was careful to avoid taking full responsibility for policies not defined by royal decrees or contrary to them. To immunize himself, at least partially, against the anger of the king and the Council for disobeying royal law, he often convoked a junta of the chief administrative, military, and religious leaders of the colony. This body acted as the governor's unofficial advisory council and decided or affirmed policies to be carried out in emergencies or in cases when the required action deviated from normal procedures. The junta ordinarily consisted of the governor, treasurer, accountant, sergeant major, auxiliary bishop, curate of the church, guardian of the convent, an infantry captain, an infantry lieutenant, three second lieutenants, and a military engineer.[84] Membership on the junta varied according to the wishes of the governor or the availability of certain officials, but it usually represented all groups within the colony.

Under the law the junta had no real power or no official standing except in two cases. In 1702 the king empowered the junta to choose agents (*situadistas*) to go to New Spain to collect the yearly subsidy.[85] In 1740 the junta also obtained the right to pick the emissary who went to Cuba annually to bargain with Havana Company, a trading enterprise responsible for providing the Florida garrison with food and supplies.[86] Otherwise the junta had no rights or permanent status. It met at the whim of the governor, who dissolved it after its deliberations were concluded.

In practice, however, the junta was a significant political institution. The governor inevitably called this body together in extreme crises and in cases where it was clear he would have to strain royal law severely or disregard it completely. For the governor the approval of his actions by the junta was absolutely essential if he was to avoid being charged with disloyalty for disobedience of the king's decrees. If challenged by his superiors on this score, he could claim his policy was based on the junta's decision, not purely on his own responsibility. Working with a junta he could avoid taking individual responsibility. Trading with Carolinians to obtain badly needed supplies,[87] requesting arms and ammunition from the French in Mobile,[88] and misappropriat-

84. AGI, Santo Domingo, Legajo 845. Testimonio de diferentes instrumentos que remitén a S. M. y sus oficiales de su Real y Supremo Consejo de estas Indias, el Gobernador y Oficiales Reales del Presidio de la Florida, Nov. 23, 1734. This was the makeup of the *junta* which met on that date.

85. AGI, Santo Domingo, Legajo 843. Real cédula, Madrid, March 8, 1702. See also Gabriel Cárdenas y Cano, *Ensayo cronológico para la historia general de la Florida* (Madrid, 1829), II, 349-354.

86. AGI, Santo Domingo, Legajo 838. Consulta del Consejo de las Indias, May 27, 1741.

87. AGI, Santo Domingo, Legajo 842. Carta del gobernador interino de la Florida al rey, Nov. 22, 1717.

88. AGI, Santo Domingo, Legajo 842. Carta del gobernador de la Florida al rey,

ing funds from the treasury[89] were actions which defied established law; and in each case a junta supported the governor by approving his actions.

The governor, of course, did not intend to share his wide powers with such a council, but this was the practical result of his use of the junta system. The junta met often enough to become an established political institution. Since the governor needed the agreement of prominent colonial leaders for any irregular practices, the junta was both a reassuring and necessary convenience that enabled the governor to pose a stronger case in vindication or extenuation should his behavior be challenged by his superiors in Spain. For this protection the governor had to share some of his extensive authority. Use of the junta tempered his one-man rule in the colony and extended political power to various officials in Saint Augustine, who came to have at least a partial voice in colonial politics.

[*Attempts at Democratic Reform*]

To some residents of the Florida capital, the junta was a poor substitute for the town council (*cabildo*), a venerable political institution with permanent standing. In most areas of the Spanish Empire the *cabildo* was the local governing body, consisting of two popularly elected magistrates (*alcaldes*) and four to six councilors (*regidores*). Its functions included distribution of land, imposition of a few selected local taxes, provision for police, regulation of holidays, inspection of jails and hospitals, granting of building licenses, and other local duties. Sometimes the *cabildo* served judicially as an appeal body for the local court system. Usually the deliberations of the town council were secret, but in emergencies it often became an open meeting (*cabildo abierto*). In extreme crises residents of the town met in common assembly to discuss and to vote on a course of action very similar to the town meeting system in colonial Massachusetts.[90]

The *cabildo* made only one brief appearance in Florida. Pedro Menéndez de Avilés established a town council in Saint Augustine almost immediately after he arrived and used it as a governing body

---

June 16, 1725. Two *juntas* met to discuss this problem on Oct. 6, 1723, and April 15, 1724.

89. AGI, Santo Domingo, Legajo 854. Carta de los oficiales reales de la Florida al rey, June 1, 1722.

90. W. W. Pierson, "Some Reflections on the Cabildo as an Institution," *Hispanic American Historical Review*, V (1922), 573-596.

while he was absent from the colony. When most of the original migration left Florida in 1570, however, the *cabildo* disappeared and did not reappear despite periodic agitation for its revival. One of these vain attempts occurred in the late 1750's when a group of colonists and clergymen began a drive for re-establishment of the town council. Resentful of the governor's arbitrary rule, they hoped to restrict his wide power by establishing a *cabildo*. Authorities in Spain began investigating this possibility in 1759, and in February, 1761, the order went out setting up such a body in Saint Augustine. Charles III called for a town council of nine members—two magistrates, six councilors, and one clergyman (*padre de minores*). Although in some areas of the Indies these council members were popularly elected, in Florida the king preferred that they be appointed by the governor.[91]

The ensuing events present an interesting commentary, first, on the methods used by colonial administrators to block execution of royal edicts, and second, on the quality of personnel in Florida. Upon receiving the *cédula*, the temporary governor, Alonso de Cárdenas, refused to establish the *cabildo*. The law, he pointed out in a return letter to the king, stated that only distinguished men with a long record of community service were fit to serve on the town council. In his search for qualified appointees, he had found no residents who met this requirement; hence he could not fill the nine seats on the *cabildo*. Rather than press the matter, Charles III accepted Cárdenas' decision, at least for a time. Postponing execution of the *cédula*, the king ordered the governor to make continuous surveys of the Florida population. When enough qualified men became available, Cárdenas was to form a *cabildo*.[92] In the end, however, nothing came of the plan. Florida fell under English control in 1763 before another quest for competent officials could begin. It seems probable too that the governor would have ignored the king's order in any case. It was far more convenient to rule without the encumbrance of a meddling *cabildo*.

[*The Governor and Colonial Patronage*]

The king and the Council of the Indies held control of virtually all appointments in Florida. They picked the governor, his accountant and treasurer, and all military officers except a cavalry captain and militia captain chosen by the governor. Even then the militia captaincy was

91. AGI, Santo Domingo, Legajo 2581. Real cédula, El Pardo, Feb. 23, 1761.
92. AGI, Santo Domingo, Legajo 2581. Carta del gobernador interino de la Florida al rey, Dec. 22, 1761. Real cédula, San Lorenzo, Nov. 12, 1762.

purely an honorary post with no financial advantage accruing to its holder. This seemingly left the governor with little power over the patronage. He could appoint a cavalry captain, but decades might pass before this post fell vacant, leaving some governors without authority to choose any of their associates. Appointive power thus seemed to rest firmly in the hands of the governor's superiors in Spain, not with him in Saint Augustine.

But again theory and practice diverged. In reality the governor had wide influence over appointments despite his seeming impotence under the law. When an office fell vacant (usually because of sickness, incompetence, transfer, or death), the governor played a key role in filling the post. He immediately appointed an associate to take the office temporarily, then notified the Council of the Indies of the opening. At the same time he included his personal recommendation, invariably his temporary choice. With few exceptions the king and the Council of the Indies approved the governor's appointee. It was not worth their time and trouble to nominate and approve a new man for infantry captain, treasurer, or accountant. For the Floridians reaffirmation of the governor's temporary appointment came with such predictable regularity that it must have been obvious that his favor was essential in order to secure a permanent post.[93]

The governor's grip on appointments did not always go unchallenged. In 1720 the accountant at Saint Augustine, Francisco Menéndez Marqués, proposed a new method for filling his position. He wanted the privilege of naming his own successor. In this way, he explained, he could keep the office out of the hands of an incompetent interim appointee; he could train his own replacement in accountancy techniques and save the governor the embarrassment over a possible poor temporary choice.[94] When this proposal reached Spain, however, it failed to impress the king and the Council of the Indies, who saw no reason to change existing methods. They saw his plan either as a scheme to obtain retirement funds by peddling his office to the highest bidder or as a conspiracy to take power properly belonging to the governor and his Spanish superiors. The king flatly rejected the accountant's request and continued to use ordinary appointive procedures. The king would

93. There are many instances of this procedure. See particularly, AGI, Santo Domingo, Legajo 2534. Provisiones de empleos, mercedes, y gracias: años de 1730 a 1778.

94. AGI, Santo Domingo, Legajo 847. Carta del contador de la Florida al rey, Feb. 23, 1720.

choose all officials in Florida upon recommendation of the governor in Saint Augustine and the Council of the Indies.[95]

One position, the public secretaryship, was not appointive but salable. This official (*escribano público*) was the governor's scrivener. He wrote dispatches, filed correspondence, and performed other clerical chores in the colony. Once he had assumed his position, the secretary usually served until his death, a period that might last fifty or sixty years, and the problem of filling the office rarely arose. In September, 1727, however, the death of the public secretary, Juan Solana, left Governor Benavides with the task of securing a replacement. It was particularly vexing first because no resident of Saint Augustine desired the job badly enough to pay the minimum price of three hundred pesos and second because few Floridians were qualified to fill the post. Those able to read and to write already held responsible positions and were not anxious to become the governor's clerk, particularly at a cost of three hundred pesos.

Benavides realized he would have difficulty finding Solana's successor and took steps to secure one elsewhere. With his own colonists either too poor or illiterate to take the position, the governor asked the Council of the Indies to seek a secretary in Havana.[96] Sympathetic to Benavides' plight, the Council ordered the governor of Cuba to send a public secretary to Florida.[97] In the meantime, however, Benavides became impatient. Having heard no word from either Spain or Cuba about the Council's decision, he finally set up the machinery for selling the secretaryship in Saint Augustine.

The events that followed resembled a comic opera. On May 23, 1730, an auctioneer, Francisco Ponce de León, an infantry private in the garrison at Fort San Marcos, opened the bidding for the office. Three times that day he urged the curious populace assembled in the public square of the Florida capital to bid; three times they met his entreaties with stony, perhaps amused, silence. Benavides blamed Ponce for the lack of results and the next day replaced him with a drummer from the fort, Antonio de Fuentes. At first he was as unsuccessful as his predecessor. For ten days he futilely asked for a bid. On the

95. AGI, Santo Domingo, Legajo 847. Despacho del rey al contador de la Florida, Sept. 5, 1721.

96. AGI, Santo Domingo, Legajo 844. Carta del gobernador de la Florida al rey, Sept. 28, 1727.

97. AGI, Santo Domingo, Legajo 837. Despacho del rey al gobernador de Cuba, April 16, 1729.

eleventh day, however, Francisco Ponce de León, the original auctioneer, shattered the silence with a bid of one hundred pesos, short of the minimum sale price but enough to give Fuentes some hope. Then four more days without another offer led the drummer-auctioneer back into despair. Finally, however, on June 17 Ponce added fifty pesos to his original offer, stating that this was absolutely his last bid. At this the discouraged Fuentes closed the auction. Eighteen days of shouting had elicited two bids, both inadequate.[98] Benavides, however, decided to forward Ponce's offer to Spain, where the king might decide that half a loaf was better than none and confirm Ponce in office. In this the governor proved correct. Happy to secure the 150 pesos for the royal treasury, Philip V approved Ponce in the secretaryship, despite the fact he had ordered the governor of Cuba to fill the office.[99]

Then the drama became even more ludicrous. Ponce de León had evidently viewed the entire episode as a joke. Perhaps he had bid on a dare by his fellow soldiers. Perhaps he had a spontaneous urge to break the terrible monotony of a bidless auction. After all Ponce himself had experienced a futile one-day stand as auctioneer and realized something of Fuentes' frustration. Possibly the governor prompted Ponce to start bidding in the hope that it would inspire another offer for the full purchase price. In any event, when Ponce received word of his appointment, he was outraged. In a heated conversation with Governor Benavides he claimed that he was merely a simple soldier, qualified only for that profession, and that he could not possibly become secretary.[100] Refusing on the basis of ill-health, Ponce managed to avoid taking the position.[101]

By this time six years had passed since Solana's death. Hopefully Benavides set up machinery for a second auction in December, 1733. Like the first it was initially unsuccessful. Thirteen days passed without a single bid from the Floridians. On the fourteenth day, however, the treasurer and the accountant submitted a bid of 150 pesos on behalf of the infantry lieutenant Bartolomé Nieto de Carvajal, probably the result of a deal between Nieto, the governor, and the two treasury

98. AGI, Santo Domingo, Legajo 844. Carta del gobernador de la Florida al rey, July 16, 1730.
99. AGI, Santo Domingo, Legajo 844. Carta del gobernador de la Florida al rey, Oct. 15, 1731.
100. AGI, Santo Domingo, Legajo 844. Carta del gobernador de la Florida al rey, Oct. 15, 1731.
101. AGI, Santo Domingo, Legajo 844. Auto de pregón del oficio de escribano público, July 29, 1734.

officials who agreed among themselves to pay the required three hundred pesos. On the following day when no counter-offer came, the treasurer and the accountant added 150 pesos to their original bid, enough to purchase the secretaryship for Nieto. Benavides then closed the bidding and installed the infantry captain as secretary pending royal confirmation.[102]

Once again the matter seemed settled. Nieto would become public secretary at Saint Augustine; the governor would have a competent clerk; and the king could add three hundred pesos to the royal treasury. But unfortunately the case became even more confused. In Havana, Francisco de Castilla, with both the qualifications and the money to fill the office, petitioned the governor of Cuba for the secretaryship.[103] This request then went to Philip V, who, unaware of what had gone on in Florida, confirmed Castilla's appointment. A short time later when the king heard of Nieto's installation, he refused to approve the Floridian and ordered Governor Montiano to take Castilla, who left Havana for Saint Augustine late in 1737.[104]

Once again the problem seemed resolved, but this time Montiano refused to abide by the king's decision. Rather than oust Nieto, the governor refused to accept Castilla's credentials and asked Philip V to clarify the *cédula* rescinding Nieto's appointment.[105] In the meantime Nieto continued in office while Castilla waited impatiently for the king's reply. Finally in August, 1740, over two and one-half years after Castilla's arrival in the Florida capital, the king reconfirmed the Cuban's appointment, ending the fourteen-year search for Solana's replacement.[106] Lack of administrative co-ordination, a combination of impatience and inertia on the part of Spanish officialdom, and slowness in communication had turned the simple problem of naming a secretary for the tiny Florida outpost into a major colonial crisis.

102. AGI, Santo Domingo, Legajo 844. Auto de pregón de oficio de escribano público, July 29, 1734.
103. AGI, Santo Domingo, Legajo 844. Carta del gobernador de la Florida al rey, Nov. 11, 1737.
104. AGI, Santo Domingo, Legajo 844. Carta del gobernador de la Florida al rey, July 4, 1738.
105. AGI, Santo Domingo, Legajo 844. Carta del gobernador de la Florida al rey, Nov. 11, 1737.
106. AGI, Santo Domingo, Legajo 837. Título de escribano público y de la guarnación de la ciudad de San Agustín de la Florida, Aug. 14, 1740.

[The Governorship of Florida and Opportunities
for Advancement]

With one exception all governors of Florida during the eighteenth century agreed that they served in a miserable, undesirable post. They were poorly paid, were irregularly supplied with the necessities of life, and enjoyed none of the prestige usually associated with their office. They were, in their own minds, unappreciated, abused time servers. Yet Saint Augustine was not an abysmal jumping-off place where the monarch sent his least efficient, most troublesome officers, nor was it a dead-end for Spanish colonial administrators. Service in Florida was rather a stepping stone to more alluring, more prestigious posts in other parts of the Indies. Perseverance in the governorship usually was rewarded by a promotion to a more attractive colonial office in an area where life and work were far more agreeable and satisfying.

The record of gubernatorial advancement was impressive. Zúñiga y Cerda left Florida to become the governor of Cartagena, a busy seaport on the north Colombian coast.[107] Benavides survived his operation for appendicitis and the debilitating effects of pain from old wounds to become governor of Vera Cruz, the most important harbor in New Spain.[108] After thirteen years in Saint Augustine, Manuel de Montiano went to Panama to become governor and president of the *audiencia* there.[109] Melchor de Navarrete overcame back and chest pains, particularly severe in Florida, to become governor of Yucatán.[110] His successor, Alonso Fernández de Heredia, followed the same path to Mérida.[111] The fate of the others who assumed the governorship is not clear, but it is plain from these examples that the king rewarded the patient, long-suffering administrator who had the misfortune of being sent to Saint Augustine. There is one question that emerges, however: was the reward worth the long years of personal sacrifice in Florida?

107. AGI, Santo Domingo, Legajo 836. Despacho del rey al gobernador de la Florida, Aug. 18, 1705.

108. AGI, Santo Domingo, Legajo 2541. Carta del gobernador de la Florida al rey, May 6, 1733.

109. AGI, Santo Domingo, Legajo 2541. Despacho del rey al gobernador de la Florida, Nov. 15, 1748.

110. AGI, Santo Domingo, Legajo 2542. Título de gobernador y capitán general de la Provincia y Presidio de San Agustín de la Florida para el Brigadier don Alonso Fernández de Heredia, Dec. 28, 1751.

111. AGI, Santo Domingo, Legajo 2542. Carta del gobernador de la Florida al rey, Oct. 14, 1758.

Chapter II

CHECKS ON
THE GOVERNOR

In Florida all power rested with the governor, who personally bore all administrative responsibility. Except for the junta he did not share his authority, either with local officials or with administrators or administrative councils in other parts of the Indies. He was responsible to the king and the Council of the Indies in Spain, but they were three thousand miles away. Isolated from his superiors, the governor was free to pursue an independent course, suited to the colonial environment and to his personal predilections. Still he could not proceed completely without restraint, according to his own whims or at his own discretion. Significant checks prevented unrestricted, arbitrary rule in Saint Augustine.

[*General Checks on the Governor*]

The most obvious limitation on the governor's power was royal law, the orders-in-council passed down to the governor from the king. Past and current *cédulas* regulated the governor's every activity, aiming in the final analysis at bringing him under the rigid control of his superiors in Spain. Ideally, the king and the Council of the Indies hoped to define and prescribe all gubernatorial policies and to dictate a course of action for every eventuality. They desired to set up a centralized administrative system with the king having the last word. To insure absolute conformity to the royal will, the king bound all colonial officials to the spirit and the letter of the law. In Florida, for example, the governor pledged three times in his inaugural oath to obey and to enforce royal decrees. Violation of this solemn obligation was treasonable.

A second restraint grew out of the right of all Spanish colonists to lay their grievances directly before the king. All Floridians were free to expose cases of gubernatorial graft, fraud, peculation, favoritism, inclemency, cruelty, or nepotism and to point up administrative incompetence and corruption. This practice forced the governor to maintain at least a semblance of good government if he was to avoid being caught up in a bothersome probe of his administration, or worse, in his disgraceful removal. Failure to reckon with this fact of colonial life could and did have disastrous consequences for the indiscreet colonial administrator.[1]

Of course few officials were free of criticism. Jealous or vengeful colonials often abused their right to communicate directly with the king by bringing false, unsubstantiated charges against their superiors in the Indies. Ordinarily the monarch ignored accusations based on flimsy, hearsay evidence and sometimes censured the malcontents, but an undue number of complaints concerning the conduct of a colonial official inevitably set off a royal investigation of his administration.

[*Specific Checks on the Governor: The* Visita *and the* Pesquisa]

Royal law and the privilege of Spanish colonists to air their grievances before the crown were natural restraints on the governor implicit in the colonial system. There were, however, explicit checks designed to prevent misgovernment and to insure honest, efficient colonial administration. One of these was the visitation (*visita*). Although historians have failed to agree on its character, the *visita* generally took two forms—the formal inspection of a given province and the investigation of a specific official whose activities had come under suspicion.[2] Procedures varied, but usually the king or one of his colonial subordinates chose a *visitador del juzgado* to conduct an investigation of a province or official. Occasionally the *visitador* had authority to correct abuses he uncovered or to remove an offending official, but ordinarily he only made recommendations to his superiors.[3]

Formal visitations in Florida were rare. Far from the centers of

1. For example, the extraordinary number of complaints reaching Spain concerning Governor Francisco del Moral Sánchez's conduct resulted in a secret investigation of his administration that paved the way for his ouster in 1737.

2. See Haring, *The Spanish Empire*, pp. 153-156; Guillermo Céspedes del Castillo, "La visita como institución indiana," *Anuario de Estudios Americanos*, III (1943), 984-1025.

3. Although formal visitations were unusual in Florida, the king determined conditions in the colony in other ways. Periodically the king requested the governor of Cuba to report on problems and personnel in Florida. Usually it was left to the Cuban governor to obtain his information in any way he saw fit. Ordinarily he got such reports from residents of the colony—a soldier on detached duty in Saint Augustine, a friar visiting Cuba for a chapter meeting, the auxiliary bishop, or a sea captain calling at the Florida capital. See AGI, Santo Domingo, Legajo 866. Carta del gobernador de Cuba al rey, Dec. 23, 1726. Carta del obispo de Cuba al rey, Dec. 30, 1726.

Empire, sparsely inhabited, and unproductive, the colony was not worth a *visita*. A visitor might devise ways to make more efficient use of the subsidy or prevent peculation, but strict records of receipts and disbursals and periodic auditing of subsidy accounts reduced opportunity of graft from this source. He might uncover an illicit trade venture or a morals scandal, but his findings would hardly be significant enough to warrant the expense to the crown. It was far simpler and cheaper for the king to secure information in other ways, and only once during the eighteenth century did the monarch call for an official visitation. Soon after the end of Queen Anne's War, Philip V appointed the Cuban licentiate Antonio Ponce de León as *visitador del juzgado* for Florida. He was to make a complete report on conditions in Florida for the crown.[4]

When he arrived in Saint Augustine in 1720, Ponce received a rude reception. Like any visitor he must have known that he would be unwelcome to at least some segments of the population. He was, for these people, a royal busybody prying into colonial matters that he as an outsider could neither understand nor interpret, but he was surely not prepared for the greeting that awaited him in Florida. When he reached Saint Augustine, he found rudely inscribed handbills posted in conspicuous spots about the town threatening him with death if he did not leave at once.[5]

The appearance of the handbills worried Governor Benavides. Although he too may have wished for the visitor's departure, he saw that the posting of the leaflets reflected his lack of control over the colony, and a visitation was an occasion to put his administrative talents on display. Immediately, therefore, he offered one thousand pesos to anyone naming the person who had posted the threatening notices. In this way he hoped to bring the culprit quickly to justice and to impress the visitor with his abilities.

It was an effective move. One nameless soldier evidently needed the money badly enough to turn informer and accused Bernardo Nieto Carbajal, a long-time soldier of the Florida garrison. Nieto feared that Ponce would revive charges against him for abusing the Apalache

4. AGI, Santo Domingo, Legajo 833. Consulta del Consejo de las Indias, Nov. 28, 1721.

5. AGI, Escribanía de Cámara, Legajo 153A. Consulta del Consejo de las Indias, Nov. 28, 1721. Autos efectuados por don Antonio de Benavides, Gobernador de la Florida, contra don Ignacio Rodríguez Roso y don Bernardo Nieto de Carbajal sobre sus procedimientos. Legajo 80 de Pleytos de la Florida, número 8.

Indians in 1702. By threatening the visitor's life, he hoped to intimidate Ponce into leaving. But if Nieto meant to avoid trouble, he only asked for more. Acting on the informer's testimony, Governor Benavides seized the infantry captain, confronted him with the charge of the anonymous accuser, forced a confession, and dispatched the prisoner to Cádiz for sentence. The informer, in turn, obtained five hundred of the one thousand pesos originally promised by the governor.[6] Benavides had demonstrated his competence to the visitor, and the case seemed closed.

In Spain, however, the Council of the Indies challenged the governor's handling of the Nieto affair. The Council accused Benavides of drawing up his case against the soldier improperly, of acting on information provided by a paid informer, and of not allowing Nieto to testify in his own defense. Sacrificing traditional legal practices for speed, the governor had illegally extorted a confession from the accused. As a result the Council first ordered Benavides to pay the expenses of sending Nieto to Cádiz and of returning him to Saint Augustine. Then, on second consideration, it relented. Benavides had obviously acted in good faith; forcing him to pay Nieto's expenses was too harsh a punishment. The governor's real fault, explained the report of the Council, lay in his complete ignorance "of the methods and the common legal practices of the day." He clearly needed a legal counsel. In the end the Council ordered Benavides to recover the five hundred pesos paid to the informer from the royal treasury. Then, in order to insure proper handling of criminal cases in the future, he was to remit all litigations to Havana for review by legal authorities there. Such action, it was hoped, would prevent recurrence of the legal complications involved in the Nieto case.[7]

All these events overshadowed the *visita* of Ponce, who uncovered no shocking scandals and proposed no sweeping reforms as a result of his investigation. Royal policy toward Florida remained unchanged. Benavides remained in the governorship fourteen years after Ponce left the colony; no significant changes occurred. Ponce's visitation had accomplished little, and as a force to insure efficient honest government, the *visita* failed. Its sole effect was the loss of the governor's judicial

6. AGI, Escribanía de Cámara, Legajo 153A. Carta del gobernador de la Florida al rey, Aug. 23, 1721.

7. AGI, Escribanía de Cámara, Legajo 153A. Papel del fiscal, Nov. 21, 1721. AGI, Santo Domingo, Legajo 833. Consulta del Consejo de las Indias, Nov. 28, 1721.

authority to experts in Cuba, but for this the visitor was only indirectly responsible.

A second special check on colonial officials was the *pesquisa*, the secret probe of a given province or official. In 1736 the king called for a *pesquisa* to investigate Francisco del Moral Sánchez, appointed to the governorship in 1734 and suspected of abuse of office. In Moral's case a secret investigation was imperative. An official *visitador* would only serve to put the governor on his guard; an unsuspected secret agent, however, could work more effectively and achieve more reliable results. As *pesquisador* the governor of Cuba, Francisco de Güemes y Horcasitas, appointed the Cuban engineer Antonio de Arredondo. Ostensibly he was sent to Florida to confer with the governor of Georgia, James Oglethorpe, concerning a border dispute. This, it was hoped, would disguise Arredondo's real intentions and allow him to survey conditions in Florida without arousing Moral's suspicions.[8]

Arredondo obtained strong evidence of Moral's corruption and misrule. Effectively masking his real aims from the governor, he took secret testimony from soldiers at Fort San Marcos, from friars in the Franciscan convent, and from residents of Saint Augustine. Their statements and Arredondo's own observations bore out the rumors concerning Moral's conduct in office and were decisive in convincing Governor Güemes of Moral's guilt.[9] Ultimately, the engineer's report paved the way for the governor's ouster in 1737 and formed the basis of later charges against Moral.[10]

In 1759 still a third special procedure was called into play to restrain the governor at Saint Augustine. When Floridians hurled charges of incompetence and inefficiency at Governor Lucas Fernando de Palacio, Charles III considered them serious enough to warrant investigation, yet they were not worth the expense of either a *visita* or a *pesquisa*. The king believed that a permanent resident of Florida could report on conditions there as well as a *visitador* or *pesquisador*.[11] To secure this

8. John Tate Lanning, *The Diplomatic History of Georgia* (Chapel Hill, 1936), pp. 45-46. This passage describes Arredondo's diplomatic mission. AGI, Santo Domingo, Legajo 2541. Carta del gobernador de Cuba al rey, Oct. 27, 1736. This document points out that Arredondo was serving as *pesquisador*.

9. AGI, Santo Domingo, Legajo 862. Testimony taken by Arredondo is contained in documents for the months of September and October, 1736. See, for example, Certificación de Fray Joseph de Florez Rubio, Oct. 16, 1736.

10. AGI, Santo Domingo, Legajo 862. Carta del gobernador de Cuba al rey, Nov. 27, 1736.

11. AGI, Santo Domingo, Legajo 2584. Informe de Juan Joseph Solana, April 22,

information, the king and the Council of the Indies chose the curate of
the Saint Augustine church, Juan Joseph Solana, who had already submitted an unsolicited report suggesting reforms for the province.[12]

Solana did not procrastinate, and within six months after he received
his charge, he had completed his investigation. Highly critical of
Governor Palacio, Solana pointed out that the governor had sold
the office of public secretary (again a knotty problem) for one hundred
pesos instead of the three hundred pesos required under the law. He
had levied an unduly severe tax of fifteen pesos on local shopkeepers and
tavern owners, who had paid only five pesos in the past. He had mis-
treated one hundred forced laborers and had wasted lime and stones for
a new defense line near Saint Augustine. In his dealings with the
Indians Palacio had antagonized the Caveta chief, Lagiche, by
refusing to allow the Cavetas to trade within the walls of Saint
Augustine. Then, after salving the chief's feelings with peace offerings
of rum, the governor had changed his mind and allowed the Indians to
enter the Florida capital. Those savages who staggered into town
presented a "disgusting spectacle" for which Solana held Palacio
personally responsible. In a general condemnation of the governor,
Solana asserted that Palacio lacked judgment and tact and that he
pursued a policy of "general tyranny."[13]

Despite the fact that Solana obviously bore a strong personal grudge
against the governor, the king and the Council of the Indies accepted
the curate's report. Acting to check the "general tyranny" described by
Solana, the king issued a *cédula* on February 23, 1761, providing for a
town council in Saint Augustine.[14] This, it was hoped, would check the
tendency toward arbitrary, one-man rule in Florida and divide the
governor's administrative responsibility. Ultimately, however, this
move failed. First, the interim governor Alonso de Cárdenas declared
there were no qualified persons available to sit on the *cabildo*. Then,
in 1763 Florida became a British province before the royal *cédula*
establishing the town council could be put into effect.

1759. See also Charles W. Arnade, "The Architecture of Spanish St. Augustine," *The
Americas*, XVIII (Oct. 1961), 155-161.

12. AGI, Santo Domingo, Legajo 2584. Carta del Juan Joseph Solana (cura vicar)
a don Julián de Arriaga, April 9, 1760.

13. AGI, Santo Domingo, Legajo 2584. Carta de Juan Joseph Solana al rey, Aug.
12, 1760.

14. AGI, Santo Domingo, Legajo 2581. Real cédula, El Pardo, Feb. 23, 1761.

[*Specific Checks on the Governor: The* Residencia]

The *visita, pesquisa,* or unofficial report on colonial conditions were designed to stop abuses among colonial officials, but these procedures were instituted only in exceptional cases. In Florida none of the three was a normal practice. No *visitador* or *pesquisador* visited Saint Augustine regularly; they came only in cases of flagrant gubernatorial misconduct. There was, however, a check binding all governors, no matter how competent, scrupulous, or high-minded. This was the *residencia,* the judicial review of the administrator who had completed his term in office.

Procedure for the *residencia* was rigidly set by royal statutes. No official could leave the area under his jurisdiction until a royal commissioner *(juez de residencia)* had carried out a complete investigation of his administration and taken extensive testimony from a wide sampling of colonists. All colonials had the right to bear witness against the outgoing official, a privilege also enjoyed by the Indians. The law also provided for a *residenciado,* a defense attorney to insure the rights of the official being investigated. For a governor no *residencia* could last more than sixty days. After all the evidence was compiled, the commissioner and the incoming administrator reviewed the completed file of documents and passed judgment on the departing official. It was conceivable but highly unlikely that they would find him innocent, since to do so would indicate their own lack of perspicacity and inability to ferret out the real facts of the case. They then passed sentence, either a fine, imprisonment, confiscation of property, demotion in rank, or a combination of all four. But execution of the sentence depended, in the end, upon the Council of the Indies, which reviewed all *residencia* papers and could demand a stiffer penalty, mitigate the sentence, or exonerate the official completely.[15]

Theoretically the *residencia* operated as a significant check on colonial officials. They knew that sooner or later they would get their just due, that those whom they had abused or exploited would have their turn to get final revenge. They realized that they must rule temperately within the law and for the benefit of the colonists (not always the same) to avoid being entangled in a web of charges at the close of their tenure. In addition the *residencia* ostensibly protected the king and his subjects from misgovernment, arbitrary rule, immorality, and abusive conduct on

15. *Recopilación de las Indias,* Lib. 5, tít. 15. See also, Haring, *Spanish Empire,* pp. 148-153.

the part of powerful colonial administrators and insured that justice would triumph in the end.[16]

But this seemingly strong check on colonial officialdom did not always serve its intended purpose, particularly in eighteenth-century Florida. Eight of ten governors subject to the *residencia* managed to avoid it altogether. Only Governor Joseph de Zúñiga y Cerda and Governor Francisco del Moral Sánchez had to face a *residencia*, and analysis of both cases indicates that although it was a bothersome practice it was an ineffectual check, hardly an institution promoting honest, loyal government.

[*A Case Study: The* Residencia *of Governor Joseph Zúñiga y Cerda*]

Joseph de Zúñiga y Cerda governed during the early years of Queen Anne's War, one of the most chaotic periods in the history of Spanish Florida. For a time it looked as if Spain would lose its precarious foothold in the Southeast to English and Indian invaders, but Governor Zúñiga successfully led his 1,600 colonists through the most perilous days of the war. He managed both to beat back the enemy and to prevent disease and starvation from decimating the colony. In fact, the king gave him special commendation for his efforts during the critical siege of Saint Augustine in 1702.[17] Then in 1704 the governor received an even more concrete reward. In recognition of his valorous and distinguished service, Zúñiga was appointed to the governorship of Cartagena.

Like most governors Zúñiga was eager to leave Florida, but he could not take his post on the Caribbean until he had faced a *residencia*. A royal *cédula* of February, 1703, had already set up machinery for it by appointing the public secretary in Saint Augustine as *juez de residencia*.[18] For the first time the commissioner was to come from Florida rather than from Cuba in order to save travel costs and to avoid the dangers of a wartime sea voyage.[19] Once the new governor arrived, the required judicial review could begin immediately, and Zúñiga could leave for Cartagena without a long delay.

The *cédula*, however, reached Florida in 1704, two years before

16. Haring, *Spanish Empire*, p. 152.

17. AGI, Santo Domingo, Legajo 858. Real cédula de gracias, Madrid, Oct. 5, 1703.

18. AGI, Santo Domingo, Legajo 858. Real cédula, Madrid, Feb. 10, 1703.

19. AGI, Santo Domingo, Legajo 858. Despacho del rey al gobernador de la Florida, April 28, 1703.

Zúñiga's replacement reached Saint Augustine. When Governor Francisco de Córcoles y Martínez took office in 1706, he either forgot the royal order or, more probably, ignored it. With Zúñiga anxious to leave for his new post and Córcoles eager to assume his new responsibilities, neither evidently wanted to bother with a time-consuming *residencia*. Quickly investing Córcoles with the governorship, Zúñiga sailed for Cuba on the same ship that had brought his successor to Saint Augustine. With the *cédula* of 1703 lying neglected in his gubernatorial files, Córcoles turned to the pressing problems of his colony, probably hoping the entire matter of the *residencia* was closed.

This attempt to avoid the *residencia* requirement failed. Refusing to let Zúñiga and Córcoles make a mockery of royal law, the newly crowned Philip V demanded a review of Zúñiga's administration, despite the fact the former governor had departed for Cartagena.[20] In Florida, however, Córcoles refused to act and frankly told his superiors that he was too busy fighting hostile Indians to be bothered with a troublesome *residencia*.[21] But this candid reply only convinced the king and the Council of the Indies of Córcoles' arrogance, and they sternly ordered him to set up the machinery for the *residencia* without further delay.[22] Reluctantly Córcoles appointed the constable Juan Ruiz to act as *juez de residencia*, and on January 12, 1707, posted notices in five conspicuous spots in Saint Augustine, announcing *residencia* hearings.[23]

The constable posed thirty-three questions concerning Zúñiga's administration. Had the former governor obeyed royal law? Had he played favorites in making appointments? Had he administered justice fairly? Had he collected fines properly and deposited the money in the public treasury? Had he seduced married women whose husbands were away fighting the English and the Indians, and had he fathered the child of an attractive mulatto woman in Saint Augustine? Had he sold pole wood allocated for the defenses of the Florida capital? Other questions concerned treatment of the Indians, handling of supplies for the garrison at Fort San Marcos, illegal trade practices, conduct during

20. AGI, Santo Domingo, Legajo 858. Carta del gobernador de la Florida al rey, Sept. 30, 1706.
21. AGI, Santo Domingo, Legajo 841. Certificación por escribano público sobre las causas que han vistos para no haber entrado a tomar la residencia, Sept. 20, 1706.
22. AGI, Santo Domingo, Legajo 841. Carta del gobernador de la Florida al rey, Nov. 30, 1707.
23. AGI, Santo Domingo, Legajo 858. Residencia de don Joseph de Zúñiga y Cerda: año de 1707. Quaderno 2.

the siege of 1702, the care of the poor and the needy, attention to defense, and his other activities as governor.[24]

The witnesses who appeared before Ruiz told different stories. Some had no answer for the constable's thirty-three questions and indicated they had no way of ascertaining the facts. Others were less restrained, despite the fact they had little evidence on which to base their statements. From gossip or hearsay many witnesses glibly substantiated the tales of Zúñiga's amorous adventures that had been circulating in the colony. Invariably, however, those testifying gave conflicting versions or disagreed on minor points that could have built a strong case against the governor.

A convincing defense of Zúñiga by his *residenciado*, Bernardo Nieto Carbajal, only added to the confusing maze of claims and counterclaims. Nieto pointed out—with supporting testimony—that the governor had administered justice fairly, punishing all criminal offenses in accordance with the law, even to the point of exiling one resident found guilty of stealing flour and bacon from a royal warehouse. Zúñiga, argued Nieto, had always provided for his colonists, although at critical times it had been necessary to trade illicitly to keep his province from perishing. Supply ships had been delayed as long as eighteen months, and then when a supply vessel finally put in at Saint Augustine, the food on board proved to be inedible, "putrefied with cockroaches." If Zúñiga was guilty of obtaining supplies illegally, his acts were necessary to keep the Floridians alive. In addition, the governor had attended to widows and orphans (a chronic problem), and despite lack of funds, had strengthened the fortifications of Saint Augustine. He had treated the clergy "with courtesy, benevolence, and attention" and had maintained high morale among the residents of Saint Augustine huddled beneath the walls of Fort San Marcos during the siege of 1702. Faithful to his instructions, the governor had made a personal visitation of Guale and had dispatched a lieutenant to Apalache to make a similar inspection there. Zúñiga had also taken the *residencia* of his predecessor, Laureano de Torres y Ayala.[25]

If Nieto's defense was persuasive, it was not persuasive enough to bring about Zúñiga's exoneration. From the testimony taken in the colony and from the *residenciado's* statements and counter-testimony,

24. AGI, Santo Domingo, Legajo 858. Residencia de don Joseph de Zúñiga y Cerda: año de 1707. Quaderno 2.

25. AGI, Santo Domingo, Legajo 858. Defensa del gobernador don Joseph de Zúñiga y Cerda por capitán Bernardo Nieto de Carbajal, Feb., 1707.

Ruiz drew up eleven charges. First, in a case involving a Negro slave who had murdered an Apalache Indian, the governor had assessed a fine of thirty pesos rather than administering corporal punishment as required by law. Then, instead of depositing the thirty pesos in the treasury, the governor had given the money to the chaplain of Fort San Marcos to say Mass for the dead Indian and his assailant (who had died in the meantime).[26] Another charge involved the infantry squad captain, Juan Lorenzo, who had whipped his wild thirteen-year-old daughter Marianna and put irons on her feet. As punishment Zúñiga fined Lorenzo and placed Marianna in a foster home. The governor, claimed the punctilious Ruiz, was at fault for not imprisoning the squad captain as prescribed by law.[27]

The remaining charges covered a wide range of activities. Disgracing his office, Zúñiga had carried on lurid affairs with various women in Saint Augustine in a manner somewhat resembling David's affair with Bathsheba. Zúñiga had not punished certain "public sins" such as drunkenness, indecent dancing, and adultery, which had appreciably lowered moral standards in the colony. In Indian affairs his abuse of Lorenzo de Santiago, chief of the Tama, had caused the defection of that tribe. At the same time Zúñiga had neglected to keep the weapons of his soldiers clean and in good repair and had provided the garrison with wet powder and useless supplies. Buildings, bridges, and earthwork defenses had deteriorated during his tenure in office, and he had not taken proper precautions to prevent the loss of two supply ships to four English men-of-war that entered the Saint Augustine harbor in 1702. Tempestuous Marianna figured in still another charge when she fled her foster home to seek new thrills in English Charleston; Ruiz held the governor responsible for her flight. Finally, the meticulous *juez de residencia* charged Zúñiga with illicit trading and with showing favoritism toward a certain Captain Lorenzo Arias.[28]

His task completed, Ruiz submitted the eleven charges to Governor Córcoles for review and sentence. After consideration of the documents the governor found Zúñiga guilty of all but three charges—those

26. AGI, Santo Domingo, Legajo 841. Sentencia de la residencia se tomó a el Maestro del Campo General Don Joseph de Zúñiga y Cerda, Gobernador y Capitán General de las Provincias de San Agustín de la Florida, Aug. 1, 1710.

27. AGI, Santo Domingo, Legajo 858. Auto sobre los grillos de la hija de Juan Lorenzo, June 22, 1705.

28. AGI, Santo Domingo, Legajo 841. Sentencia de la residencia se tomó a el Maestro del Campo General Don Joseph de Zúñiga y Cerda, Gobernador y Capitán General de las Provincias de San Agustín de la Florida, Aug. 1, 1710.

involving the Tama Indian chief, Zúñiga's alleged adultery with the women of Saint Augustine, and his handling of "public sins." On the other eight Córcoles was convinced of Zúñiga's guilt and levied a total fine of 1,104 pesos 4 reales. The largest assessment, 500 pesos, was for furnishing wet powder and bad-quality supplies to his soldiers; the smallest, 27 pesos, was for his action in the Apalache Indian murder case.[29]

With the review completed in Florida, Zúñiga's fate lay in the hands of the Council of the Indies, but this body could not act immediately. Claiming that no ships called at Saint Augustine to carry the documents back to Spain, Córcoles kept the *residencia* files in Florida a year and a half after he had pronounced sentence.[30] It was not until late in 1708 that he sent the trunk of papers to Havana, where a ship might be more easily found to take the papers to Cádiz.[31] But even in this busy seaport there was some delay, and it was not until July, 1710, that the *residencia* files reached the Council tables.[32]

Review of his case in Spain proved advantageous to Zúñiga. After examining the testimony, the Council rejected the findings of Ruiz and Córcoles, absolved Zúñiga of guilt on all eleven counts, and reduced his fine to one hundred pesos, probably a token payment to help defray the costs of his case.[33] This decision might have ended the matter once and for all, but like most Spanish officials, Zúñiga was jealous of his honor and reputation.[34] Exoneration by the Council of the Indies was not sufficient vindication. Córcoles and Ruiz had tarnished his good name, and he meant to get revenge on them. He therefore embarked upon a rigorous campaign to malign Córcoles and to bring him under royal suspicion. In an acrimonious letter to Philip V, Zúñiga pointed out that

29. AGI, Santo Domingo, Legajo 841. Sentencia de la residencia se tomó a el Maestro del Campo General Don Joseph de Zúñiga y Cerda, Gobernador y Capitán General de las Provincias de San Agustín de la Florida, Aug. 1, 1710.

30. AGI, Santo Domingo, Legajo 858. Carta del gobernador de la Florida al rey, Jan. 8, 1708. Carta del gobernador de la Florida al rey, April 18, 1708.

31. AGI, Santo Domingo, Legajo 858. Carta del gobernador de la Florida al rey, December 12, 1708.

32. The *residencia* documents arrived in Spain early in July in the care of a certain Agustín de Jevallos.

33. AGI, Santo Domingo, Legajo 841. Sentencia de la residencia se tomó a el Maestro del Campo General Don Joseph de Zúñiga y Cerda, Gobernador y Capitán General de las Provincias de San Agustín de la Florida, Aug. 1, 1710.

34. For most Spaniards, states Pedro Calderón de la Barca in his play, *The Mayor of Zalamea*, "honour is the patrimony of the soul." Certainly Zúñiga meant to protect his honor and his reputation. See Salvador de Madariaga, *Spain* (London, 1931), pp. 48-49.

his successor had misappropriated subsidy money and had become personally rich through peculation and graft. Florida, claimed Zúñiga from his post far away in Cartagena, had fallen into a lamentable state because of Córcoles' mismanagement of the annual subsidy.[35]

Initially Zúñiga was successful in persuading his superiors of the ineptness and corruption of the Florida governor. In fact soon after the Council received Zúñiga's report, it recommended to Philip V that Córcoles be relieved and that his administration be carefully investigated.[36] Shortly afterwards, however, a closer look at Zúñiga's charges indicated that no irregularities had occurred in Florida. A legal adviser for the Council painstakingly audited all Florida accounts for the years 1706 to 1710 and found them in perfect order. Even for the year 1709, on which the former governor's accusations had centered, the accounts showed no discrepancies. Moreover, the report of the legal adviser pointed out that Córcoles had provided for the defense and welfare of the colony and was a model of gubernatorial virtue.[37] Córcoles thus lingered in office until 1716 without any further encounters with his superiors in Spain; Zúñiga, serving in Cartagena, was unsuccessful in getting revenge on his successor for besmirching his reputation.

[A Case Study: The Residencia of Governor Francisco del Moral Sánchez]

No governor of Florida during the eighteenth century held out more promise than Francisco del Moral Sánchez, yet none created more problems and unrest. An appointee of the governor of Cuba, Moral obtained his post on the strength of thirty years of outstanding military service on the island. As an army officer he had demonstrated those qualities essential to success in Florida—loyalty, initiative, and ability to command—and these qualities won him the governorship. During his first few months in office, he seemed to bear out the governor of Cuba's high estimate of his talents. Moral's proposals for the development of pearl fishing, silver mining, farming, and shipbuilding all showed an enthusiastic concern for the economic future of Florida. In a strong letter to Philip V he asked for a number of hard-working Spanish immigrants who would be willing to bend their efforts to these new enter-

35. AGI, Santo Domingo, Legajo 836. Consulta del Consejo de las Indias, Aug. 17, 1713. This document discusses Zúñiga's charges against Benavides.

36. AGI, Santo Domingo, Legajo 836. Consulta del Consejo de las Indias, Aug. 17, 1713.

37. AGI, Santo Domingo, Legajo 836. Consulta del Consejo de las Indias, Sept. 22, 1713.

prises and revive the colony. In his view immigrants would stop the expansion of the "ambitious and covetous" English settlers in the Southeast and pave the way for a renewal of mission work among the Indians.[38]

These early proposals gave Moral's superiors confidence that the Cuban governor had made an able choice, but later reports from the colony changed this view. In May, 1735, the treasurer and the accountant at Saint Augustine accused Moral of abusing his office. The governor, they stated vaguely, burned with "the fire of insatiable avarice."[39] Another report from a Franciscan friar, Pablo Rodríguez, accused Moral of slighting the Indians of Palica and of alienating their chief by cutting off their supplies.[40] An infantry officer, Lamberto Benedit Horruitiner, charged Moral with beginning an illicit trade with the English.[41] Seven Franciscans bore out this accusation when they indicated that only English goods could be purchased in the shops of Saint Augustine.[42] Compounding the offense, Moral had evidently allowed Englishmen to walk about the town freely, surveying the fortifications and spreading Protestant heresies. At the same time, Moral was himself selling English goods at high profits.[43] But this was not all.   He had evidently neglected the garrison in Apalache,[44] was misappropriating funds from the annual subsidy,[45] and had failed to stop the erection of an English blockhouse on San Juan Island twelve leagues north of Saint Augustine.[46] He was abusing the auxiliary bishop, recently assigned to Florida, and took sides in a quarrel between the Creole and Spanish Franciscans, rather than maintaining a dis-

38. AGI, Santo Domingo, Legajo 2541. Carta del gobernador de la Florida al rey, Aug. 31, 1734.

39. AGI, Santo Domingo, Legajo 862. Copia de la carta de los officiales reales al gobernador de Vera Cruz (Benavides), May 23, 1735.

40. AGI, Santo Domingo, Legajo 862. Copia de la carta de Fray Pablo Rodríguez al gobernador de Vera Cruz, April 14, 1735.

41. AGI, Santo Domingo, Legajo 862. Copia de la carta de Lamberto Benedit Horruitiner al gobernador de Vera Cruz, April 18, 1735.

42. AGI, Santo Domingo, Legajo 862. Copia de la carta de los capellanes (7) de la Florida al gobernador de Vera Cruz, May 17, 1735.

43. AGI, Santo Domingo, Legajo 862. Carta de los oficiales reales de la Florida al rey, Oct. 12, 1735.

44. AGI, Santo Domingo, Legajo 862. Copia de la carta de Ignacio Rodríguez Rozo al gobernador de Vera Cruz, May 3, 1735.

45. AGI, Santo Domingo, Legajo 837. Copias de cartas escritas en derechura a S. M. por los oficiales reales y otros sujetos de presidio de San Agustín de la Florida, Oct., 1735.

46. AGI, Santo Domingo, Legajo 862. Certificación de Fray Francisco Gómez, predicador misionero de la Florida y comisario provincial, Oct. 7, 1736.

passionate, Olympian position implicit in his office as royal vice patron of the church.[47]

In 1736 Moral's position grew weaker, when, in his desperation to stay in power he made arbitrary arrests of key citizens who opposed his regime in Florida. The governor first seized Felipe de Iturrieta, commander of a Cuban infantry company on detached service in Florida. According to Moral, the Cuban officer had willfully disregarded his orders and urged all Cuban soldiers to ignore the governor's commands that they take their turn at guard duty alongside the Florida regulars.[48]

In a second case Moral impulsively arrested the able soldier Sebastián López de Toledo. One night in the spring of 1736 the governor and eight grenadiers were making a late-evening inspection of Saint Augustine when they encountered López heading toward the Franciscan convent. Moral stopped the officer and demanded to know why López walked the streets so late in the evening. The soldier replied with some irritation that he was on his way to talk with his son, a friar in the convent, in the hope that he could convince him to resolve the unhealthy quarrel between the Creole and Spanish Franciscans. At this the governor may have colored, for he had already become deeply involved on the Creole side. In any event Moral told López sharply not to meddle in business that did not concern him. The officer replied angrily that the welfare of his son assuredly was his business. Besides, as royal vice patron of the church, Moral should have settled the controversy long ago. This impudence was more than the governor could take. In a fury he ordered his eight grenadiers to seize López and place him under arrest.[49]

In still another case Moral clashed with his sergeant major, Ignacio Rodríguez Rozo. Rumor had reached the governor that his second-in-command had been critical of gubernatorial policies and was conspiring to overthrow Moral. Deciding to approach his aide directly, the governor confronted him with the rumor and asked Rodríguez how he would change these policies. If possible, stated Moral sweetly, he would redress any legitimate grievance. Rodríguez retorted curtly that

47. AGI, Santo Domingo, Legajo 862. Carta de los oficiales reales de la Florida al rey, Oct. 12, 1735.

48. AGI, Escribanía de Cámara, Legajo 157B. Testimonio de los autos que don Francisco del Moral formó contra el capitán de granaderos, Don Phelipe Iturrieta: año de 1737. AGI, Santo Domingo, Legajo 2541. Carta del capitán de granaderos, don Phelipe de Iturrieta al gobernador de Cuba, Aug. 28, 1736.

49. AGI, Escribanía de Cámara, Legajo 157B. Testigo de don Antonio Eligio de la Puente, n.d.

he had no grievances. Again the governor repeated his question and again Rodríguez came back with the same reply. Moral, who probably hoped to get his sergeant major to reveal facts concerning a possible conspiracy against him, became angry and seized Rodríguez on the charge of treason. Five other arrests followed a similar pattern, keeping the Saint Augustine jail well filled with colonial dignitaries.[50]

The steady stream of reports concerning Moral's abuse of office was decisive in spurring his superiors to action.[51] In April, 1736, convinced of the governor's guilt, Philip V ordered the governor of Cuba, Francisco Güemes y Horcasitas, to replace Moral immediately. Removing all obstacles to quick action, the king sent a blank dispatch of title to Havana affixed with the proper seals and the royal signature. All Güemes had to do was name a replacement.[52] The king also ordered the Cuban governor to make a complete investigation of Moral's administration and send his report to Spain immediately.[53]

Colonial officials always exercised a great deal of personal discretion in carrying out the king's commands. In naming a successor for Moral, Güemes followed his own pattern. Rather than appoint a replacement immediately, he decided to proceed first with the investigation of Moral's administration. Then, if the facts warranted, he would name a successor.[54] To secure this evidence, he appointed the engineer Antonio de Arredondo as *pesquisador*.[55] Güemes also took steps to placate his superiors in Spain. He stated in a letter to them that he had delayed naming Moral's successor until he received reports from Arredondo, Iturrieta, and Auxiliary Bishop Francisco de San Buenaventura. This, declared the governor, would prevent any injustice to the Florida governor who might be innocent of the charges being made against

50. AGI, Escribanía, de Cámara, Legajo 157B. Testigo de la secreta del capitán de infantería, don Diego Pablo de Escobar, n.d.

51. Apparently Moral imposed a rigid censorship on communications leaving Saint Augustine. The early reports of his misrule came principally from Vera Cruz, where Benavides, the ex-governor, built up a lengthy file of accusing letters. He probably obtained them from the *situadista*, the agent sent from Florida to obtain the annual subsidy. See AGI, Santo Domingo, Legajo 847. Copia de la carta del gobernador de Vera Cruz al virrey de Nueva España, Jan. 16, 1736. AGI, Santo Domingo, Legajo 862. Extracto de los excesos que cometé el gobernador de la Florida, que se remitió al gobernador de la Havana y corregidor de Vera Cruz, para que informen de ellos en justificación, May 13, 1736.

52. AGI, Santo Domingo, Legajo 2541. Carta del gobernador de Cuba al rey, Oct. 22, 1736.

53. AGI, Santo Domingo, Legajo 862. Real cédula, Aranjuez, May 13, 1736.

54. AGI, Santo Domingo, Legajo 2541. Carta del gobernador de Cuba al rey, Oct. 22, 1736.

55. See p. 37.

him.[56] Güemes was also careful to point out that he was maintaining the status quo in Saint Augustine until completion of his probe and that he had already denied Moral's request for reinforcements and forced laborers.[57]

Upon his return to Cuba late in November, 1736, Arredondo confirmed the rumors concerning Moral's conduct in Florida. The engineer had uncovered evidence of fraud, peculation, favoritism, and flagrant disobedience of royal law on the part of the governor. Güemes was astounded at Arredondo's findings. In a strong letter to authorities in Spain he wrote there were "such scandalous excesses in the manner of living of that governor, that they [the residents of Saint Augustine] have no decent words with which to describe them." The imprisonment of Felipe Iturrieta was particularly distressing to Güemes, who trusted the Cuban officer implicitly as a "man of honor" and "distinguished character." That Moral could throw this loyal subject in prison for treason was inconceivable to Güemes.[58]

While the web of incriminating evidence against Moral grew, he frantically sought to maintain his precarious position. Desperately he cast about for allies to support him in the governorship. He had already won over the Creoles in the Franciscan order by taking their side in a fight with the Spanish Franciscans and by giving the Creole friars complete control of the religious subsidy. In return for these favors, the Creoles had extolled Moral's virtues in letters to his Spanish superiors.[59] In Apalache Moral found a champion in the chaplain of the garrison at Fort San Marcos who claimed that Moral's generosity could not be surpassed. Apalache, stated the cleric, had never experienced a food shortage or been neglected as Moral's opponents claimed.[60]

Moral was also active in his own defense. In his correspondence with the king and the Council of the Indies, he described a nepotistical chain of fathers, sons, brothers, uncles, and nephews combining with the

56. AGI, Santo Domingo, Legajo 2541. Carta del gobernador de Cuba al rey, Oct. 22, 1736.

57. AGI, Santo Domingo, Legajo 2541. Carta del gobernador de Cuba al rey, Oct. 22, 1736. The Cuban governor seemed at first reluctant to believe Moral guilty of the charges being made against him. Iturrieta's arrest was crucial, however.

58. AGI, Santo Domingo, Legajo 862. Carta del gobernador de Cuba al rey, Nov. 27, 1736. One month later Güemes' attitude had changed completely. With Arredondo's reports before him, he had become convinced of Moral's guilt.

59. AGI, Escribanía de Cámara, Legajo 157B. Carta de los religiosos de San Francisco de la Florida (18) al Audiencia de Santo Domingo, Dec. 20, 1736.

60. AGI, Escribanía de Cámara, Legajo 157C. Carta del capellan de San Marcos de Apalache a la Audiencia de Santo Domingo, Dec. 20, 1736.

auxiliary bishop and a scheming band of Spanish friars in a conspiracy against him. He had also been beset by problems over which he had no control. Surely, he claimed with some justice, the colonists could not blame him personally for the non-arrival of the subsidy ship in 1735, the cause of most of his troubles. If he had obtained supplies from English traders, he had done so because it was absolutely essential to keep his people from starving. Why, cried Moral, were individuals and circumstances unfairly conspiring to bring him down?[61]

His pleas for understanding and the adulatory letters of his few supporters failed to save the unfortunate governor. Arredondo's damning reports, the seizure of Iturrieta, and the stream of letters from discontented Floridians had built too strong a case against Moral. By February, 1737, the governor of Cuba had finally signed a new name in the blank dispatch of title, Joseph de Justís, a trusted soldier and former sergeant major of the garrison at Santiago.[62]

The arrival of Justís in Saint Augustine on March 11 set the stage for a major crisis in the colony. According to his instructions Justís was to present his credentials to Moral, assume the interim governorship, and send Moral to Cuba while the case was being drawn up against him. Thus, on the morning of March 12 Justís appeared before Moral requesting him to surrender his office. Moral was openly hostile. He adamantly refused to honor the new governor's dispatch of title or to hand over the keys to the fort and the town and audaciously suggested that Justís disregard his instructions and go back to Cuba where he belonged. Shocked and alarmed, Justís refused to be intimidated and reboarded his ship to lay new plans. In the meantime Moral proclaimed Justís an intruder, called the city to arms, and doubled the guard around his own residence.[63]

Justís' next move was to approach the governor as if the first incident had never occurred. Undeterred by Moral's intransigent position, the new governor went to him a second time, repeating the initial request for certification of credentials. Again the Florida governor refused, but this time he commanded his soldiers to seize Justís and to imprison him on Santa Anastasia Island, a crucial step for Moral in his shaky position. If his grenadiers carried out his orders, he could,

61. AGI, Escribanía de Cámara, Legajo 157C. Carta del gobernador de la Florida al rey, Jan. 7, 1737.

62. AGI, Santo Domingo, Legajo 2541. Carta del gobernador de Cuba al rey, May 24, 1737.

63. AGI, Santo Domingo, Legajo 862. Carta del gobernador interino de la Florida al rey, March 22, 1737.

perhaps, remain in the governorship, at least for a time. If they refused, he would be finished in Florida. In the end the regulars refused to rally to Moral's support and left Justís at large, a clear sign that Moral's fall was imminent. They did not, however, commit themselves to the new governor.

Justís had won the second round in his fight to take the governorship, but the battle was not over. He still needed military support to seize Moral and assume his new office. Although the Florida regulars refused to back the governor, they had not as yet agreed to lend their support to his Cuban replacement; and to become governor, Justís had to have help. Finally, Auxiliary Bishop Buenaventura, offered Justís a solution. He suggested that the new governor attempt to free all colonial leaders incarcerated by Moral during the purge in 1736. Respected officers like Iturrieta, Rodriguez Rozo, and López de Toledo might form a strong nucleus of support for Justís and might be useful in persuading undecided soldiers and colonists to join the new governor against Moral. Convinced that the plan was sound, Justís managed to bring the Saint Augustine jailors over to his side and to free the imprisoned officers.[64]

This move was crucial in breaking Moral's hold on Florida. By the morning of March 13 virtually the entire colony had deserted him. Moral stood practically alone against the people of Saint Augustine, the soldiers at Fort San Marcos, and the Cuban officer who had come to replace him. Still he would not give up. When Justís again demanded the keys to the fort and the town, Moral again refused, but this time he did not respond with threats or bribes. Instead, he fled to the sanctuary of the Franciscan convent, where he would be temporarily safe from his persecutors and could lay new plans. In the meantime, Justís took formal possession of the governorship from the treasurer and the accountant.[65]

With Moral still at large, Justís still had a real problem. Enjoying ecclesiastical sanctuary in the convent, Moral could not be extricated by force and might remain there permanently. There was also danger that he would escape under cover of darkness and flee to Georgia. Justís thus surrounded the convent with twenty-four grenadiers under the command of Felipe de Iturrieta, who was certain to carry out his

64. AGI, Santo Domingo, Legajo 862. Carta del gobernador interino de la Florida al rey, March 22, 1737.

65. AGI, Santo Domingo, Legajo 862. Carta del gobernador interino de la Florida al rey, March 22, 1737.

assignment with a vengeance. At the same time the new governor sent word into the convent asking Moral to give himself up. Speaking through a friar, Moral replied that Justís had misconstrued his visit to the convent. He was not seeking sanctuary, as most Floridians had assumed; he was carrying on colonial business with the Franciscans. He promised to leave but at his own good pleasure.

At this Justís lost patience. In strong terms he told Moral's spokesman that he would seize the former governor forcibly if he did not come out immediately, even if it meant violating the sanctity of the convent. He was through bickering with Moral. The Franciscan, however, was not intimidated by this threat. He asserted calmly that any attempt by the governor's soldiers to take Moral within the walls of the friary would be considered a usurpation of clerical rights and reported to authorities in Spain.

A man of action, Justís was not deterred by arguments concerning ecclesiastical rights and privileges that stood as unnecessary obstacles in the way of a solution to his problem. He meant to extricate Moral from the convent by force and announced his intention to Auxiliary Bishop Buenaventura, his ally and adviser. Fearful that such action would stir up a civil-religious controversy, the cleric rushed to the convent to begin negotiations there. After some discussion he evidently persuaded the friars (and Moral) to give in to Justís, for soon after Buenaventura's visit Moral emerged from the convent, protesting all the while that he had not sought ecclesiatical sanctuary among the Franciscans. Justís seized Moral, sequestered his papers and his property, and put him on a ship bound for Havana.[66] On June 23, 1737, after a two-month stay in a cell at Morro Castle, Moral left for Spain. Once he reached the mother country, he was thrown into Santa Catalina prison at Cádiz while a full investigation was being made of his administration.

In the Indies investigations had already begun. The governor of Cuba had appointed a three-man commission to probe Moral's rule in Florida—a judge (*oidor*) and a lawyer (*fiscal*) from the Audiencia of Santo Domingo and an accountant from Havana.[67] In Saint Augustine Manuel de Montiano, Moral's permanent replacement, was taking the

66. Justís seized 33,427 pesos worth of specie and property belonging to Moral. See AGI, Santo Domingo, Legajo 2541. Inventario de los papeles y vienes que pertenecer a Don Francisco del Moral Sánchez, March 14, 1737.

67. AGI, Santo Domingo, Legajo 862. Carta del gobernador de Cuba al rey, May 24, 1737. It appears that this commission never set foot in Florida. The case against Moral stemmed principally from the *residencia* testimony taken by Governor Manuel de Montiano.

former governor's *residencia*, based on thirty-nine questions concerning Moral's administration. Like those drawn up for Zúñiga, the queries covered all of Moral's activities as governor—Indian affairs, trade, the subsidy, the poor and needy, defense, administration of justice, and the clergy. Other questions involved Moral's personal life and the charges made by various Floridians in their letters to the king.[68] As Moral's *residenciado* Montiano chose the former governor's nephew, Romulado Ruiz del Moral, who obtained twenty-one testimonies favorable to his uncle and made an estimable defense in a seemingly hopeless case.[69]

In the end, Moral had to face eleven charges. Surprisingly none of them seemed as serious as the accusations leveled at him during his tenure as governor. Moral had mitigated fines levied by his predecessor, Antonio de Benavides. He had used 1,693 pesos in fines for other ends than those set down by the king. He had allowed the English to trade illicitly in Florida and permitted English merchants to sell their wares on the streets of Saint Augustine. In collusion with these heretical traders, he had stored supplies in his own residence, intending to sell them later for personal profit. He had arrested colonial officials without sufficient evidence and had shown favoritism by conferring the captaincy of a small brigantine on an undeserving friend. He had misappropriated 5,851 pesos from the *situado* and improperly abused the clerical privileges of Auxiliary Bishop Buenaventura. Moral had neglected 488 muskets under his care and had not handed the governorship over to Justís as the king had instructed. He had also permitted the Englishman Carlos Densi (Charles Dempsey) to travel through Florida without restraint.[70]

The case was much too serious, however, for Montiano to pass sentence. It was now a *cause célèbre*, too weighty for a man in his position to decide. Probably, too, he did not want to risk being refuted or chastised by the Council of the Indies. It was far easier to let the

68. AGI, Santo Domingo, Legajo 862. Despacho del rey al gobernador de Cuba, May 27, 1737.

69. AGI, Escribanía de Cámara, Legajo 157B. Prueba del defensor. This 816-page document is contained in the Autos de residencia tomada en virtud de reales ordenes por el señor coronel don Manuel de Montiano. Gobernador y Capitán General de esta Plaza de San Agustín de la Florida y sus provincias a Don Francisco del Moral Sánchez del tiempo que la governó.

70. An English translation of these charges appears in John Tate Lanning, "The Legend that Governor Moral Sánchez was Hanged," *Georgia Historical Quarterly*, XXXVIII (1954), 352-353. See also AGI, Escribanía de Cámara, Legajo 157B. Quaderno de comprabaciones de la residencia de Don Francisco del Moral Sánchez; año de 1738.

Council review the documents and pass sentence, especially in view of the special report being prepared by the three-man committee appointed by the governor of Cuba. By mid-1739, therefore, most of the documents had reached Spain, leaving the key to Moral's fate with the king and the Council of the Indies.

In the meantime Moral had been working feverishly to extricate himself from his uncomfortable cell in Santa Catalina prison. Initially he pressed the Council of the Indies with petitions protesting his innocence, complaining that he had been victimized by his enemies on the basis of inconclusive evidence.[71] When the Council refused to release him,[72] he tried a different tack. Near Christmas of 1739, the prison doctor, Alonso García, and a member of the Cádiz *protomedicato*,[73] López de Peralta, certified that Moral suffered piles, colic, and a periodic impediment of the urinary tract. These ailments, asserted the two physicians, would continue as long as Moral remained in his cell at Santa Catalina. In a strong recommendation (prompted perhaps by a bribe from Moral), they asked that the former governor be removed to a more salubrious environment.[74] Again the Council refused to free Moral, but in 1740 a third attempt by the former governor was more successful. In May the prison doctor reaffirmed the earlier list of complaints and added two new ones—dysentery and fever. This time the Council proved more compassionate, granting Moral permission to leave his cell in Cádiz for Madrid, where he had complete freedom as long as he remained within the confines of the Spanish capital.[75]

For Moral this was a stroke of good fortune. In Madrid he was free to work for his vindication from an extremely advantageous position. From the open files of the *residencia*, he could build a better case in his own defense by picking out inconsistencies in the testimonies

71. AGI, Santo Domingo, Legajo 862. Memorial de Moral Sánchez al Señor Presidente de Casa de Contratación de Cádiz (Francisco de Varas y Valdes), Oct. 2, 1737. AGI, Santo Domingo, Legajo 838. Carta del don Francisco de Varas y Valdes al Consejo de las Indias, October 12, 1737.

72. AGI, Santo Domingo, Legajo 833. Consulta del Consejo de las Indias, Feb. 25, 1738.

73. The *protomedicato* was a medical society of doctors established to examine and license druggists, physicians, surgeons, and bleeders. It also performed, as in this case, administrative, judicial, and scientific duties connected with medicine and medical practice.

74. AGI, Escribanía de Cámara, Legajo 157B. Certificación de Don Alonso García, Médico, y Don Roque López de Peralta, Cirjuano por el protomedicato, Dec. 20, 1739.

75. AGI, Santo Domingo, Legajo 862. Certificación de Don Alonso García, médico revalidado por el real protomedicato, May 9, 1740. Despacho del rey al Señor Don Francisco de Varas y Valdes, June 7, 1740.

taken against him. In addition, his most vociferous critics were far away in Florida or Cuba. Only their written accusations stood to bear witness against him, and Moral could easily find flaws and contradictions in this testimony. Moreover, three years had passed since Moral's removal. The heat and excitement of 1737 had waned, and the case was not likely to stimulate the interest of the Council's prosecuting attorney, who was already overburdened with legal work. With a personal stake in securing his exoneration, Moral was bound to be more enthusiastic and tenacious in dealing with the litigation.[76]

Time was also on Moral's side. Hearings dragged on over three years from February 10, 1741, until April 20, 1744, and even then the Council could reach no decision. Evidence was so contradictory and the documentation so immense that its members ultimately gave up trying to determine Moral's guilt or innocence and turned the case over to a special panel of judges for its verdict. This body acted more speedily. Within three months on July 10, 1744, the special court found Moral guilty on all eleven charges and sentenced him to four three-year tours of duty with the Spanish army, probably in an undesirable outpost in Africa. He also had to pay a fine of 2,000 pesos and the costs of his trial, which surely must have been considerable.[77]

This might have closed the whole affair, but Moral was irrepressible. Refusing to accept the court's judgment, he appealed his case to the Council of the Indies, which showed an amazing penchant for both patience and justice in agreeing to his request. For two years its lawyers again grappled with the *residencia* papers, now swollen with the record of the hearings on Moral's litigation.[78] In the end they were so overwhelmed and so confused by the mass of documents that they could make no recommendation to their superiors. On October

76. AGI, Escribanía de Cámara, Legajo 157C. *Memorial adjustado de los autos de pesquisa hechos en virtud de reales ordenes contra don Francisco del Moral Sánchez, Gobernador y Capitán General que fué de San Agustín de la Florida, en los Reynos de las Indias, desde fin de Marzo del año pasado de 1734 hasta 12 de Marzo de 1737 sobre excesos cometidos en el tiempo de su gobierno. Hecho con asistencia de las partes, y citación del señor Fiscal del Consejo, a pedimiento del expresado Don Francisco, y en virtud de Decreto del Consejo de 25 de Octubre del año pasado de 1746.* This printed document contains a brief resumé of the entire case.

77. AGI, Escribanía de Cámara, Legajo 157B. Copia de la sentencia, pronunciación, y notificaciones, Madrid, July 10, 1744.

78. AGI, Escribanía de Cámara, Legajo 157C. *Memorial ajustado de los autos de pesquisa hechose en virtud de reales ordenes contra don Francisco del Moral Sánchez . . .,* p. 5.

25, 1746, therefore, the Council ordered a printed resumé of the case in the hope of clarifying the issues and insuring justice for Moral.[79]

Once again events favored the former governor, for as it was finally printed, the resumé put him in a favorable light. Not only did the condensed version of the *residencia* fail to recapture the vehement anti-Moral tone of the original documents, but it also pictured him as a martyr, bandied about and abused by the confused machinations of Spanish justice. Moral, it appeared, had suffered greatly from the delays encountered in deciding his fate. In any event, on July 10, 1748, the Council finally handed down its decision. It absolved Moral of all guilt, granted him the right to bring suit against his accusers, and restored the property Justís had sequestered in 1737.[80] Moral's persistence had combined with the ponderous machinery of Spanish justice to exonerate the former governor and to demonstrate once again the failure of the *residencia* system.

[*The* Residencia: *A Check on the Governor?*]

Analysis of the *residencia* in eighteenth-century Florida indicates that this practice was not a significant check on colonial officials. It was effective only in so far as the fear of an investigation at the close of his administration restrained the governor and kept him from abusing his office. Otherwise, it did not achieve its purpose since most governors managed to avoid the *residencia* entirely. Probably by a mutual agreement with their successors, eight of ten governors ignored the requirement and proceeded to their new assignments without facing a *residencia*. By the time authorities in Spain became aware of this laxity, it was usually too costly or too late to bother with a judicial review of an official who had long since departed the colony. Ultimately the king stepped in to force a *residencia* in only two cases, and for both there was a special explanation. In 1706 Philip V demanded a review of Zúñiga's administration in order to assert his royal prerogatives in the Empire. As the new Bourbon king of Spain, he was eager to impose his will on his colonial subjects and to demonstrate royal supremacy over his colonial dominions. In Moral's situation, evidence of corruption

---

79. The decree of October 25, 1746, ordering the printed resumé seems strong evidence that two years of investigation had failed to establish Moral's guilt or innocence. Two years of additional hearings had evidently only confused the case further.

80. AGI, Escribanía de Cámara, Legajo 157B. Concuerdia con la sentencia de revista y pronunciación originales, July 10, 1748. For the English translation, see Lanning, "The Legend that Governor Moral Sánchez was Hanged," pp. 354-355.

and misrule was so overwhelming that the *residencia* could not have been ignored. It was absolutely necessary as part of the process of bringing the governor to justice.

Still another reason for the ineffectiveness of the *residencia* as a check on the governor was that sentences imposed on those leaving office were never carried out. Those charged and sentenced in the Indies found the Council of the Indies in Spain more lenient than their peers in the New World and were exonerated by authorities in the mother country. Both Zúñiga and Moral faced serious charges uncovered during their *residencia*, yet both were absolved of all guilt once their files reached Spain. Surely colonial officials realized that even if they had to endure an onerous investigation of their administration, they would, in the end, avoid a severe rebuke or punishment by those who counted most—the king and his Council of the Indies.

Chapter III

THE GOVERNOR
ADMINISTERS JUSTICE

The governor of Florida had many varied duties. In vital matters such as defense and military organization, his experience on the battlefields of Europe, Africa, and the Indies served him well; but for other administrative tasks he was not so well qualified. Military training simply did not equip him to assume all his responsibilities. In the administration of justice he was particularly inadequate. Acquainted only with the military style of justice, the governor had no training in civil or criminal law as practiced in civilian courts. He lived in a world where military law prevailed, where justice was both stern and simple. The complicated legalistic procedures of civilian courts were outside the governor's experience, and administration of justice ultimately proved one of his most bewildering and troublesome tasks.

[The Theory and Practice of the Administration
of Justice in Florida]

Spanish law painstakingly laid down a judicial system for the entire colonial empire. The most important judicial body in the colonies was the *audiencia*, a court of twelve judges (more or less) sitting in criminal and civil sections (*salas*). During the colonial period *audiencias* were established in Santo Domingo, Lima, Cuzco, Chile, Quito, Buenos Aires, Charcas, Caracas, New Granada, Mexico, Guatemala, Panama, Guadalajara, and Manila. These courts had original jurisdiction over the limited areas in which they sat, heard appeals from lesser colonial courts, and served as an advisory body for viceroys, captains general, and governors. Technically Florida fell under the jurisdiction of the Audiencia of Santo Domingo, but actually the legal connection was tenuous. Appeals from Saint Augustine usually went directly to the Council of the Indies in Spain, bypassing the appeals court in Santo Domingo.[1]

1. *Recopilación de las Indias*, Lib. 2, tít. 15, ley 2.

There was also provision for the administration of justice in towns, villages, and municipalities. Two magistrates *(alcaldes)* of the town council served as judges in the first hearing of both civil and criminal cases. A legal counsel *(fiscal)*, similar to the English solicitor, and a prosecuting attorney *(procurador)* drew up and tried criminal cases. A defense attorney *(defensor)* acted for the accused. Lesser functionaries such as the constable *(alguacil mayor)*, fine collector *(receptor de peñas)*, and the legal secretary *(escribano)* performed obvious tasks.[2] In addition, an assessor *(asesor)* interpreted military law and drew up cases against soldiers;[3] an auditor *(auditor de guerra)* served as a kind of provost marshal, advising local military authorities on legal questions and soldiers' rights.[4]

In Florida the judicial system bore little resemblance to that set up by royal law. In Saint Augustine there was no town council with magistrates to give first hearings on civil and criminal cases. No citizens or soldiers were qualified to fill the positions of prosecutor, defender, solicitor, assessor, or auditor, leaving the governor to provide makeshift substitutes. Usually the governor himself played the role of judge and prosecuting attorney (which surely must have given him an enviable record of convictions), and occasionally he called in a reluctant infantry, cavalry, or artillery captain to act as defense attorney. An infantry lieutenant or a squad of grenadiers served his purposes as a constable, and the public secretary—already overburdened with work—took depositions and transcribed testimony. But no substitutes were available for the assessor or the auditor, fundamental in a military outpost like Florida. These two officials absolutely required legal training, and no resident of Saint Augustine, including the governor, had even a smattering of the necessary legal experience.

This expediential arrangement for administering justice was a constant source of gubernatorial complaint. When Governor Benavides was chastised for his mishandling of the Nieto case in 1721, he argued, in his own defense, that it might not have occurred if he had had a qualified legal counsel to draw up the litigation.[5] Later, in 1728, he decried the lack of an assessor in Saint Augustine. With no one to help him in legal matters, he declared, he was bound to make judicial

2. Haring, *Spanish Empire*, pp. 162, 168.
3. *Recopilación de las Indias*, Lib. 3, tít. 11, ley 4.
4. Haring, *Spanish Empire*, p. 124.
5. AGI, Santo Domingo, Legajo 857. Carta del gobernador de la Florida al rey, March 5, 1725.

errors.[6] Eight years later Governor Moral requested an auditor for his colony. He pointed out that he had followed the practice of sending all legal documents to Cuba for review by judicial experts there, but long delays had occurred before Cuban lawyers had acted. With an auditor he could draw up the cases more speedily himself. A year later, having received no reply to his first plea, he repeated the same request with the same result.[7] In 1750 Governor Melchor de Navarrete complained that many criminals filled his jail but that he could not bring them to trial without the help of a legal adviser to draw up a formal case. His answer to this problem was to train his sergeant major, his company captains, and other military officers by holding formal classes in law at Saint Augustine. Once the course was completed, its graduates could serve as magistrates, prosecutors, defenders, and auditors and insure justice to the accused, but again nothing came of this scheme.[8]

Not all complaints came from the governor. In 1741 Philip V received an anonymous letter from a few dissatisfied residents of Saint Augustine requesting two magistrates to administer justice in Florida. These malcontents believed Governor Montiano held too much arbitrary judicial power. Two new magistrates, trained in the law, they stated, could judge more fairly. If this was not feasible, stated the residents, Florida needed at least some sort of trained legal official to curb Montiano's wide judicial powers.[9] In 1759 the bishop of Cuba complained about the same problem but on different grounds. He too deplored the lack of qualified lawyers but believed that it led to moral laxity and looseness in Saint Augustine. The governor simply left many crimes unpunished. Under the restricting arm of the magistrates of a town council or the sharp eyes of an auditor, he could properly punish all offenders and administer justice more efficiently.[10]

No amount of complaint or suggestion stirred the king or the Council into remedying the weaknesses of the Florida judicial system. No auditor, magistrate, or provost ever appeared in Saint Augustine to aid the governor in administering justice or in bringing order to the

6. AGI, Santo Domingo, Legajo 857. Carta del gobernador de la Florida al rey, Jan. 23, 1728.

7. AGI, Santo Domingo, Legajo 2541. Carta del gobernador de la Florida al rey, March 3, 1735. Carta del gobernador de la Florida al rey, April 21, 1736.

8. AGI, Santo Domingo, Legajo 2584. Carta del gobernador de la Florida al rey, July 4, 1750.

9. AGI, Santo Domingo, Legajo 2541. Carta de los vecinos de la Florida al rey, Sept. 15, 1741.

10. AGI, Santo Domingo, Legajo 2584. Carta del obispo de Cuba al rey, Oct. 8, 1759.

judicial process. No classes in law were ever set up to train officers of the Florida garrison, and they remained unschooled in legal procedures. Throughout the eighteenth century the governor himself bore the responsibility of grappling with litigation after litigation without the advice or assistance of an experienced lawyer. Blundering through most cases, the governor found it difficult to administer justice according to traditional legal procedures. For their part the king and the Council did little to relieve this situation. They seemed to find it easier to censure the governor for his blunders than to give him the assistance needed to avoid them.

[*The Governor Punishes Petty Offenders*]

The methods used by the governor to judge and punish petty criminals is not absolutely clear from the documents. For offenses like street fighting, drunkenness, or petty thievery, litigations were seldom formalized, and only a few clues are available to indicate how such cases were handled. Generally, however, it appears that the governor followed this pattern. He himself acted as the chief judicial officer and carried out a variety of tasks. He investigated the crime, took testimony from witnesses, heard the defendant, and passed judgment. If he found the accused guilty, he levied a fine, imposed a prison sentence, administered corporal punishment, condemned the offender to hard labor, or banished him from the colony. For such criminals there were no appeals, either to the Audiencia of Santo Domingo or to the Council of the Indies.[11]

This military summary court-martial was entirely compatible with the governor's experience and training. Using the military style of justice, he stayed on familiar ground where he was not likely to become confounded by civilian legal procedures. He did not have to draw up a great mass of certified documents, nor did he have to press his unwilling soldiers into service in an unfamiliar courtroom. Since trial proceedings were seldom recorded, there was little danger that the governor's superiors would question his methods or his decisions. He thus found the summary court convenient, safe, time-saving, and inexpensive. It also allowed his biases and prejudices free reign. Capriciously he could dismiss or ignore those cases and crimes involving friends and vindic-

11. Because there were no appeals from cases tried in the governor's summary court, there was no elaborate documentation submitted to higher judicial bodies from which to determine the exact methods and procedure used by the governor.

tively incriminate and condemn his enemies, although this was not common in Saint Augustine.

Evidence on the type and severity of sentences imposed on petty offenders is scanty, but it appears that each governor punished these criminals at his own discretion. Fines, for example, varied greatly from governor to governor. Between 1690 and 1707 (a period for which there are records), treasury officials collected 1,436 pesos.[12] Over two-thirds of this amount, however, was for two large fines—one for 687 pesos and the other for 372 pesos. Twelve other fines totaled only 367 pesos, an average of little more than 30 pesos per criminal or 20 pesos a year for the eighteen-year period audited.[13] On the other hand, in his three-year tenure as governor, Moral Sánchez collected 1,693 pesos, an average of 565 pesos a year.[14] This is twenty-eight times greater than the yearly average for the period 1690-1707, indicating that both the amount and the number of fines depended upon the governor in office.

To what extent the governor imposed corporal punishment, exile, or imprisonment is again not clear. Imprisonment of petty criminals evidently was rare;[15] only one such case emerges from the documents in the eighteenth century. In the fall of 1752 interim Governor Fulgencio García de Solís jailed the soldier Antonio Regidor for disturbing the peace. Don Antonio, it appears, was unhappy in Saint Augustine, frequently attempting to forget his woes in spirituous liquors. One morning, after an all-night drinking bout in which he had not successfully drowned his sorrows, he came to the gubernatorial palace, demanding loudly to see the governor. An aide, recognizing that Regidor was too inebriated to talk coherently, told the soldier that García was busy but would be glad to confer with him later. Regidor, however, refused to be put off. With vociferous "threats, words, and admonitions," he insisted on an interview. In the meantime his noisy demonstration attracted the governor's attention, and when he appeared, Regidor became violent. He first thrust his hand under his coat as if to reach for a pistol, and then, thinking better of such an act, began gesticulating obscenely toward the governor.

12. AGI, Santo Domingo, Legajo 841. Carta de los oficiales reales de la Florida al rey, Oct. 29, 1708.

13. AGI, Santo Domingo, Legajo 841. Certificación de los oficiales reales de la Florida, Oct. 13, 1708.

14. AGI, Escribanía de Cámara, Legajo 157B. Quaderno de comprobaciones de la residencia de Don Francisco del Moral Sánchez: año de 1738.

15. During his administration Moral imprisoned many colonial leaders who, he thought, were conspiring against him, but this was not a common occurrence.

García never lost his self-possession. He grabbed the drunken soldier by the shoulders and tried to induce him to stop his obscene display. At the same time the governor's aide, who had gone for help, returned with two soldiers, who promptly dragged the unfortunate Regidor to jail. Later the governor brought charges against the soldier for disorderly conduct and disturbing the peace. During the trial Regidor claimed, probably in truth, that he could not remember a single incident of the eventful morning, but a few months in the Saint Augustine jail gave him some time to reconstruct the events that led to his imprisonment.[16]

The governor also used the summary court to dispense justice to second-class citizens—Negroes, Indians, and forced laborers. Sentences imposed on second-class citizens in the summary court usually bore little relation to the crime committed. Governor Zúñiga, for example, levied a thirty-peso fine on the Negro slave, Juan Francisco del Cierro, who murdered the Apalache Indian Vicente.[17] The same governor, however, exiled a forced laborer caught stealing a bit of flour and bacon from the royal warehouses at Saint Augustine.[18] A few decades later Governor Navarrete sentenced three Negroes to three years at hard labor for petty thievery.[19] The details in these three cases are not clear, but it seems apparent that the severity of the sentence depended almost completely upon the governor's whims.

The records of still a fourth case indicate that the circumstances under which the crime was committed also determined the degree of punishment. In 1760 the forced laborer, Joseph de la Paz, murdered his Spanish overseer, Blas de Ortega, stabbing him seven times in the mouth, breast, and back during a fight at a quarry near Apalache. In this affair the governor demanded immediate retribution. Unlike the Negro slave of Zúñiga's time, Paz had killed a Spaniard with some official standing.

Justice moved swiftly. Paz confessed his crime and was sentenced to death by the governor's summary court. But on this occasion death

16. AGI, Santo Domingo, Legajo 846. Testimonio de los autos obrados contra don Antonio Regidor, Dec. 1, 1752.

17. AGI, Santo Domingo, Legajo 853. Defensa del gobernador Don Joseph de Zúñiga y Cerda por capitán Bernardo Nieto de Carvajal, Feb., 1707.

18. AGI, Santo Domingo, Legajo 841. Sentencia de la residencia se tomó a el Maestro del Campo Don Joseph de Zúñiga y Cerda, Gobernador y Capitán General de las Provincias de San Agustín de la Florida, Aug. 1, 1710.

19. AGI, Santo Domingo, Legajo 846. Carta del gobernador interino de la Florida al rey, June 16, 1753.

was not a severe enough penalty. Governor Palacio ordered Paz's head and hands severed from his body. He then commanded that the head and one hand be placed at the site of the murder to serve as a sober reminder to other forced laborers who might entertain similar ideas. The other hand was put on display at Fort San Marcos de Apalache as another grim momento of the misdeed.[20]

The summary court thus served the governor in two ways—to judge petty offenders and to deal with Negroes, forced laborers, and Indians. It was convenient and workable and enabled him to proceed in the military style with which he was familiar. It meant, however, that there was no established pattern of justice for petty criminals or second-class citizens, who were completely at the governor's mercy. He was supreme and his decisions were final; fair administration of justice depended solely upon his fancies.

[*Formalization of the Judicial Process: The Ayala-Pedroso Case*]

Spanish veneration for the spirit of the law and the sanctity of the judicial process is not apparent from the methods used to try petty offenders and second-class citizens. Judged arbitrarily and peremptorily, criminals of these types obtained justice in the military style. Occasionally, however, the governor had to use traditional civilian legal practices in drawing up a litigation, and for serious offenses involving leading Floridians he had to formalize his case. He had to tread on unfamiliar ground, where his military training and experience did not equip him adequately and where he could get no help from his advisers in Saint Augustine. Sometimes the results were disastrous, both for the governor and those charged by him.

In the eighteenth century Governor Benavides was most active in drawing up formal cases against Floridians. A vigorous, efficient man with dictatorial tendencies, he was eager to bring the colony rigidly under his personal control. To do this, he meant to purge those who, on the surface, seemed certain to oppose his policies as governor. Within ten days after his arrival in Saint Augustine in the summer of 1718, he began the expulsion. On meager evidence obtained from a few soldiers at the garrison at Fort San Marcos, Benavides indicted Joseph Pedroso, his treasurer, and Juan de Ayala Escobar, his sergeant major

20. AGI, Santo Domingo, Legajo 2584. Carta del gobernador de la Florida a don Julián de Arriaga, Aug. 4, 1760.

and the former interim governor, on charges of illicit trade and general misconduct. The governor had both men seized and sent immediately to Cuba, where they were imprisoned while their cases were being determined.[21]

Ayala and Pedroso were both taken by surprise at their sudden removal from Florida. Ayala was almost ninety years old with a long record of distinguished service in the colony. Now within three weeks he had been relegated from the governor's residence to a damp prison cell in Havana, accused by a new governor who knew little about Florida and its personnel. Besides, the indignities of a long imprisonment and trial might be more than a man of his age could bear. Pedroso was also anxious about his situation. After over three decades of military service in Saint Augustine, he had won the treasurer's post. Now after only four years in that office, he saw the office slipping from him. Angrily both Pedroso and Ayala submitted memorials to the Council of the Indies, charging Benavides with conspiring against them unfairly.[22]

In Spain the case immediately aroused the interest of the Council of the Indies. It appointed a *fiscal* to investigate the case, and he reported that the governor's accusations were "vague, general, and irregular,"[23] prompting the Council to ask the king for a complete probe of the charges.[24] Unfortunately for the two prisoners impatiently awaiting a decision, Philip V took two years to act, and it was not until December 19, 1721, that he finally ordered Juan Félix García Chicano, a Havana auditor, to go to Florida to investigate the Pedroso-Ayala litigation.[25]

Today a brief sojourn in sunny Florida might prove exceedingly attractive to an office-bound bureaucrat, but for the eighteenth-century Spanish colonial administrator, service in Saint Augustine was closely akin to service in hell. Chicano dreaded the assignment and hoped to avoid it. In his reply to the king, he asked to be relieved of his task, arguing that Benavides must be replaced before he could carry on any impartial investigation. No residents of Florida, he stated, would

21. AGI, Santo Domingo, Legajo 843. Carta del gobernador de la Florida al rey, Aug. 12, 1718.

22. AGI, Santo Domingo, Legajo 833. Consulta del Consejo de las Indias, Sept. 15, 1719.

23. AGI, Santo Domingo, Legajo 859. Dictamen del fiscal, Sept. 4, 1719.

24. AGI, Santo Domingo, Legajo 833. Consulta del Consejo de las Indias, Sept. 15, 1719.

25. AGI, Santo Domingo, Legajo 837. Despacho del rey al gobernador de Cuba, Dec. 19, 1721.

testify truthfully about the Ayala-Pedroso case because of fear of reprisals by the governor.[26]

It was not long before Chicano received a strong reply. Irked by the Cuban auditor's attempt to avoid his responsibilities, the king ordered Chicano to go to Florida "without making any further excuses whatsoever." The *cédula* of December 19, 1721, required the auditor to investigate the Ayala-Pedroso case, and as king, Philip V meant to have such commands carried out.[27] In any case the king's order evoked a meek reply from Chicano, who promised faithfully to make the voyage to Saint Augustine.[28]

For Ayala and Pedroso the long waiting period had different effects. Pedroso was at first anxious to be restored to his post in Florida. He had been charged unfairly and wanted his treasurer's job back.[29] But as the years passed, he mellowed in Cuba. He evidently came to enjoy life away from Florida and ultimately asked Philip V for a new post (hopefully at court in Spain) and the right to name his successor in Saint Augustine.[30] Ayala, on the other hand, began to fail. Although he had received permission to return to Saint Augustine, early in 1727, eight years after his banishment from Florida, he died. Whether his death came from the strain and tension caused by his exile and impending trial or from old age is a matter for conjecture. Unfortunately, the aged sergeant major had died with the stigma of the governor's accusations still upon him.

Ayala's death was crucial, for it gave Chicano still another excuse to postpone his voyage to Florida. Two years had passed since he had made his solemn promise to Philip V to investigate the Ayala-Pedroso case, but in two years he had done nothing. Now, in November, 1727, he used Ayala's death as the basis for canceling his investigation. Boldly, Chicano suggested that with Ayala dead and Pedroso too ill to resume his job as treasurer (this was probably not true), there was no need for him to go to Florida.[31] But again authorities in Spain would not be

26. AGI, Santo Domingo, Legajo 859. Carta de don Juan Félix García Chicano al rey, June 30, 1722.

27. AGI, Santo Domingo, Legajo 837. Despacho del rey a don Juan Félix García Chicano, Feb. 17, 1724.

28. AGI, Santo Domingo, Legajo 837. Carta de don Juan Félix García Chicano al rey, July 22, 1725.

29. AGI, Santo Domingo, Legajo 859. Carta de don Joseph Pedroso a Andrés Paz, June 12, 1721. Carta de don Joseph Pedroso al rey, July 12, 1721.

30. AGI, Santo Domingo, Legajo 833. Consulta del Consejo de las Indias, June 7, 1724.

31. AGI, Santo Domingo, Legajo 859. Carta de don Juan Félix García Chicano al rey, Nov. 15, 1727.

persuaded by the auditor's new proposal. In a fury the Council of the Indies ordered Chicano a third time to carry out his duties. This time it put additional pressure on him. Chicano could not assume his recently awarded judgeship on the Audiencia of Santo Domingo until he made his investigation. Ridding the auditor of still another excuse—lack of funds to make the trip—the Council awarded him 1,000 pesos to cover the costs of his voyage to Saint Augustine.[32]

These measures seemed to remove all obstacles to Chicano's investigation. He had received the funds to go to Florida and had been blocked from taking his seat on the Audiencia of Santo Domingo until he carried out the king's order. But the wily auditor had delayed just long enough. In January, 1728, Governor Benavides stepped in to ask suspension of Chicano's investigation. The governor believed that trouble would result from a probe. A smallpox epidemic had swept through Saint Augustine late in 1727, leaving three hundred dead in its wake. The coming of a royal investigator prying into an old legal matter, stated the governor, would only retard the rehabilitation of this colony and create more unrest. Candidly Benavides admitted drawing up the case against both Ayala and Pedroso without proper substantiation of the evidence. He hoped, however, that the years had dispelled the king's anger at his indiscriminate action. After all, when he charged Ayala and Pedroso in 1718, he was new in the governorship and unacquainted with established judicial practices. Pedroso, stated the repentant Benavides, should be restored to his post as treasurer immediately. He had already suffered a great deal in his eight (really ten) -year exile in Cuba.[33]

Benavides' self-effacement did not at first move the Council of the Indies. The governor had admittedly accused Ayala and Pedroso without sufficient proof. Ayala had died with the charges still hanging over him; Pedroso had already endured a humiliating ten-year banishment. Unmoved by the governor's request for suspension of Chicano's investigation, a *fiscal* for the Council advised that the Cuban auditor go to Florida immediately. Benavides' contrite plea, he stated, was not warranted.[34] A year-and-a-half later the Council concurred with the *fiscal*

32. AGI, Santo Domingo, Legajo 837. Despacho del rey a don Félix García Chicano, June 20, 1728. See also AGI, Santo Domingo, Legajo 833. Consulta del Consejo de las Indias, July 19, 1730.

33. AGI, Santo Domingo, Legajo 859. Carta del gobernador de la Florida al rey, Jan. 23, 1728.

34. AGI, Santo Domingo, Legajo 859. Dictamen del fiscal, Dec. 19, 1728.

and for the fourth time ordered Chicano to go to Saint Augustine.[35] A month later, however, for no apparent reason, the Council reversed itself and canceled the probe once and for all.[36] On March 2, 1731, the king informed Benavides of this decision,[37] and two years later ordered the viceroy of New Spain to reimburse Pedroso with full salary for the years he had spent in exile in Havana.[38] The treasurer finally returned to Florida to assume the duties he had left behind fourteen years before, ending the affair.

[*Governor Benavides Administers Justice: The Nieto-Rozo Case*]

Not long after Benavides became embroiled in the Pedroso-Ayala case, he instituted another purge by the same methods he had used previously. He indicted two long-time captains of the Florida garrison —Ignacio Rodríguez Rozo and Bernardo Nieto Carbajal on charges that on the surface seemed serious. Nieto was indicted for threatening the life of the royal visitor, Antonio Ponce de León, and on an old charge (1701) of abusing the Apalache Indians.[39] Rozo was accused of cowardice, illicit trade, and inciting a mutiny. First, as commander of one hundred soldiers sent out to rout a party of twenty to thirty Indians, he had lost six of his men unnecessarily and allowed the entire band of savages to escape when he delayed his attack. Second, Rozo had traded illicitly with English sailors and had conspired with an English sea captain to sell illegal supplies in Saint Augustine. Third, he had ordered soldiers under his command to disregard strict military discipline and to ignore existing bans on marriage with the Florida women.[40]

As part of the purge which included Ayala and Pedroso, Benavides sent Nieto and Rozo to Spain for trial and sentencing, but here the machinery of justice moved more rapidly than in the Indies. The

35. AGI, Santo Domingo, Legajo 859. Consulta del Consejo de las Indias, June 16, 1730.

36. AGI, Santo Domingo, Legajo 833. Consulta del Consejo de las Indias, July 19, 1730.

37. AGI, Santo Domingo, Legajo 837. Despacho del rey al gobernador de la Florida, March 2, 1731.

38. AGI, Santo Domingo, Legajo 837. Despacho del rey al virrey de Nueva España, Oct. 4, 1733.

39. See pp. 35-36.

40. AGI, Escribanía de Cámara, Legajo 153A, Ramo I. Consulta del Consejo de las Indias, Nov. 28, 1721. See also AGI, Escribanía de Cámara, Legajo 153A, Ramo II. Autos efectuados por Don Antonio de Benavides Gobernador de la Florida contra Don Ignacio Roso sobre la mala disposición que tubo para embarazar la entrada de Indio enemigos auxiliados de Ingleses de San Jorge en el lugar de Ayachin, n.d.

Council of the Indies immediately surveyed the documents submitted by Benavides and concluded that the governor had not used proper legal procedures in drawing up his case against Nieto and Rozo. He had not notarized the testimonies, and most of them had been reduced to vague summaries. In addition neither officer had been given a chance to testify in his own defense. The Council's first inclination was to punish Benavides by forcing him to pay the costs of sending the two soldiers to Spain and back to Florida. It finally relented, however, believing that Benavides had acted in good faith. The governor obviously lacked experience and training in judicial processes and could hardly be expected to follow standard legal procedures. Still, in order to avoid future irregularities, the Council required the governor to submit all legal documents to the governor of Cuba for review by legal authorities in Havana. They would pass on the judicial methods used in Saint Augustine and authorize appeals.[41]

After the Council had settled the matter of Benavides' handling of the Nieto-Rozo case, it turned to the matter of judging the two officers, who might still be guilty despite the governor's imprudence. The king thus ordered the two defendants back to Cuba and commanded the governor in Havana to render a verdict in their case.[42] Three years later he reached a decision. Fortified—or confused—by 626 pages of conflicting testimony, the Cuban governor found Ignacio Rodríguez Rozo innocent. He did not, however, pass judgment on Nieto. The infantry captain had died on the return voyage from Spain, and the governor did not see any need to decide Nieto's case.[43]

Rozo ultimately went back to Saint Augustine, where he resumed his duties as the senior military officer in the garrison. Benavides evidently accepted Rozo's return without argument or recriminations. When Benavides left for Cuba to undergo surgery in 1726, he appointed Rozo to the interim governorship with no apparent qualms. Later in 1727 Rozo replaced Juan de Ayala Escobar as sergeant major and served in that capacity until his altercation with Governor Moral in 1736.

41. AGI, Santo Domingo, Legajo 833. Consulta del Consejo de las Indias, Nov. 28, 1721.
42. AGI, Escribanía de Cámara, Legajo 153B, Ramo II. Carta del gobernador de Cuba al rey, June 21, 1724.
43. AGI, Escribanía de Cámara, Legajo 153B, Ramo II. Carta del gobernador de Cuba al rey, June 21, 1724.

[Governor Benavides Administers Justice:
The Primo de Rivera Case]

Benavides, it appears, intended to purge all those who might oppose him, even if this meant the use of extralegal tactics. As governor he was determined to assert his mastery in Florida and found the judicial process a convenient means by which to rid the colony of possible critics and enemies. Rigging testimony, refusing the accused a chance to defend himself, and deviating from the standard judicial procedures, he was able to eliminate potential opponents like Ayala, Pedroso, Nieto, and Rozo. All four had been influential leaders in the colony; all four were purged by the governor.

But still another antagonist remained in the colony—the cavalry captain, Joseph Primo de Rivera. Primo had come to Saint Augustine during Queen Anne's War in command of a detachment of Cuban infantrymen. At the close of the war when his men returned to Havana, he chose to stay on in Florida, where he became captain of a newly formed cavalry company. In 1720 he assumed a new post. Upon Benavides' recommendation the viceroy of New Spain appointed Primo governor of a tiny outpost on Saint Joseph's Bay between Apalache and Pensacola.

The governor apparently recommended his cavalry captain for one of two reasons. Either Primo was well-fitted for the post, or more likely, it was a move by Benavides to get rid of the able Cuban soldier. In any event, as soon as Primo assumed his post in the undermanned, ill-supplied blockhouse on the Gulf of Mexico, the governor submitted incriminating memorials to the viceroy of New Spain concerning Don Joseph. Benavides charged Primo with illicit trade, collaborating with the French at Mobile, and negligence for allowing his soldiers and forced laborers to desert their posts at Saint Joseph's.[44]

The viceroy was taken in by Benavides' charges and drew up charges against Primo. As a pretense to get him to Mexico, the viceroy sent word to Saint Joseph's that he wished to transact important business with the commandant in New Spain. Probably expecting another promotion, Primo took a small boat for Vera Cruz, but here he received a rude shock. As he debarked, the viceroy's agents seized him and threw

44. AGI, Santo Domingo, Legajo 849. Carta de Joseph Primo de Rivera al rey, May 24, 1723.

him into prison. Finally after five months the viceroy ordered him to Mexico City for trial.[45]

Early in the fall of 1723 hearings opened on Primo's case. Initially the viceroy's counsel confronted the cavalry captain with Benavides' accusations, questioning him closely concerning the three charges. Primo, however, made a convincing defense. He claimed that Benavides had based his accusations on hearsay evidence. If his soldiers and forced laborers had deserted, sickness, lack of supplies, and lack of encouragement from Saint Augustine and Mexico City had led to their failure at Saint Joseph's. The other charges, he stated, were not true. He had given long, faithful, and obedient service to both the king and the governor. The viceroy accepted this explanation and absolved Primo of the charges against him. The cavalry captain was then awarded back pay for the time he had spent in prison in New Spain and late in the fall of 1723 returned to Saint Augustine.[46] Evidently he worked his way back into the governor's good graces, for in 1726-1727 he became Benavides' choice to negotiate a boundary dispute with the English in Charleston, and he continued to be a key official in the Florida colony.

Benavides thus made a shambles of the judicial process in Florida. When he abandoned the informal summary court in favor of more formal civilian-style justice, he proved inept. Review of his methods by his superiors revealed his glaring inadequacies as a judicial officer. Benavides had submitted false evidence, reduced testimony to mere summaries, failed to allow defense witnesses, and drawn up trial documents without proper certification and notarization. At times he seemed to act in good faith and to attempt, within the limits of his experience, to draw up his cases according to established procedures, but for the most part he knowingly and deliberately abused justice to eliminate his opponents from Florida. In the end the Council of the Indies censured the governor for his shoddy practices and reduced his judicial power, yet for him it was probably worth the Council's reprimand to eliminate possible troublemakers from his colony.

[*The Governor Punishes Illicit Traders*]

Spanish law minutely regulated trade within the Empire. All goods coming into Florida, for example, had to be carried on licensed Spanish

45. AGI, Santo Domingo, Legajo 849. Carta de Joseph Primo de Rivera al rey, Oct. 16, 1723.

46. AGI, Santo Domingo, Legajo 849. Carta de Joseph Primo de Rivera al rey, Oct. 16, 1723.

ships and sold in Saint Augustine by licensed Spanish merchants. No foreign ships, no foreign goods, and no foreign merchants might enter the Florida capital. The law provided severe punishment for those who violated these prohibitions, and it was the governor's duty to enforce the law. For the most part, however, he ignored this obligation. In fact, when it became necessary to feed his needy colonists, he himself became a party to illegal commerce. Córcoles, Ayala, Benavides, Moral, Montiano, and others often sought goods from English merchants when the colony was in need. Seldom did any governor bring charges against those bringing goods into Florida illicitly. The province was too far removed from the mainstream of trade, and, like Buenos Aires, somehow had to obtain the necessities of life.

Interim Governor Fulgencio García de Solís was an exception, a rare example of one who took action against illicit traders. In April, 1753, John Hume, a Charleston sea captain, sailed his *Isabel* into Saint Augustine harbor intending to recover three of his Negro slaves. Three years earlier Hume had called at the Florida capital (probably to sell his English wares), and during his stay the three Negroes had robbed a resident of the town. Governor Navarrete had summarily condemned the trio to three years at hard labor on the fortifications of Saint Augustine. Now that they had served their sentences, Hume wanted them back.[47] As he made arrangements with the governor for their return, one of his passengers on the *Isabel*, an erstwhile French surgeon named Guillaume Ambland, disembarked and entered the town with a trunkful of choice articles to sell to the residents. While he was peddling his wares on the streets of Saint Augustine, a detachment of troops seized him and placed him in prison.[48]

Ambland had clearly disobeyed Spanish law prohibiting foreign traders in Saint Augustine, and García easily established the surgeon's guilt. Using the summary court, he first sentenced Ambland to perpetual banishment from all Spanish domains. Then the governor confiscated and sold the Frenchman's trunk of goods, realizing a profit of 1,294 pesos four reales for use in rebuilding the sea wall around Saint Augustine. Captain Hume was not involved, but García returned only one of the three Negroes. Two of the slaves had embraced Roman Catholicism during their stay in Saint Augustine and were granted their

47. AGI, Santo Domingo, Legajo 846. Carta del gobernador interino de la Florida al rey, June 16, 1754.
48. AGI, Santo Domingo, Legajo 838. Consulta del Consejo de las Indias, April 1, 1754.

freedom. The third Negro, however, either had not wanted freedom or preferred life with his old master and sailed with Hume on the *Isabel*.[49] To all these preceedings the king and the Council of the Indies gave their approval, but refused to allow the entire amount realized from the sale of Ambland's articles to be used for building the sea wall: one-sixth of the 1,294 pesos rightfully belonged to the crown, and the king insisted that this be sent to Spain immediately.[50]

[Governor Fernández de Heredia Uncovers an Illicit Trade Scandal]

Not long after the Ambland affair, another illicit trade scandal broke in Florida. Actually the affair did not directly involve any Floridians except the governor, who exercised his judicial prerogatives and tried the illicit traders in his Florida court. But it was a significant event, and Governor Fernández laid bare an illegal commercial enterprise that implicated many Cubans, including the governor in Havana.

The unlawful trade that Fernández exposed had evidently been common practice for some time. Cuban sea captains, it appears, received licenses from the governor to fish from four to six months in waters off Nova Scotia and Newfoundland. This, however, had become a cover for clandestine trade activities. Leaving Cuba with hidden cargoes of tobacco or sugar, Cuban sailors sailed for Charleston or another convenient harbor, where they exchanged their tobacco or sugar for goods likes dishes, clothes, or furniture. They then went to another out-of-the-way port. Here they sold these articles for specie. With enough time still remaining to fulfil the terms of their license, the Cuban mariners sailed north to net a few cod and returned to Havana within the time prescribed by the governor's license.

Governor Fernández revealed this practice to his superiors in Spain when he brought the Cuban Captain Blas Angel to trial in 1756. Angel was master of the schooner *Nuestra Señora de la Luz*, which left Havana in the spring with a permit from the governor of Cuba to fish for four months in vaguely defined northern waters. Before departing, however, Angel had hidden 190 bags *(zurrones)* of Cuban tobacco on board his vessel. Initially things went well for him. The Cuban captain managed to slip his cargo out of Havana and to exchange it in

49. AGI, Santo Domingo, Legajo 2530. Carta del gobernador de la Florida al virrey de Nueva España, June 16, 1753.

50. AGI, Santo Domingo, Legajo 2530. Despacho del rey al gobernador de la Florida, May 23, 1754.

Charleston for clothes, blankets, silverware, crystal, china, foodstuffs, mirrors, and other articles.[51]

All might have gone well for Angel if he had not chosen Saint Augustine as the outlet of the goods obtained in Charleston. On the surface the Florida capital seemed a perfect market—an easy voyage from the Carolinas and a town removed from the principal avenues of Spanish colonial trade where the people would welcome his niceties. But Angel did not or could not reckon with Governor Fernández. Unlike his predecessors he was not willing to ignore illicit trade activities in his colony. He had high hopes of securing a seat on the Council of the Indies and meant to adhere to the letter of the law while he was in Florida.[52] This would solidify his claims on the office and show his superiors his loyalty and talent for administration.

When the *Nuestra Señora de la Luz* and a second vessel, the *San Joseph*, appeared at the mouth of Saint Augustine Harbor, Fernández acted immediately. Concluding that the vessels contained illicit cargoes, he ordered an aide, Domingo Pérez, to take sixty men in two launches to investigate the cargoes and manifests of both ships in order to determine their reasons for entering the harbor. The ships were obviously not regularly scheduled vessels of the Havana Company carrying the subsidy to Florida, and Fernández meant to establish their purpose in calling at Saint Augustine. When Pérez and his men boarded the two vessels, it became immediately obvious that both contained articles of illicit trade that in no way agreed with the cargoes listed on their manifests. The sixty soldiers seized the six crewmen and four passengers and confiscated a variety of goods valued at 4,487 pesos.[53] Fernández imprisoned Angel and his crew, but the four passengers somehow managed to escape to the Franciscan convent, where they obtained ecclesiastical sanctuary.[54]

Blas Angel and his mate, Alberto Andrade, came to trial before the Florida governor and confessed their crime. The two admitted that they had sailed for Charleston with the 190 bags of tobacco hidden in their

51. AGI, Santo Domingo, Legajo 846. Testimonio de los autos del comiso de la goleta nombrada Nuestra Señora de la Luz y la valandra titulada San Joseph, Oct. 18, 1756.

52. AGI, Santo Domingo, Legajo 2542. Carta del gobernador de la Florida al rey, April 17, 1756. Carta del gobernador de la Florida al rey, June 12, 1756.

53. AGI, Santo Domingo, Legajo 846. Testimonio de los autos del comiso de la goleta nombrada Nuestra Señora de la Luz y la valandra titulada San Joseph, Oct. 18, 1756.

54. AGI, Santo Domingo, Legajo 833. Consulta del Consejo de las Indias, July 5, 1758.

holds and had exchanged this for the articles Fernández had seized on the two vessels. They explained further that the four-month license granted to them by the governor of Cuba gave them ample time to carry on their illegal trade and still fulfil the terms of the license. The other crew members and the four passengers, however, did not join Angel and Andrade in their confession. They feigned ignorance of the laws against the trade being carried on by their superiors and implored Fernández to absolve them of complicity. They had wives and children in Havana who were going hungry while they were away.[55]

The governor was not appreciably moved by their protestations of ignorance or their pleas for mercy. He first condemned both Angel and his mate to six years of hard labor on the fortifications at Saint Augustine. After completion of this sentence, both men were required to serve in Spanish presidios in Africa. Neither might ever sail his own ship again. The master of the San Joseph and three of his four passengers received four years at hard labor in the Florida capital, while the other passenger and the remaining crewmen were sentenced to three years.[56] One can only speculate whether the flight of the four passengers to the convent and the need for their forcible extraction made the governor less merciful.

Fernández had dealt vigorously with the illicit traders, or so it seemed. He had proved his diligence and vigilance to the crown and demonstrated why he deserved a seat on the Council of the Indies. In Spain, however, events took their usual turn; the Council disapproved sharply of the governor's actions. Its members believed that Angel and his cohorts deserved more severe sentences, more compatible with the grave crime they had committed. In addition, Fernández had wrongfully seized the four passengers who had taken refuge in the convent. By extricating them forcibly he had desecrated the sacred rights and privileges of the Franciscans.[57] Once again the governor had attempted to administer justice; once again he had received a reprimand from his superiors in Spain. He had violated the rights of ecclesiastical sanctuary and mitigated the sentences imposed on Angel and his crew. In its dis-

55. AGI, Santo Domingo, Legajo 846. Testimonio de los autos en que se procedió contra las personas de los pasajeros y la tripulación de la goleta nombrada Nuestra Señora de la Luz y la valandra titulada San Joseph que se han comisado con los efectos de su carga, Oct. 18, 1756.

56. AGI, Santo Domingo, Legajo 833. Consulta del Consejo de las Indias, July 5, 1758.

57. AGI, Santo Domingo, Legajo 833. Consulta del Consejo de las Indias, July 5, 1758.

patch to Fernández this seemed far more important than the governor's vigorous efforts to expose the illicit trade scandal and to bring the guilty parties to justice.

In Cuba there were serious repercussions from the Angel affair. The Council censured the Cuban governor for allowing his captains to abuse their licenses to fish. In the future, ordered the Council, he must concede licenses only for the time necessary to carry out the specific provisions of the ships' manifests.[58] A royal *cédula* of September 25, 1760, later confirmed the Council's order. This specifically forbade the governor in Havana to issue licenses to Cuban mariners for periods that would enable them to trade illicitly in foreign ports.[59]

[*The Governor Administers Justice: A Critique*]

The judicial process in Florida was clearly a makeshift arrangement. The governor administered justice at his own discretion and seldom adhered to normal judicial procedures laid down by Spanish law. If there was a basis for his methods, it could be found in his military experience, where the summary court-martial was common practice. Actually the military style of justice served well. It was both simple and expeditious and fitted the realities of colonial life. When the governor saw fit to use more formal procedures, the results were disastrous. When his superiors reviewed his attempts to administer justice according to normal practice, they found the litigations shot through with blunders, inadequacies, and illegalities that were the antithesis of justice. For the most part the governor was not responsible for his ineptitude. He had no trained lawyers or solicitors, no *fiscales*, auditors, or assessors to help him with his civil and criminal cases; and without legal training himself, he was severely hampered in his attempts to proceed according to the law. Justice ran its course in Florida, but the way was rough, circuitous, and full of pitfalls.

58. AGI, Santo Domingo, Legajo 833. Consulta del Consejo de las Indias, July 5, 1758.
59. AGI, Santo Domingo, Legajo 2581. Real cédula, Buen Retiro, Sept. 25, 1760.

Chapter IV

ECONOMIC PROBLEMS OF
THE GOVERNOR

M any problems plagued the governor, but none were more perplex-
ing than the economic plight of his settlement. As a poverty-
stricken outpost on the northeastern fringe of New Spain, Florida
maintained no mining, agricultural, or commercial enterprises and was
wholly dependent upon outside aid for its existence. The remote
province was an abysmal place where want, misery, and destitution
characterized the lot of soldiers and their families. Securing money and
supplies was the governor's greatest single responsibility. No colonial
question received closer attention.[1]

[*The Subsidy*]

Sole means of support for Florida came from an annual subsidy
(*situado*), paid before 1702 from the royal treasury in Mexico City.
Each year the governor and his *junta* chose an agent (*situadista*) to go
to New Spain to collect this subvention. In the viceregal capital this
agent presented the governor's certified statements of the needs of the
colony and bargained with the viceroy's representatives for the required
specie and supplies. These goods were then carried overland by pack
train to Vera Cruz and put on ships bound for Havana. From Cuba the
money and supplies were transshipped to Saint Augustine, where the
governor and his treasury officials distributed them among the garrison
and its families.[2]

The number of soldiers, friars, and royal officials serving in Florida
determined the amount of the yearly subsidy. At the death of Pedro
Menéndez de Avilés in 1574, the annual grant for 150 soldiers totaled
24,000 ducats (approximately 33,000 pesos) and came from Central
America. In 1578 when Philip II doubled the Saint Augustine garrison,

1. For the period 1700-1763 correspondence on economic matters far outweighed
the documents on any other colonial question.
2. AGI, Santo Domingo, Legajo 843. Real cédula, Madrid, March 8, 1702.

this amount increased to 35,000 ducats (approximately 48,000 pesos) and came from New Spain, the source of the subsidy throughout the remainder of the colonial period. Rising steadily, the *situado* amounted to 65,000 pesos in 1660.[3] At the opening of the eighteenth century 350 soldiers, their families, the friars, and a few royal functionaries— close to 1,600 residents—required approximately 81,000 pesos yearly.[4]

In theory the subsidy was adequate to maintain the colony, but in practice many evils occurred in its administration and distribution. The viceroy often delayed payment of the *situado*, sometimes for several consecutive years. Adept at making excuses, the viceroy claimed either that he had no ships in Vera Cruz to carry the subsidy to Cuba or that he had no precise information on the exact number of soldiers serving in Saint Augustine, a figure necessary to determine the amount of the annual grant. Sometimes the viceroy stated that he simply could not raise the subsidy in Mexico. As a result, the viceroy came to owe a large debt to the Florida colony. In 1662 it was 202,654 pesos; by 1703 it amounted to 456,959 pesos.[5]

A second abuse developed out of dilatory payment of the *situado*. Shortages often forced the governor to secure food and supplies elsewhere, usually in Cuba. Here, however, he was forced to pay high interest rates on the money he borrowed and high prices for the necessities he obtained on credit. Then, when the subsidy finally reached Saint Augustine, he had to pay out most of the available specie to usurious Havana merchants.[6] Additional delays in remitting the annual subvention to Florida started another, similar cycle.

The price and quality of supplies obtained in New Spain created other problems for the governor. He needed specie to pay his soldiers and purchase the necessary articles for his Floridians. If the governor's *situadista* to New Spain could obtain good-quality supplies at low prices, more money remained for salaries and other pressing colonial needs. For the most part, however, the *situadista* could make few bargains.

3. Jeannette Thurber Connor, trans. and ed., *Colonial Records of Spanish Florida* (Deland, 1925-1930), II, 245.

4. AGI, Santo Domingo, Legajo 836. Despacho del rey al gobernador de la Florida, May 28, 1700. The exact amount was 80,842 pesos sixteen maravedís.

5. Photostat of document from Archivo General de Indias, 58-2-29, Carta del gobernador Alonso de Aranguiz y Cotes al rey, Oct. 10, 1662, in the Spanish Records of the North Carolina Historical Commission, 1535-1802. AGI, Santo Domingo, Legajo 853. Testimonio de los autos fechos sobre la paga de San Agustín de la Florida: año de 1703.

6. AGI, Santo Domingo, Legajo 840. Carta del provincial de la Florida Fr. Simón de Salas del orden de San Francisco al rey, June 14, 1705.

The viceroy's agents, probably in collusion with merchants in Mexico City and Vera Cruz, charged exorbitant prices for their goods, exorbitant even for inflation-ridden New Spain. At the same time, foodstuffs sold to the *situadista* were often of inferior quality, and it was common to find wormy flour and rancid pork among the items destined for Saint Augustine.[7] If foodstuffs were not contaminated at the time of purchase, a few months on the wharves at humid Vera Cruz considerably abetted the molding process. Lack of ships was usually responsible for these delays and led to the contamination of goods obtained in Mexico. The high costs (approximately 18,000 pesos) of shipping the specie and supplies by land from Mexico City to the Gulf and by sea from Vera Cruz to Saint Augustine drained still more pesos from the subsidy allocated to Florida and added to the governor's woes.

[Governor Zúñiga Seeks Additional Help in Spain]

The many abuses in administration of the subsidy system placed heavy burdens upon the governor. Without money and supplies he could not provide his soldiers with money, food, uniforms, or proper weapons. He could not maintain the defenses of Saint Augustine, pacify the Indians, or support a vigorous mission program. In fact, his entire colonial program depended upon the annual subsidy. Without it he was helpless. Governor Zúñiga complained in October, 1701, for example, that his colony was starving. Soldiers, their families, cripples, widows, and orphans were all begging him for food, which had become scarce in Saint Augustine.[8] The arrival of the *situado* ship two months later gave some help to the hard-pressed Floridians, but the governor believed this was only temporary relief and that his colony was in danger of perishing if something were not done to ease his situation.[9]

Since Zúñiga believed there was little chance that he could get help from Mexico, he decided upon a direct appeal to authorities in the mother country. In the spring of 1702, shortly before the outbreak of Queen Anne's War, he sent his personal emissary to Spain to explain the plight of the Florida settlement and to seek aid. This agent, Juan de Ayala Escobar, carried with him a long list of requests. For colonial defenses he asked for twenty-eight cannon—sixteen four pound-

7. AGI, Santo Domingo, Legajo 836. Despacho del rey al gobernador de la Florida, May 22, 1702.

8. AGI, Santo Domingo, Legajo 840. Carta del gobernador de la Florida al rey, Oct. 24, 1701.

9. AGI, Santo Domingo, Legajo 840. Carta del gobernador de la Florida al rey, Dec. 28, 1701. The *situado* ship arrived on Christmas Day, 1701.

ers, six twelve pounders, and six eighteen pounders. For the garrison he requested two hundred muskets, two hundred arquebuses, two hundred pikes, two hundred lances, and one thousand grenades.[10] Ayala also requested reinforcements amounting to 150 additional men and an appropriation of 7,000 to 8,000 ducats in *vellon*[11] to undertake public works projects such as the reconstruction of the sea walls at Saint Augustine. As a further protection for Spanish ships and crews plying the Bahama Channel, Ayala asked funds for the erection of a new blockhouse at Ais (near present-day Cape Canaveral), to be garrisoned by Spanish soldiers and at least two friars. His most radical request, however, was for remission of the subsidy to Florida entirely in hard money rather than in food and supplies.[12]

Initially Ayala could not get help in Spain, but when news of the English siege of Saint Augustine reached Madrid late in 1702, his pleas took on a new significance. In January, 1703, the Spanish *Junta de Guerra*[13] declared that the House of Trade (*Casa de Contratación*) should fill Zúñiga's requests without delay,[14] and within two months the Council of the Indies had awarded Ayala a ship of 150 nautical tons and 4,000 pesos for supplies.[15] Philip V lent his assistance by ordering the viceroy of New Spain to send fifty soldiers to Saint Augustine and by commanding the governor of Cuba to dispatch four engineers and a surgeon to the province. Twice the Spanish monarch issued orders to the viceroy and the governor in Havana to furnish Zúñiga with gunpowder. Most significant, however, was a royal *cédula* requiring the viceroy to release 20,000 pesos from the vacant bishoprics of Puebla, Guadalajara, and Guatemala for rebuilding the church, convent, and other buildings of Saint Augustine, devastated

10. AGI, Santo Domingo, Legajo 840. Carta del gobernador de la Florida al rey, March 25, 1702.

11. Copper coins or coins of copper-silver alloys used in place of gold and silver coins.

12. AGI, Santo Domingo, Legajo 840. Instrucción de lo que ha de representar a Su Magistad y señores ministros de Indias el Capitán Don Juan de Ayala Escobar, del orden del Gobernador de la Florida que se como sigue, n.d.

13. The Junta de Guerra (after 1600) was a Council composed of a president, three members of the Council of the Indies, and four members of the Council of War of Castile. It dealt almost solely with military and naval affairs. See Haring, *Spanish Empire*, p. 108.

14. AGI, Santo Domingo, Legajo 833. Consulta de la Junta de Guerra, January 31, 1703.

15. AGI, Santo Domingo, Legajo 833. Consulta del Consejo de las Indias, March 26, 1703.

during the siege. To this amount he added 6,000 pesos for the care of the indigent.[16]

Ayala's pleas, coinciding with the English attack on Florida, emphasized the importance of the colony in the growing competition for empire in the Southeast and made the agent's task easier. Yet despite the generosity of his benefactors, Ayala found it difficult to obtain what had been granted him in royal and conciliar decrees.[17] Those responsible for providing him with artillery could not find suitable cannon in Spain to fill his needs and furnished the Floridian with only six ten-pounders out of the twenty-eight originally requested. In small arms he obtained 250 rusty muskets and arquebuses—hardly fit for use—and two hundred pikes and one thousand grenades in better condition.[18] A one-year search turned up a seventy-four ton vessel, half the size of the ship originally intended for Ayala. Of the 150 Spanish soldiers ordered to Saint Augustine, only twenty unfortunates were ready to sail by September, 1704, the time of Ayala's departure, and they had to be forcibly detained in temporary prisons to keep them from deserting.[19]

Still, by Florida standards Ayala's mission could be counted a success. He had obtained men, ships, money, and supplies from the king and the Council of the Indies, who were now aware of the conditions in the colony and its place in the contest for the Southeast. The new king had also ordered aid to Florida from the wealthier provinces of New Spain and Cuba in an attempt to bolster the struggling colony. Misfortune—the English siege of 1702—had, it appeared, brought the Floridians good fortune. The assault had renewed the interest of officials in both Spain and the Indies over the fate of Florida.

16. AGI, Santo Domingo, Legajo 840. Memoria de los triplicados de despachos que han manado de los cartas que el Capitán Don Juan de Ayala Escobar, que lo es mas antiguo de las companias de infantería española del Presidio de San Agustín de la Florida presentó en el Consejo y le entregó el Maestro del Campo Don Joseph de Zúñiga y Cerda, Gobernador actual de aquellas Provincias y a su instancia mandó el Consejo por acuerdo de 30 de Marzo se le diesan y asimismo otros despachos que ordenó el Señor Don Manuel de Aperregui, n.d.

17. AGI, Santo Domingo, Legajo 836. Consulta del Consejo de las Indias, April 12, 1703. AGI, Santo Domingo, Legajo 833. Consulta del Consejo de las Indias, April 30, 1703.

18. AGI, Santo Domingo, Legajo 836. Despacho del rey a don Francisco de San Millán y Cevallos, Sept. 16, 1704.

19. AGI, Santo Domingo, Legajo 836. Consulta del Consejo de las Indias, Sept. 16, 1704. AGI, Santo Domingo, Legajo 833. Consulta de la Junta de Guerra, Sept. 16, 1704.

[Revision of the Subsidy System]

In another effort to aid the province, the king and the Council of the Indies made significant changes in the subsidy system, the first since 1578. Aware of the governor's economic problems, in March, 1702, Philip V ordered the annual *situado* paid from the sales taxes (*alcabalas*) of Puebla de los Angeles, a city situated southeast of Mexico City on the road to Vera Cruz. Administration of the subsidy was taken out of the viceroy's hands and given to the Bishop of Puebla, who received authority to release the money and to buy the supplies requested annually by the Florida *situadista*. Under the new order at least half of every subsidy had to be paid in specie. To prevent delays in delivery of the *situado*, the agent was instructed to spend no more than six months in Puebla carrying out his duties.[20] The bishop also had to remit annually 25 percent of the subsidy in specie over and above the total amount of each *situado* in order to retire the large debt owing Florida from past subsidies, an amount exceeding 400,000 pesos.[21]

Several advantages apparently accrued to Florida as a result of the change. Since the annual income from the Puebla sales taxes was almost 140,000 pesos and the Florida subsidy was only 80,000 pesos, there was now a reliable, steady source of income for the subsidy.[22] Prices were purportedly lower in Puebla than in Mexico City, and the journey to Vera Cruz was shorter and less costly than from the viceregal capital.[23] For the king and the Council there may also have been hope that a religious official would administer the subsidy more equitably and more efficiently than the viceroy had done in the past.

Finally established in 1707, the new system seemed at least a partial improvement over the old method. Ships carrying the subsidy from Puebla regularly entered the Saint Augustine harbor after 1707, bringing the Floridians their yearly quota of money and food. In ten years (to 1716), 912,290 pesos in specie and supplies left New Spain for Florida, an average of 91,229 pesos a year.[24] The payments added to the regular subsidy to retire the old debt also helped relieve the

20. AGI, Santo Domingo, Legajo 843. Real cédula, Madrid, March 8, 1702. See also Cárdenas y Cano, *Ensayo cronológico*, II, 349-354.

21. AGI, Santo Domingo, Legajo 843. Despacho del rey a los oficiales reales de la real hacienda de la ciudad de Mexico en Nueva España, Jan. 13, 1702.

22. AGI, Santo Domingo, Legajo 836. Consulta del Consejo de las Indias, Aug. 29, 1710.

23. Cárdenas y Cano, *Ensayo cronológico*, II, 356.

24. AGI, Santo Domingo, Legajo 854. Carta del gobernador de Cuba al rey, Jan. 20, 1719.

governor of his obligations to Cuban merchants, and despite Queen Anne's War, economic conditions in Florida improved considerably. At the same time the viceroy's debt diminished greatly. In 1703 (according to the governor) it was 456,959 pesos.[25] By 1709 it amounted to 273,479 pesos[26] and had fallen to 211,290 pesos by 1714, evidence that the new system of repayment was operating efficiently.[27]

[*Reappearance of the Old Abuses*]

Initially, Floridians were optimistic that the new method of securing the subsidy would end their economic woes, but it was not long before the old abuses reappeared. Although the Bishop of Puebla was more conscientious than the viceroy in releasing money and supplies, delivery was still irregular, and foodstuffs failed to improve in quality. Governor Córcoles reported in 1710 that the "intolerable corruption" of corn and flour shipped to Florida cut his soldiers' rations in half.[28] In the spring of 1712 English seizure of a *situado* ship made cats, dogs, and horses real delicacies at Saint Augustine supper tables.[29]

At the same time, some Floridians like Juan de Ayala Escobar, were using these conditions to their own advantage. Ayala illegally procured several boatloads of food, probably from the English in Charleston, and placed these commodities on sale in Saint Augustine. Tired of their domestic-animal fare, the soldiers of the garrison and their wives flocked to Ayala's shop to purchase his meat and flour, despite his high prices. As payment they used the few pesos they had managed to save from their meager earnings or received credit in lieu of future salary payments.[30] For his part Ayala took full advantage of conditions in Florida to reap high profits. In his market one real bought only a bit of corn; in Havana the same amount (it was claimed) bought one and one-half bushels. Meat priced by Ayala at nineteen pesos cost only two

25. AGI, Santo Domingo, Legajo 853. Testimonio de los autos fechos sobre la paga de San Agustín de la Florida: año de 1703.

26. AGI, Santo Domingo, Legajo 853. Informe de los oficiales reales de la Florida, Aug. 17, 1712.

27. AGI, Santo Domingo, Legajo 854. Carta del gobernador de la Florida al rey, April 24, 1714.

28. AGI, Santo Domingo, Legajo 841, Carta del gobernador, los oficiales reales, y los soldados de la Florida al rey, Feb. 27, 1710.

29. AGI, Santo Domingo, Legajo 848. Testimonio en relación sobre la buen obra del señor gobernador y capitán general Don Francisco de Córcoles y Martínez, Dec. 20, 1715.

30. AGI, Santo Domingo, Legajo 837. Consulta del Consejo de las Indias, Feb. 12, 1715.

pesos in Cuba, or nine and one-half times as much in Saint Augustine as in Havana.

Governor Córcoles was unable to stop Ayala's activities, despite their illegality. When the governor attempted to arrest his second-in-command in the spring of 1712, the entire colony threatened to mutiny if he were not allowed to continue his activities and keep his freedom. In fact almost the entire town turned out in June, 1712, to force Córcoles to dismiss charges against Ayala. Acquiescing to their wishes and threats in the public square at Saint Augustine, Córcoles induced wild cheers when he announced that he would not move against Ayala. The crowd saw the sergeant major as a benefactor, and they meant to show their appreciation. After all what had Córcoles done to relieve their hunger?[31]

In Puebla the governor's agents soon began to experience difficulty in securing the full amount of the subsidy. Joseph Benedit Horruitiner, dispatched to Mexico in 1712, found he could not obtain his quota of money and supplies because of other warrants on the Puebla sales taxes that had drained this source of revenue. In all there was a shortage of 13,000 pesos in the subsidy. The bishop's agents, however, offered him a solution to the problem. They induced Horruitiner—against his will —to accept as a substitute for the money, fine china, silk, and woolen cloth, valued at 13,000 pesos. These articles, they claimed, could easily be sold for this amount to merchants in Vera Cruz. Reluctantly Horruitiner made his way to the coast, but there he found no one to buy his niceties, and he had to return to Florida with the unwanted dishes and cloth—and a shortage of 13,000 pesos in his accounts. Córcoles, who needed pesos, not table service or a dress coat, was so angry he threw Horruitiner in prison for dereliction of duty. From all reports the *situadista* was not a model prisoner.[32]

Such occurrences were symptomatic of other evils in the administration of the subsidy in Puebla, many of them common under the old system. In 1715 there were complaints concerning inferior supplies and

31. AGI, Santo Domingo, Legajo 841. Consulta de la Junta de Guerra, July 11, 1713. See also AGI, Santo Domingo, Legajo 847. Carta del contador de la Florida (Francisco Menéndez Marqués) al rey, June 6, 1712.

32. AGI, Santo Domingo, Legajo 848. El señor fiscal del Consejo de las Indias contra el capitán Don Joseph Benedit Horruitiner a cuyo cargo fué el situado a la plaza de San Agustín de la Florida sobre haber dicho capitán empleado el caudal de el en generos y mercaderias y paga a los soldados de aquel presidio . . . , n.d. AGI, Santo Domingo, Legajo 848. Carta del gobernador de la Florida al rey, Feb. 9, 1713. AGI, Santo Domingo, Legajo 843. Carta del gobernador de la Florida al rey, April 23, 1714.

delays encountered by the *situadista* in both the City of the Angels and Vera Cruz.[33] In 1716 and 1717 it took twenty-one months to get the subsidy from Mexico to Florida. As a result the daily ration for residents of Saint Augustine was reduced to less than two pounds of flour.[34] If prices had been exorbitant in Mexico City, they were just as high or higher in Puebla. Governor Benavides complained in 1720 that the price of food in Puebla and of conducting the *situado* to Florida were too expensive, suggesting again that the new system had failed to relieve the old abuses.[35] In 1723 he repeated this complaint and suggested that the viceroy pay the costs of shipping the subsidy to Saint Augustine.[36]

Governor Moral was equally critical of the administration of the *situado* system. He went so far as to accuse the Bishop of Puebla of peculation, charging the prelate with deliberately buying supplies of low quality at a low price and charging the Florida account twice as much as their real value. Prices, claimed Moral, were 50 to 80 per cent higher for Floridians than for Pueblans. Six bushels of wheat, for example, cost eight pesos in New Spain; his *situadista* paid twelve pesos or more. For other articles, he stated, the difference in price was even greater.[37] To add to Moral's troubles, the English seized a *situado* ship carrying 97,000 pesos worth of money and supplies, leaving the governor without specie to pay his soldiers.[38] Moral, however, was always resourceful. In what he considered to be a discreet move, he paid his men in rum. If he could not assuage their hunger or pay their salaries, he at least hoped to provide the means whereby they could forget their woes—at least temporarily. But in the end this caused him nothing but trouble.[39]

Within a few years, therefore, the abuses that had prevailed before

33. AGI, Santo Domingo, Legajo 854. Carta del gobernador de la Florida al rey, Dec. 3, 1715.

34. AGI, Santo Domingo, Legajo 854. Carta del gobernador de la Florida al rey, June 22, 1716. AGI, Santo Domingo Legajo 843. Carta del gobernador interino de la Florida al rey, Nov. 22, 1717.

35. AGI, Santo Domingo, Legajo 854. Carta del gobernador de la Florida al rey, April 24, 1720.

36. AGI, Santo Domingo, Legajo 842. Carta del gobernador de la Florida al rey, June 24, 1723.

37. AGI, Santo Domingo, Legajo 2530. Carta del gobernador de la Florida al rey, March 6, 1735.

38. AGI, Santo Domingo, Legajo 845. Carta del gobernador de la Florida al virrey de Nueva España, March 26, 1743.

39. AGI, Santo Domingo, Legajo 848. Carta del obispo auxiliar de Cuba al gobernador de Cuba, Dec. 22, 1736.

the reform of 1702 reappeared. Delays, shortages, exorbitant prices, high shipping costs, inferior supplies, price discrimination, and seizures by foreign corsairs all left their mark on the Florida economy. In Puebla the bishop claimed, with some justice, that recurrence of these evils was not his fault. Lack of ships at Vera Cruz to carry the *situado* to Florida caused spoilage of foodstuffs and increased storage costs.[40] Even royal pressure on behalf of the Floridians failed to improve the situation. In December, 1721, the king's order to the bishop to purchase untainted, high-quality supplies for the Florida garrison accomplished little.[41] The Puebla system simply did not work well. It had failed to provide a regular source of money and supplies for the Florida colony. Even royal prodding did little to remedy the basic defects in the administration of the subsidy.

[*The Governor Suggests Economic Reforms*]

Besides complaining about their economic woes the governors of Florida suggested various panaceas which they hoped would bring the colony out of the economic doldrums. These proposals took different directions. Some requested basic changes in administration of the subsidy; others recommended a complete change in the economic life of the colony; but if adopted, all promised a better existence for the beleaguered province.

Zúñiga hoped to ease his economic problems in several ways. In 1702 he sought direct aid from Spain and sent Ayala to the mother country with requests for men, money, arms supplies, and ships. As has been recounted, Ayala was partially successful, but Zúñiga's action could hardly be classified as a fundamental reform. The governor did, however, propose that the subsidy be sent to Florida entirely in hard money. Gold and silver, he claimed, would enable him to bargain for supplies more advantageously with Cuban merchants and eliminate the problems of spoiled food and high-priced goods.[42]

His successor, Francisco de Córcoles y Martínez, presented another plan for solving the economic problems of the colony. Córcoles pointed out that Spaniards in Florida had been unable to grow their own food

40. AGI, Santo Domingo, Legajo 854. Carta del obispo de Puebla de los Angeles al rey, Jan. 5, 1715.

41. AGI, Santo Domingo, Legajo 837. Despacho del rey al obispo de Puebla de los Angeles, Dec. 19, 1721.

42. AGI, Santo Domingo, Legajo 840. Carta del gobernador de la Florida al rey, March 25, 1702.

and that all attempts at farming or fruit culture had been abortive. Predatory Indians had torn up seed beds, burned maturing crops, and murdered innovators who planted in the sandy soil near Saint Augustine. These Indians had also prevented lone hunters and fishermen from adding variety to the monotonous diets of the Floridians. The only farmers who succeeded at all were those who tilled small plots under the protective cannon of Fort San Marcos and the few Christian Indians who cultivated land in the fertile areas near Apalache.[43] These two sources, however, provided only a scanty, undependable food supply.[44] It would be advantageous, stated Córcoles, to settle two hundred Galician families in Florida to farm the rich land in Apalache. Since Galicia[45] was an unproductive, poverty-stricken province, the inhabitants would surely welcome the opportunity to make a new start in northwest Florida, a land flowing with milk and honey. Once these immigrants began farming, they would relieve the perpetual food shortage and increase the amount of specie available from the subsidy. This could be used to strengthen the defenses of the colony. At the same time a large Spanish population in Apalache would serve as a bulwark against English encroachments on the Gulf Coast. Córcoles, however, did not reckon with the attitude of the Galicians, who proved extremely reluctant to take up the plan. Later, even when presented with the crown's offer of free passage and aid in money, seeds, implements, and tax relief, they refused to go to Saint Augustine. They claimed they would rather die of hunger at home in Spain than far away in Florida.[46] And probably they were right.

Governor Benavides had other suggestions. He wanted to relieve the Bishop of Puebla of his responsibility for administering the subsidy. The prelate, stated the governor, was too busy with his episcopal duties to oversee the *situado*. Benavides hoped that the high sheriff of Puebla could assume this duty and suggested also that the viceroy pay all costs of shipping the subsidy to Florida.[47] In 1724 the governor requested

43. In the seventeenth century the Indians of Apalache produced considerable quantities of corn and beans. Some years they shipped as many as 3,000 to 4,000 bushels of these commodities to Saint Augustine. See Bolton and Ross, *The Debatable Land*, p. 26.

44. Between 1704 and 1718 the Spaniards had no presidio in Apalache and abandoned the province. See pp. 113-116.

45. A province in northwestern Spain.

46. AGI, Santo Domingo, Legajo 2530. Consulta del Consejo de las Indias, July 15, 1739.

47. AGI, Santo Domingo, Legajo 854. Carta del gobernador de la Florida al rey, April 24, 1720.

that the Bishop of Puebla send the entire subsidy to Saint Augustine by land. This step, he asserted, would eliminate the delays caused by a shortage of ships in Vera Cruz and cut the costs of delivering the annual grant. The governor envisaged a chain of Spanish presidios on the Gulf Coast, stretching from Vera Cruz to Apalache, that would protect Spanish caravans moving between Florida and New Spain. These proposed outposts would also reinforce Spanish pretensions on the Gulf of Mexico and keep it a Spanish lake.[48]

Moral Sánchez proved especially adept at reviving previous proposals for economic reform. On June 24, 1734, a month after he had taken office, Moral asked Philip V to reconsider Córcoles' immigration scheme. Like his predecessor, Moral proposed the repopulation of Apalache and its agricultural development, not by Galicians but by Canary Islanders. Development of Apalache, he believed, would serve both as an economic boon to Florida and as a defensive measure against further encroachments by the English, whose Indians were already active in the area. Moral also saw the possibility of building up a profitable fur trade in Apalache.[49] In addition the governor wanted to revive Zúñiga's scheme of obtaining the entire subsidy in hard money. If Florida could get its yearly grant in specie, he claimed he could secure supplies at lower prices in Havana, Campeche, and Vera Cruz, breaking the monopoly of Puebla merchants, who charged such exorbitant prices to his *situadista*.[50]

On the surface, Moral's proposals appeared sound, but his motives were apparently less than noble. During his administration Saint Augustine had become the center of illicit trade. English traders from the Carolinas had begun to pour their goods onto the Florida market in 1735 and 1736 and to sell them to Spanish soldiers and their wives, all with the governor's approval. During this period one resident observed that English merchants walked the streets of the Florida capital as if they were in London.[51] Another informer reported seeing six English vessels moored in the harbor at one time during 1736.[52] Still

48. AGI, Santo Domingo, Legajo 865. El acuerdo del Consejo de las Indias, n.d., 1724.

49. AGI, Santo Domingo, Legajo 2532. Carta del gobernador de la Florida al rey, June 30, 1734.

50. AGI, Santo Domingo, Legajo 444. Carta del gobernador de la Florida al rey, June 30, 1734.

51. AGI, Santo Domingo, Legajo 862. Carta del don Philipe de Yturrieta al gobernador de Cuba, Aug. 28, 1736.

52. AGI, Santo Domingo, Legajo 862. Carta del gobernador de Cuba al obispo de Cuba, Oct. 26, 1736.

a third pointed out that English traders had driven Spanish shopkeepers out of business with their cheaper goods.[53] Apparently, therefore, Moral hoped to get the *situado* entirely in hard money to stimulate this trade further and to get cheaper, higher quality goods from
the Carolinians.[54]

The forthright Manuel de Montiano advocated several startling
innovations to relieve the miserable lot of his Floridians. In 1744 he
shocked the king and the Council of the Indies with the news that the
Bishop of Puebla owed his colony 530,140 pesos. To repay this debt,
Montiano suggested a unique scheme for debasing the currency. He
asked that 132,523 pesos be minted in special coins solely for use in
Florida. Their value in relation to Mexican specie was set at four to
one; that is, the silver in one Mexican peso would make four Florida
pesos. Montiano hoped, however, that in Saint Augustine the Florida
peso would be equal *in value* to the Mexican peso. This scheme, he
stated, had definite advantages. The new coins would serve to confuse
English merchants and make illicit trade difficult. Since he proposed
that the money would have no value outside Florida, the new monetary
plan would prevent the flight of hard money from the colony. It
could also be used to pay off the bishop's debt to Florida with only one-
quarter of the amount actually owed. In Florida Montiano planned
to use this money for the needy, construction of new buildings, repair
of the defenses battered during the English siege of 1740, and debts
to Cuban merchants.[55]

In Spain Montiano's scheme intrigued the Council of the Indies. It
agreed that a change in the intrinsic value of money was always a
"delicate matter," but the Council saw a chance to eliminate illicit trade
and to retire an outstanding debt with only a quarter of the sum due.

53. AGI, Santo Domingo, Legajo 848. Carta del obispo auxiliar de Cuba al
gobernador de Cuba, Dec. 22, 1736. The bishop reported that during a seventeen-
month span, dating back from his letter, thirty-eight to forty English ships had
entered the harbor at Saint Augustine with illicit goods.

54. Although nothing was done to carry through Moral's plans, many of them
were adopted by his successors. Between 1757 and 1761 over seven hundred Canary
Islanders entered Florida to populate and develop Apalache. See Francisco Morales
Padrón, "Colonos canarios en Indias," *Anuario de estudios americanos*, VII (1951),
429. Governor Montiano set up a trading post in Apalache in 1738 to stimulate the
fur trade and Governor Alonso Fernández de Heredia revived the naval stores industry
that Moral began during his governorship. Even Moral's free-trade activities were
adopted in a modified form by the Havana Company, which had the responsibility of
supplying Florida after 1740.

55. AGI, Santo Domingo, Legajo 849. Carta del gobernador de la Florida al rey,
Feb. 8, 1744.

In February, 1746, therefore, upon recommendation of the Council, the king ordered the viceroy to mint specie worth 150,000 pesos in Mexico (to be valued in Florida at 600,000 pesos). Engraved on one side of these new coins was to be the coat of arms of Philip V and on the other a nosegay of flowers. There were to be three denominations of gold coins, worth 100,000 pesos, and three denominations of silver coins, worth 50,000 pesos. When this new money reached Florida, residents were to exchange the old money for the new. If a Floridian left the colony, the royal treasury officials in Saint Augustine would exchange his Florida money for the usual colonial pesos, held on deposit after the original exchange process occurred.[56] For some reason, the 150,000 pesos never reached Florida. Either the viceroy ignored the *cédula* ordering the new coins or else the ship carrying the money went to the bottom of the Bahama Channel; despite the support of the king and the Council, nothing came of Montiano's debasement plan.

Two years after making his debasement proposal, Montiano raised the royal eyebrows with another plan. This time the governor argued that the economic condition of those serving under him could be alleviated only by free trade with the English colonies in America. Certain obvious advantages would result. First, goods brought into Saint Augustine on English ships removed all risks and costs now burdening the Spaniards. Moldy bread, wormy flour, rancid meat, rusty arms, and wet gunpowder would no longer be a problem, since the governor and his agents could examine all supplies before making a purchase. In addition, English traders sold goods cheaper than their Spanish counterparts. Twenty-five pounds of English flour cost eleven reales; the same amount cost sixteen reales in New Spain. In order to prevent the spread of heretical Protestant ideas that might result from contact with English merchants, the governor suggested that all exchanges be made on Santa Anastasia Island across the river from Saint Augustine. In this way he could protect the residents against contamination by heretical English sailors. Montiano also indicated that quick discharge of English cargoes would eliminate the possibility of any social intercourse between the Floridians and the Carolinians.[57]

The practical arguments put forward by Montiano were difficult to refute, but principle, law, and tradition were too deeply rooted among

56. AGI, Papeles Procedentes de Cuba, Legajo 2263. Real cédula, El Pardo, Feb. 24, 1746.

57. AGI, Santo Domingo, Legajo 848. Carta del gobernador de la Florida al rey, April 15, 1746.

his superiors. Neither Ferdinand VI nor his councilors were prepared to take such a bold step; they were content to allow the colony to pursue its previous policies, trading occasionally with the English to obtain needed supplies but doing so without royal sanctions. The policy proposed by Montiano was far too radical, too great a change from the established system. It was up to Charles III to make these radical innovations.

[*The Colony Survives through Expedients:
Misapplication of Funds*]

Abuses within the subsidy system created insoluble problems for the governor, whose suggestions, complaints, entreaties, detailed plans, or angry letters failed to move his superiors in Spain or New Spain. The *situado* continued to arrive irregularly. Supplies were in poor condition, prices were high, and shortages in the yearly grant were commonplace. All of this forced the governor to resort to expedients to sustain those serving under him. To pay his soldiers and keep their families alive, he had to misapply funds allocated to Florida for building or other special purposes and use this money for salaries or food.

Not long after the turn of the century, the governor turned to this expedient in order to keep his colony from perishing. In 1702 soldiers and Indians from Carolina had swept down on Saint Augustine and destroyed more than forty buildings, including the parish church, convent, and homes of the leading civil and military officials. This forced many residents of the Florida capital into rude tents, makeshift huts, or crowded quarters at Fort San Marcos. To relieve these conditions Zúñiga begged the king for aid.[58] With Ayala in Spain to fortify Zúñiga's claim, the request was answered with unusual dispatch, at least by eighteenth-century standards. In the summer of 1703 Philip V ordered 20,000 pesos freed from the vacant bishoprics of Puebla, Guatemala, and Guadalajara, each contributing one-third for the rebuilding of the church, convent, and other edifices. The king also released 6,000 pesos from New Spain for distribution among the needy.[59] The 26,000 pesos arrived in Florida in December, 1707.

Governor Córcoles would not and could not use the money for the purposes laid down by the king. The governor needed the money to

58. AGI, Santo Domingo, Legajo 836. Consulta del Consejo de las Indias, April 23, 1703. This letter was dated Jan. 6, 1703.
59. AGI, Santo Domingo, Legajo 836. Despacho del rey al virrey de Nueva España, Oct. 18, 1703.

buy food and clothing for the residents, to strengthen colonial defenses, and to pay salaries owing his soldiers. This, he believed, was absolutely essential if the colony was to survive. Reconstruction of the town would have to come later.[60] Córcoles was careful, though, to consult the principal regular and secular clergymen in Florida, including the new Auxiliary Bishop Dionisio Resino, before taking such action, and they consented to postpone rebuilding of the church and convent until other more pressing colonial needs had been met.[61]

Córcoles quickly spent the 26,000 pesos and soon began requesting more. In August, 1709, he presented a claim of 56,520 pesos, the value of the buildings leveled in 1702, and asked the king to provide additional funds for reconstruction. Using Zúñiga's techniques, Córcoles painted a dismal picture of families forced to live in temporary quarters, in crowded conditions at Fort San Marcos, or in the homes of friends and relatives.[62] His plea was successful. Philip V granted Córcoles an additional 20,000 pesos to carry out plans to rebuild Saint Augustine. Again the king tapped the three vacant sees of Puebla, Guatemala, and Guadalajara to finance the reconstruction,[63] and by the end of 1716 money from this new allocation had arrived in Saint Augustine.

The new building fund dwindled as quickly as the previous one. By the time Benavides assumed the governorship in 1718, all but 6,000 of the 20,000 pesos was gone. Inspection of the town revealed that the church, convent, and other buildings for which the money had been released had not been erected. Indignant over the lack of money in the treasury and eager to put his own efficiency on display, Benavides accused Córcoles, Pedro de Olivera y Fullana, and interim governor Juan de Ayala Escobar of disobedience to the king's *cédulas*.[64]

In Spain Benavides' revelations struck like a thunderbolt, not over the failure to comply with the *cédulas* but over the loss of the 40,000 pesos. The king and the Council realized that the money allocated for poor relief would be spent quickly, but they hardly expected the building funds to be used for projects other than those specified by the king.

60. AGI, Santo Domingo, Legajo 841. Carta del gobernador de la Florida al rey, Jan. 2, 1708.
61. AGI, Santo Domingo, Legajo 843. El acuerdo de la junta de la Florida, July 2, 1709.
62. AGI, Santo Domingo, Legajo 841. Carta del gobernador de la Florida al rey, Aug. 13, 1709.
63. AGI, Santo Domingo, Legajo 836. Carta del virrey de Nueva España al rey, Dec. 20, 1714.
64. AGI, Santo Domingo, Legajo 843. Carta del gobernador de la Florida al rey, Sept. 30, 1718.

In an angry letter Philip V commanded Benavides to determine exactly how the 34,000 pesos, then unaccounted for, had been spent. In his audit the governor found little to incriminate his predecessors. Although they had not rebuilt the church and the convent, the three governors had used the money for colonial needs—food, arms, powder, salaries, and fortifications.[65] Apparently satisfied that there had been no peculation, the king then outlined a means by which the 34,000 pesos could find their way back into the Florida treasury. In November, 1720, he ordered Benavides and his two treasury officials to separate a small sum from each annual subsidy solely for use on projects proposed in his earlier *cédulas*, until the entire 34,000 pesos was reintegrated.[66]

Poor Benavides was thoroughly discouraged over the course of events. He now found himself paying for the sins of his predecessors. Although he agreed to reintegrate the 34,000 pesos by the process the king had ordered, he pointed out that this new demand on the *situado* would only serve to increase the hardships in his colony. In fact, stated the governor, the *cédula* of November, 1720, might result in the loss of Florida to the English.[67] As further demonstration of his desperate economic condition, Benavides asked permission to use the 6,000 pesos remaining in the building fund for fortifications rather than for a new church or convent. After all, observed the harried governor drily, dead men could not attend Mass, and his Floridians would surely perish if he did not attend to the defenses of the colony.[68] To this Philip V gave his grudging approval, but he once again refused to relent on his order requiring the reintegration of the 34,000 pesos into the Florida treasury.[69]

Benavides' use of the remaining 6,000 pesos for bolstering the defenses of Saint Augustine left his treasury empty. For the first time in twenty years, the governor was without a contingency fund for use in emergencies. Keenly aware of his plight, Benavides was anxious to

65. By the time Benavides turned in this audit, he had become more sympathetic with the problems of his predecessors and was less strident in his criticism and condemnation of their use of the money.
66. AGI, Santo Domingo, Legajo 854. Carta del gobernador de la Florida al rey, Dec. 6, 1721. The *cédula* was dated November 7, 1720.
67. AGI, Santo Domingo, Legajo 854. Carta del gobernador de la Florida al rey, Dec. 6, 1721.
68. AGI, Santo Domingo, Legajo 854. Carta del gobernador de la Florida al rey, April 24, 1722. Benavides stated also that he used 13,254 pesos from *comisos* (money obtained from seizure and sale of illicit goods) to aid in the building projects.
69. AGI, Santo Domingo, Legajo 837. Despacho del rey al gobernador de la Florida, Dec. 23, 1724.

build up a new reserve that he could call upon when the *situado* did not arrive or in times of sudden crises. Undeterred by the king's *cédula* of November, 1720, Benavides again requested money to rebuild the buildings destroyed in the siege of Saint Augustine twenty-four years before.[70] Similar pleas had won 26,000 pesos for Zúñiga and 20,000 for Córcoles, and Benavides evidently had a slim hope that they might still be persuasive.[71] This time, however, Philip V refused. In September, 1726, he turned down the governor's request and reiterated his order calling for the creation of a new building fund out of small sums from the yearly *situado*.[72]

Failure to get help from Spain forced Benavides to call a junta, an indication of the seriousness of his economic situation. After inspecting the royal storehouses and surveying the general economic condition of the colony, the junta concluded that it would be impossible for Benavides to comply with the *cédula* of November, 1720. Since the *situado* could not even meet the ordinary needs of the colony, taking money from the subsidy for a building program would leave the soldiers without pay and their families without food. The junta estimated too that 60,656 pesos would be necessary for rebuilding Saint Augustine.[73] A short time later Benavides reaffirmed the position of his junta and pointed out that the subsidy was not large enough to maintain his colony. In one optimistic note, he pointed out that the church and convent were now half-finished but that the 1,952 pesos remaining at his disposal were not enough to complete the structures.[74] In the end private donations furnished the funds for completing the church and the convent. In 1735 Auxiliary Bishop Francisco de San Buenaventura y Tejada arrived in Saint Augustine to set off a religious revival. One of its most tangible results was the number of gifts he elicited for reconstruction of the religious edifices, which were completed during his stay in Florida.[75]

70. These projects included stone redoubts to encircle Saint Augustine, the city gates, and adjacent walls. See Chatelain, *The Defenses of Spanish Florida*, p. 86.

71. AGI, Santo Domingo, Legajo 854. Memorial de la junta general de la Florida, June 10, 1726.

72. AGI, Santo Domingo, Legajo 854. Real cédula, San Ildefonso, Sept. 21, 1726.

73. AGI, Santo Domingo, Legajo 844. Testimonio de autos, junta, y demás diligencias sobre el Contenido de una Real Cédula de Su Magistad sobre que el situado de la infantería se remplazen los quarenta y ocho mil pesos que Su Magistad libró para fabricar de iglesia y casas quemadas . . . , July 22, 1727.

74. AGI, Santo Domingo, Legajo 844. Carta del gobernador de la Florida al rey, Sept. 25, 1727.

75. See Wilbur M. Siebert, "Some Church History of Saint Augustine during the Spanish Regime," *Florida Historical Quarterly*, IX (Oct., 1930), 121. See also

In the meantime, the king took pity on the Floridians. He abrogated his *cédula* of 1720, and in 1731 released a new contingency fund for Benavides to draw upon in time of need. Under the terms of the grant the viceroy of New Spain was to send 12,000 pesos worth of specie and supplies to Saint Augustine for use in emergencies. The governor could use the fund when he thought necessary, but he was solemnly bound to reintegrate the money and goods he withdrew when the subsidy arrived in Saint Augustine. In this way the king hoped to insure a perpetual contingency fund, a permanent reserve for use in crises on the Florida frontier.[76] Among the goods shipped to Florida in February, 1733, under this grant were grain, cattle feed, pork, lead, candle wax, candle wicks, and 4,495 pesos in specie.[77]

If experience had been a teacher, it had shown that such a fund simply could not last in Florida, no matter what strictures the king might apply. Florida was continually in need and perennially in an economic crisis. In fact, within four years the money and supplies were gone. By the time Governor Montiano took office in 1737 only a "little suet lead, and few candle wicks" remained from the shipment of 1733. Montiano also reported that he had found no accounts verifying the use of the fund.[78]

Montiano's report rankled the Council of the Indies. Once again the governor had misappropriated money in the Florida treasury. Members of the Council angrily demanded an immediate audit of the emergency fund to ascertain where the food, supplies, and money had gone. Montiano dutifully carried out the audit but found no irregularities. Benavides had used the money to pay his soldiers and the supplies to maintain a band of slaves and forced laborers. When the subsidy arrived from Cuba late in 1733, Benavides had replaced every peso and candle wick he had withdrawn. Moral, however, once again proved a convenient scapegoat. He had spent the money and used the supplies after English pirates seized the *situado* ship in 1735. Not only had he exhausted the emergency fund, but he had also failed to make an accounting of his use of the 12,000 pesos.[79]

Cathedral Records, Saint Augustine Parish, photostatic copies in the Saint Augustine Historical Society, p. 131.

76. AGI, Santo Domingo, Legajo 837. Despacho del rey al gobernador de la Florida, Jan. 31, 1731.

77. AGI, Escribanía de Cámara, Legajo 153B. Carta del gobernador de la Florida al Marqués de Torrenueva, June 15, 1738.

78. AGI, Escribanía de Cámara, Legajo 153B. Carta del gobernador de la Florida al rey, Nov. 11, 1737.

79. AGI, Santo Domingo, Legajo 2541. Testimonio de un decreto y de dos informes

Blaming Moral for the disappearance of the 12,000 pesos did not satisfy the Council. Moral had only signed the warrants releasing the money and supplies. His treasurer and accountant had issued the goods and specie and were responsible for keeping accounts of expenditures. This made the two treasury officials equally culpable. At this juncture, however, it was not feasible to indict them for negligence. Moral's treasurer, Salvador García de Villegas, and his accountant, Francisco Menéndez Marqués, were dead. Their successors, Juan Esteban de Peña and Francisco de Castilla, could hardly be held responsible.[80] Still, the Council hoped to prevent a recurrence of such behavior. On February 16, 1740, it ordered Montiano and his two treasury officials to replace the 12,000 pesos from the first *situado* reaching the Florida capital. It also commanded the governor and his two aides to return to the three-key system of withdrawing specie from the Saint Augustine treasury. All public money arriving in Florida was to be placed in a three-lock chest to which the governor, accountant, and treasurer each had a key. When money was withdrawn, all three had to be present. No money could be extracted without full knowledge of all three; each bore equal responsibility for all expenditures.[81]

In October, 1740, the Council modified this order. Believing it was an undue hardship on Montiano to force him to repay money spent by Moral in 1735, the Council ordered the viceroy of New Spain to send an additional 12,000 pesos to Florida. The provision for the three-key chests, however, was retained, with the two treasury officials getting special authority to check the governor's misuse of the fund. If the governor used the money for purposes that did not qualify as colonial emergencies, the accountant and treasurer were sworn to warn him "one, two, and three times." If he persisted in this illicit spending, they were to inform the king.[82] Relieved that he did not have to reintegrate the 12,000 pesos into the treasury, Montiano approved of the new plan in April, 1742.[83]

dados por los oficiales reales de este presidio en asunto de los doce mil pesos de repuesto, mandos por S.M. remitir a el para sus urgencias, que pasa a sus Reales Manos: año de 1738.

80. AGI, Santo Domingo, Legajo 2530. Carta de los oficiales reales de la Florida al rey, April 18, 1742.

81. AGI, Santo Domingo, Legajo 833. Consulta del Consejo de las Indias, Feb. 16, 1740.

82. AGI, Santo Domingo, Legajo 833. Consulta del Consejo de las Indias, Oct. 22, 1740.

83. AGI, Santo Domingo, Legajo 2584. Carta de los oficiales reales de la Florida al rey, April 20, 1742.

The 12,000 pesos, like the building fund, served the colony in time of need. The extra pesos and supplies lying conveniently at hand in Saint Augustine sustained the colony when the subsidy failed to arrive and provided necessities when emergencies occurred. The governor had no other recourse than to use the funds available in his treasury. In the end the king and the Council of the Indies grudgingly countenanced the losses but not without half-hearted attempts to get the money back or to regulate the distribution of emergency funds. For the most part, however, these efforts were fruitless.

[The Reform of 1740: The Royal Havana Company]

The economic trials and tribulations endured by Florida finally brought about a fundamental change in the subsidy system. The Puebla scheme of 1702 had clearly failed. The bishop had never been able to eliminate the old evils—delays, high prices, high shipping costs, and low-quality supplies—and all of these had continued to work innumerable hardships on the Floridians. In 1740, therefore, the king instituted a change in the method of supplying Florida with its annual needs.

The reform was closely tied to the establishment of the Havana Company, a joint stock enterprise similar to the British East India Company. Chartered in December, 1740, this venture aimed at stimulating Cuban trade with Spain and at promoting the royal tobacco monopoly on the island. The Caracas Company, founded twelve years earlier to increase the Spanish cacao supply, was a convenient model. For a time, at least, this enterprise had been profitable. Its stock had paid lucrative dividends, the cacao supply had increased in Spain, and it had eliminated the necessity for a *situado* in the Caracas area.[84] Undoubtedly the king, the Council of the Indies, and stockholders in the Havana Company hoped to obtain similar results in Cuba and Florida.

Philip V issued the royal *cédula* setting up the Havana Company on December 18, 1740. The venture had a total capitalization of one million pesos in shares of five hundred pesos each. The king, a leading subscriber, bought one hundred shares. The company agreed to maintain a coast guard around Cuba, to repress smuggling, to carry military goods free of charge to military and naval bases in the Caribbean, to build its own ships at its own cost, and to furnish Florida its annual quota of money and supplies. In return the company received special privi-

84. Roland Dennis Hussey, *The Caracas Company, 1728-1784* (Cambridge, 1934), *passim*.

leges. It obtained a monopoly over the Cuban tobacco trade with Spain, exemption from port taxes, and the right to enter Spanish ports duty free with Cuban sugar and hides. These same vessels could also carry flour, flagstones, and shipbuilding materials without imposts. For fourteen years ships of the Havana Company could transport rum and wine duty free.[85]

In May, 1741, the Council of the Indies set down the responsibilities of the Havana Company toward Florida. It required that the entire subsidy from Puebla be sent to Havana in hard money on the ships of the Windward Squadron (Armada de Barlovento). With these funds officials of the company were to buy supplies and food for Florida. In order to determine the price and amount of the goods needed, a company agent was to consult with the governor and his junta in Saint Augustine. Together they would draw up a contract. Officials of the company would then ship the necessary supplies and remaining specie to the Florida capital. If the governor and his junta could prove that the colony was in "dire necessity," the company had to furnish food and other articles one year in advance, in lieu of the arrival of the situado from New Spain. The principal source for the subsidy remained the Puebla sales taxes, but since income from the alcabalas had diminished since 1702, the viceroy was ordered to make up the difference between the income produced in Puebla and the amount requested by the governor in Florida. It was left to the governor in Saint Augustine to submit a certified statement of this amount to the viceroy.[86]

Despite these elaborate preparations the new system was not at first a success. In the winter of 1742, when the Havana Company sent its first agent, Domingo Reborato y Solar, to Florida to draw up a contract, it proved a task to try the keenest bargainer. Initially, Montiano and his junta put off the agent, refusing to confer with him. Then, on January 31, 1742, the governor convoked his junta, which agreed to a contract.[87] Reborato found that the Floridians drove a hard bargain. Immediately they insisted upon invoking Article Twenty-Nine of the charter, requiring the company to furnish supplies one year in advance. At the same time Montiano and his junta gave Reborato the responsibility of collecting a debt of 250,000 pesos from the viceroy, owing Florida from

85. Hussey, The Caracas Company, pp. 207-210.
86. AGI, Santo Domingo, Legajo 838. Consulta del Consejo de las Indias, May 27, 1741.
87. AGI, Santo Domingo, Legajo 863. Carta del gobernador de la Florida al presidente y los directores de la Real Compañía de la Havana, March 10, 1742.

past subsidies. The Floridians, of course, expected to draw upon this account at will.[88]

Thoroughly outmaneuvered by Montiano and his cohorts, Reborato returned to Havana, where his superiors were furious. Their agent had unwisely agreed to provide supplies for Montiano under Article Twenty-Nine with no proof that Florida was in desperate condition. In addition, Reborato had agreed to assume the responsibility for collecting the huge debt owing to the province. With little likelihood that even a small part of it would ever be repaid, this was far too heavy a burden for the company to bear, especially in its first years of operation. For this reason the directors of the company immediately abrogated the contract and requested that a new one be drawn up.[89]

With the whole affair at an impasse, both Montiano and the company took their cases to the Council of the Indies. The governor stressed the fact that for three years no subsidy had reached Florida. This, he believed, was reason enough to invoke Article Twenty-Nine. He pointed out also that his colony had reached such straits that he had dispatched an agent to Puebla to collect the *situado* under the old system.[90] In its arguments the company emphasized that it too had not received the subsidy from New Spain. Without it, the directors could not pay for the supplies required by the garrison in Florida. Without the *situado*, stated the report of the company, it could not act, even under Article Twenty-Nine.[91]

In Spain the king and the Council of the Indies pursued a middle course in mediating the dispute. A *fiscal* of the Council pointed out in August, 1742, that forcing the Havana Company to supply Florida on a credit basis was an undue financial hardship on the new enterprise. He also suggested that the term "dire necessity" or "extraordinary emergency" be more specifically defined so that it would be absolutely clear when Article Twenty-Nine should be invoked.[92] A month later the king

88. AGI, Santo Domingo, Legajo 863, Carta del gobernador y los oficiales reales de la Florida al rey, April 16, 1742.

89. AGI, Santo Domingo, Legajo 863. Carta de los directores de la Real Compañía de la Havana al gobernador de la Florida, April 18, 1742.

90. AGI, Santo Domingo, Legajo 863. Carta del gobernador los oficiales reales de la Florida al rey, May 22, 1742. Testimonio de los papeles en que consta haverse negado le Real Compañía de la Havana al cumplimiento de la contrata celebrada entre su comisario y la junta del presidio de la Florida, sobre la provisión de viveres de el ante dicho Presidio: año de 1742.

91. AGI, Santo Domingo, Legajo 863. Testimonio de autos formados sobre la contrata celebrada con la Real Compañía de Havana obligandose a proveer este Presidio de viveres y demas efectos: año de 1742.

92. AGI, Santo Domingo, Legajo 863. Dictamen del fiscal, Aug. 11, 1742.

chided both parties for their inability to agree on a contract. In a bit of wishful thinking by which Philip V may have hoped to soften the directors of the company, he stated that the missing subsidies for 1740 and 1741 were bound to arrive in Cuba soon. They would provide funds for supplies the company might ship to Florida in the meantime; but he did not directly order such action.[93] To Montiano the king was sharper. Philip V admonished the governor and his junta to act with "more mature judgment" in making supply contracts with the Cuban agent. The king also justified the action of the company in withholding supplies and in abrogating the first supply contract.[94]

While the king and his Council were trying to settle the dispute in Spain, the governor and officials of the Havana Company managed to resolve their differences. In June, 1742, six months after Reborato had signed the first contract, a new agreement was reached, apparently on the basis of a partial subsidy that had finally reached Havana.[95] This evidently provided funds to buy supplies needed in Florida and partially relieved tensions between Montiano and the directors of the company.[96] Still, the governor was determined to prevent any recurrence of difficulties over Article Twenty-Nine. In a dispatch to Philip V he emphasized the suffering and misery in Florida, brought about by delays, shortages, or non-delivery of the subsidy. Together, claimed Montiano, the viceroy of New Spain and the bishop of Puebla owed his colony 194,000 pesos. Except for the few supplies that had reached Saint Augustine in 1742, "not one real" of the *situados* for 1739, 1740, or 1741 had been delivered. In strong terms Montiano asserted, "Saint Augustine, Florida, is the most odious and abhorrent name heard in New Spain and Havana."[97] Six months later he repeated this account of conditions in Florida, continuing his drive to point up the plight of his colony to the king.[98]

93. AGI, Santo Domingo, Legajo 838. Despacho del rey al presidente y los directores de la Compañía de Havana, Sept. 9, 1742.

94. AGI, Santo Domingo, Legajo 838. Despacho del rey al gobernador y los oficiales reales de la Florida, Sept. 9, 1742.

95. AGI, Santo Domingo, Legajo 863. Carta del gobernador y los oficiales reales de la Florida al rey, June 22, 1742.

96. In April, 1742, Governor Montiano claimed that the debt owing Florida amounted to 250,000 pesos. In October of the same year he had reduced the claim to 194,000 pesos. Evidently, the 56,000 pesos arrived in Havana in the meantime and reached Florida in specie and supplies.

97. AGI, Santo Domingo, Legajo 845. Carta del gobernador de la Florida al rey, Oct. 2, 1742.

98. AGI, Santo Domingo, Legajo 2584. Carta del gobernador y los oficiales reales de la Florida al rey, March 26, 1743.

The supply contract negotiated in the summer of 1742 helped lay the way open for more workable arrangements between Florida and officials of the Havana Company. To assist the company, the governor and his junta agreed to send a list of anticipated needs to Havana, which would give officials there more time to procure the articles requested at favorable prices. The company also obtained the right to purchase supplies outside Havana and to revise prices upward if necessary. For its part the Havana Company assumed the responsibility for collecting back debts owing Florida by the viceroy of New Spain and the bishop in Puebla and agreed to use *what it obtained* for the welfare of the Floridians. The governor and the company also worked out new shipping arrangements. All Cuban ships unloading at Saint Augustine would be served by small launches working back and forth from the entrance of the harbor to the wharves. This would remove all risk of shipwreck at the shallow inlet leading into the harbor. Florida had to bear all shipping costs. Typical prices set in supply contracts were twenty-five pounds of flour, twenty reales; one and one-half bushels of corn, thirty-six reales; twenty-five pounds of pork, forty-eight reales; and a bushel and one-half of salt, twenty reales.[99]

These agreements prevented the recurrence of many of the early differences between the governor and the company, but they could not stop the emergence of former abuses, as old as the subsidy system itself. In July, 1743, for example, Montiano pled again for the prompt delivery of the subsidy and complained about the high prices being charged his colony by the Havana Company. Twenty-five pounds of flour, he stated, cost only sixteen reales in Mexico City; he paid twenty reales for the same amount.[100] Not long after, the governor pointed out that the Havana Company had shipped a cargo of spoiled meat to Saint Augustine, which the governor refused to accept. Dispatching his own agent to Havana, Montiano obtained good beef eight reales a side cheaper than the price agreed upon in his supply contract with the company.[101]

Periodic disappearance or seizure of *situado* ships was still another problem. In January, 1745, for example, a convoy of ships from New

99. AGI, Santo Domingo, Legajo 845. Testimonio de la contrata celebrada entre la Real Compañía de la Havana y la Junta del Presidio en asunto de su provisión, July 18, 1743.

100. AGI, Santo Domingo, Legajo 845. Carta del gobernador de la Florida al rey, July 18, 1743.

101. AGI, Santo Domingo, Legajo 838. Despacho del rey al gobernador de la Florida, Nov. 12, 1746.

Spain, escorted by frigates of the Windward Squadron, dropped anchor in Havana harbor, carrying the Florida subsidy in its holds. In Havana officials of the Havana Company immediately took charge of the specie and purchased the supplies requested by the governor and his junta. Co-operating closely with the Florida accountant, Francisco de Castilla, these officials then drew up a plan to carry the goods and remaining specie (worth 47,000 pesos in all) to Saint Augustine in a fleet of two small galleons, a frigate, and a brigantine.

All went well in Havana until Castilla attempted to seek a larger naval escort from the governor of Cuba, Francisco de Güemes y Horcasitas. Blocked at every turn by Güemes' supercilious secretaries, he failed to obtain an audience with the governor and ultimately had to sail for Florida without securing adequate naval protection for his two vessels.[102] Not long after the four ships left the harbor, a violent storm broke. During the tempest the foremast shattered on the small galleon carrying the 47,000 pesos, separating it from the rest of the fleet. A cannon shot fired as a distress signal failed to attract the attention of the other ships, long since out of range, and the disabled vessel had to take refuge in a sheltered inlet of one of the Bahamas. Here the captain and crew assessed the damage wrought by the storm and took stock of their predicament. Caught halfway between Saint Augustine and Havana, their ship badly in need of repair, and separated from their escort vessels, the Spanish sailors had to decide whether to proceed to Florida or to go back to Cuba, once they had put their ship in seaworthy condition. After some debate the crew voted to chance the voyage to Saint Augustine. This, the majority believed, was no more dangerous than returning to Havana, where they might also fall prey to English corsairs.

The Spanish captain never had the opportunity to know whether his men had made a wise decision. While he waited in the Bahama harbor for a favorable wind to take his ship north to Florida, an English man-of-war carrying twenty-nine men, six cannon, and smaller armaments sailed into the inlet. Initially the Spaniards resisted with a few feeble volleys from their small arms, but the English ship was undeterred and finally came close enough for its crew to throw out grappling hooks to draw the two vessels together. With the odds three-to-one against them and facing almost certain annihilation in hand-to-hand fighting, the Spaniards surrendered. The English captain then took his prize in tow to

102. AGI, Santo Domingo, Legajo 833. Expediente sobre la perdida de 47,000 pesos de S.M. que se remitián en una goleta desde Havana para socorro de la tropa del Presidio de la Florida, n.d.

Providence Island, where British authorities confiscated the supplies and money on board and released the Spanish crew, which finally made its way back to Cuba on a French vessel.[103]

Incidents like these dealt a serious blow to the hard-pressed Floridians and also set off investigations in Spain. Eager to find a scapegoat, the king and the Council of the Indies hoped to avoid a similar occurrence and to find a culpable party who might be made responsible for paying the sum which was lost. But in this case the Council could not fix the blame despite the attempt of the Florida accountant, Francisco de Castilla, to incriminate the governor of Cuba. Castilla stated that the governor should have issued specific instructions to the four ship captains in case they became separated. If Güemes had fulfilled this responsibility, claimed Castilla, the 47,000 pesos would now be resting in the treasury at Saint Augustine. Castilla also condemned Güemes for his failure to provide adequate naval protection for his ship.[104] The Council, however, did not hold the Cuban governor responsible. It was apparent that no amount of gubernatorial instructions could have controlled the vagaries of nature, and the Council finally placed the blame for the loss on the storm, requesting the viceroy to deliver an additional 47,000 pesos to Havana as soon as possible.[105] Meanwhile the Floridians suffered.

[*The Burden of Extra Expenses*]

Maintaining his regular soldiers and their families in the face of difficulties such as these was a heavy burden on the governor, but it was an even heavier one when he had to support soldiers and laborers temporarily assigned to Florida. Until 1739 the problem arose only occasionally. In 1735-1736, for example, Governor Moral had to maintain Felipe de Iturrieta's company of Cuban infantrymen on detached service in Florida, but this was uncommon, and not until the outbreak of the War of Jenkins's Ear did the problem become acute.

Governor Montiano found this responsibility particularly vexing. Administering Florida's affairs throughout the years of the War of Jenkins's Ear, he had to support a great many extra military and naval

103. AGI, Santo Domingo, Legajo 845. Consulta del Consejo de las Indias, Oct. 6, 1745.

104. AGI, Santo Domingo, Legajo 833. Expediente sobre la perdida de 47,000 pesos de S.M. que se remitián en una goleta desde Havana para socorro de la tropa del Presidio de la Florida, n.d.

105. AGI, Santo Domingo, Legajo 833. Consulta del Consejo de las Indias, Oct. 14, 1746.

men and forced laborers sent into Florida to strengthen the fortifications of the province. By 1743 these additional forces numbered over three hundred; three years later there were over seven hundred additional military men and forced laborers under Montiano's jurisdiction. To maintain them, he had received some help from the governor of Cuba, but for the most part he had provided them with food and supplies out of the subsidy shipped to his regulars from New Spain through Cuba. This meant that many of the established garrison of 350 received neither a regular salary nor a normal ration.[106]

In May, 1745, Montiano made an impassioned plea to the Havana Company to relieve this burden. Asking for an additional appropriation to provide for those on detached service in Saint Augustine, he claimed that he had no more money or supplies to care for the Cubans in his employ. If his own colony was to survive, he would need more assistance.[107] In his plea to his superiors in Spain, Montiano complained that the Havana Company was not doing its part to provide for his own garrison or the extra soldiers and sailors on detached service. In Madrid Montiano got support from a *fiscal* of the Council, who believed that refusal of the company to send aid was a breach of contract. Under their charter company officials were obligated to support the Floridians.[108] Still, this legal opinion was not enough to stimulate royal action against the Cubans, and in his reproachful dispatch to the Havana Company, the king refused to spell out the obligations of the company towards Florida.[109]

In 1749 the governor complained of other expenses which contributed to his sorry economic plight. Besides maintaining the military on detached service, he had to support a cavalry company, the organist and choir boys of the parochial church, a band of Indians, forced laborers, and the Franciscan missionaries. In addition he had to maintain a fleet of small launches for the harbor, lights for the guard house, and ornaments for the church. He also had to bear the expense of public festivals, the care of slaves, of pens, paper, horses, and of transportation costs for military officers traveling to Apalache. These expenses took

106. AGI, Santo Domingo, Legajo 845. Carta del gobernador y los oficiales reales de la Florida al rey, Nov. 23, 1743.
107. AGI, Santo Domingo, Legajo 845. Carta del gobernador y los oficiales reales de la Florida a los directores de la Real Compañía de la Havana, May 24, 1745.
108. AGI, Santo Domingo, Legajo 845. Dictamen del fiscal, Jan. 15, 1746.
109. AGI, Santo Domingo, Legajo 838. Despacho del rey al presidente y los directores de la Real Compañía de la Havana, Nov. 12, 1746.

more than a third of his annual expenditures in Florida (43,057 pesos), an amount still not covered by the annual *situado* of 116,127 pesos.[110]

[*An Economic Awakening: The Rise of a Naval Stores Industry*]

After 1750 gubernatorial complaints concerning the subsidy and the want and destitution in Florida suddenly diminished. Reasons for this phenomenon are not clear, but apparently the Havana Company had adopted a policy urged by Montiano some years before. Directors of the company evidently began to make contracts with English traders in New York and Charleston, and these merchants began calling at Saint Augustine regularly with cheaper, good-quality supplies.[111] Since company directors had obtained royal permission to purchase supplies elsewhere, if they were not available in Cuba, they took advantage of this relaxation in trade restrictions to buy low-cost goods in English colonies. They also made contracts calling for delivery of these supplies in English vessels, removing the costs and risks of carrying them to Florida on company ships.

Still another reason for the improvement in the economic situation grew out of the use of Saint Augustine as a base for Spanish privateers. These vessels ranged widely and effectively along the Atlantic coastline during the War of Jenkins's Ear and continued their depredations after the conflict ended. Bringing their prizes into Saint Augustine, these privateers provided the Floridians with another new source of supplies.[112]

For the governor this meant considerable relief for his treasury. He was now able to obtain supplies regularly at low prices. Moreover, with the supplies and food seized by privateers, he was better able to provide for the needs of his colony. His only real concern was that the subsidy would not reach Cuba from Puebla to pay for the goods purchased by the Havana Company in New York or Charleston, but Bourbon efficiency had apparently eliminated many of the previous evils.

110. AGI, Santo Domingo, Legajo 2584. Certificación de los oficiales reales de la Florida, March 15, 1749.

111. AGI, Santo Domingo, Legajo 2542. Carta del gobernador interino de la Florida al rey, July 13, 1752. In this letter the governor describes the arrival of English ships in Saint Augustine with supplies ordered by the Havana Company. The letter indicates that this practice was common.

112. Legally the governor was required to report all seizures of enemy ships to the crown and to allot a certain proportion of the amount obtained from the sale of enemy goods to the king. Apparently, although there is no conclusive evidence, the governor and his Floridians often seized English ships and supplies that they did not report to the crown and kept all profits themselves for use in the colony.

There were other signs of an economic awakening as well. In the 1750's production of naval stores on a large scale seemed a very real possibility, and many Floridians saw tar, pitch, resin, masts, and spars as the economic salvation of the colony. For all of his notoriety Governor Moral had taken the initial steps to establish the industry. In 1735 he had provided the stimulus for the production of enough pitch, tar, spars, and masts for use by Cuban shipbuilders.[113] After his departure in 1737, however, little was done to continue the experiment until 1744, when Montiano proposed to re-establish the industry on a grander scale. He wanted to erect a large factory to produce tar and pitch for the shipbuilders of the Havana Company. He also believed the tall pines in the mountains north of Apalache would make superb masts and spars, which could easily be floated to the coast on one of the many rivers flowing into the Gulf of Mexico near Apalache. As a by-product the Floridians could fashion ramrods for artillery for use all over the Indies. Montiano also believed that such a venture demanded the creation of a new company similar to the Havana Company.[114]

Montiano's enthusiasm was not contagious, however, and his superiors in Spain proved unwilling to sponsor such an enterprise. When the governor left in 1749, nothing had been done to implement his plan. But this did not end the matter. In April, 1756, Governor Alonso Fernández de Heredia induced some colonists in Saint Augustine to begin manufacture of naval stores on their own initiative and sent seventy barrels of pitch and tar to the Havana Company, which used the commodities for its shipbuilding operations. This so encouraged the governor that in a report to the king he evisaged an enlarged trade with such important shipping centers as Vera Cruz, Puertobelo, and Cartagena.[115] When Ferdinand VI received reports of these activities, he encouraged them. For the first time in almost two hundred years a productive, profit-making venture seemed possible in Florida, and in his dispatch to Saint Augustine in the fall of 1756 he enthusiastically approved the scheme. He also agreed to let the Floridians cut royal timber in the colony for masts and spars.[116]

113. AGI, Santo Domingo, Legajo 845. Informe del escribano de cámara, Sept. 27, 1743.
114. AGI, Santo Domingo, Legajo 2530. Carta del gobernador de la Florida al rey, Feb. 8, 1744.
115. AGI, Santo Domingo, Legajo 2542. Carta del gobernador de la Florida al rey, April 7, 1756.
116. AGI, Santo Domingo, Legajo 2542. Despacho del rey al gobernador de la Florida, Oct. 13, 1756. Despacho del rey al gobernador de la Florida, June 14, 1757.

With royal support Governor Fernández expanded the trade in naval stores to include New Spain. Late in 1757 or early in 1758, his first launch arrived in Vera Cruz carrying pitch and tar. In the Mexican port the appearance of this vessel both shocked and perplexed royal officials. For almost two centuries dock hands had loaded ships bound for Florida with immense quantities of money and supplies. Since 1570 more than ten million pesos in money and goods had passed through Vera Cruz on their way to Saint Augustine. Now the hitherto unimaginative Floridians had seemingly shaken off their economic lethargy and had come to Vera Cruz selling naval stores, products they had extracted from their own barren province.

For the port officials, the matter became a vexing problem. The captain of the launch claimed that the king had awarded shippers of Florida naval stores relief from all port taxes for ten years. The customs' officers at Vera Cruz, however, had received no orders to this effect and were reluctant to grant an exemption. Besides, it was hardly credible that the Floridians should have articles for sale in the first place. Clearly this was a matter that demanded a decision from the viceroy in Mexico City. In his report the viceroy suggested that an exemption from port taxes be allowed for two years but that the *alcabala* and a "moderate tax" be placed on all naval stores carried by the Floridians.[117] This, in turn, was submitted to the king before action was taken on the cargo in Vera Cruz.

Charles III pursued a middle course. In July, 1760, he granted Florida shippers relief from port taxes for ten years rather than the two years advised by the viceroy, but he ordered dealers in pitch and tar to pay the sales taxes and another "moderate tax," not clearly defined in the king's orders.[118] Thus, the way seemed open for the development of the naval stores industry now that the test case in Vera Cruz had worked out in favor of the Floridians. But not long after the king's *cédula* reached the governor in Saint Augustine, the colony shifted to English control. Hopes for an economic revival based on the naval stores industry were never realized, and the first Spanish period ended with Florida struggling to find new means of support for the colony other than the subsidy system that had maintained it for almost two hundred years.

117. AGI, Santo Domingo, Legajo 2530. Consulta del Consejo de las Indias, April 5, 1758.
118. AGI, Santo Domingo, Legajo 2530, Real cédula, San Ildefonso, July 29, 1760.

Chapter V

THE GOVERNOR AND
DEFENSE, 1700-1733

I n the eighteenth century Florida was useful to Spain almost solely as
a military outpost. The province protected the Bahama Channel on
the route of homeward-bound Spanish fleets, and with Cuba and the
eastern coast of New Spain, constituted a link in the chain of outposts
that kept the Gulf of Mexico a Spanish lake.[1] As the sole Spanish
foothold in the Southeast, Florida served as a bastion against the English
in Georgia and South Carolina and against the late-arriving French in
Mississippi and Alabama. For the king its military value was worth
the heavy drain on the royal treasury, and strategically, Florida held an
important place in the Spanish Empire in America.

[*The State of the Military and Defenses in 1700*]

In 1700 Governor Zúñiga commanded 323 men, scattered in various
outposts throughout Florida. A captain, executive officer, sergeant,
drummer, piper, page, and four squad captains formed the nucleus of
each of the three infantry companies assigned to the province. A sergeant
major—the governor's second-in-command—a lieutenant of the fort,
four adjutants, an armorer, a blacksmith, barber, and pharmacist served
at Fort San Marcos and received their salaries from the military payroll.
Small complements of artillerymen and sailors supported the three
infantry companies. In 1702 there were 137 infantrymen, twenty artillerymen, and sixteen sailors stationed in Saint Augustine proper. Thirty-
one footsoldiers garrisoned Fort San Luis de Apalache, thirteen served
in Guale mission villages, and three lived among the Timucuans near
Saint Augustine. Altogether twenty-five soldiers guarded the northern
and southern entrances to Saint Augustine (the bar of Saint Augustine
and the bar of Matanzas, respectively). Another small body of soldiers

---

1. French settlements on the Gulf Coast prevented the Spanish from maintaining
complete control of the Gulf of Mexico. Practically, however, Spain dominated the Gulf.

maintained a lonely vigil at the mouth of the Saint John's River (the bar of San Juan).[2] It was never clear how many able-bodied soldiers were actually serving in Florida. Widows and orphans of those who died in Florida and crippled or aged veterans were carried on the military rolls and were often included in the estimates of the effective fighting force available in Saint Augustine. This practice was especially odious to Zúñiga, who insisted that a five-hundred-man garrison was absolutely essential because of widows, orphans, old men, and cripples carried on the military rolls.[3]

Procuring enough seasoned men was only a part of the governor's military problems. The state of colonial defenses and the condition of war supplies were also his responsibility. Finally completed in 1687, Fort San Marcos was not as yet prepared to withstand a long siege. According to the governor, the stone structure had no adequate moat, counterscarps, or bunkers on its land side to the north and west. Of the thirty-six cannon mounted atop the fort, only eighteen were serviceable. Cannon balls were scarce, and the meager supply of powder available was hardly usable because of the excessive humidity and poor construction of the powderhouse at Fort San Marcos. It was reported also that Zúñiga's artillerymen were unable to hit a large house at ten paces, and without proper training the governor held out little hope that their aim would improve.[4] Surveying his supply of muskets, arquebuses, pikes, lances, catapults, swords, knives, mortars, and pistols, Zúñiga found that most were in poor condition—rusty, worn, or without the proper parts.[5]

Fort San Luis, the second most important outpost in Florida at the opening of the eighteenth century, was in no better condition than San Marcos. A wooden structure, located fourteen leagues northeast of the mouth of the Apalache River near present-day Tallahassee, housed four mortars, five rusty cannon, and a garrison of thirty-one soldiers. These men also maintained a perpetual lookout on the watchtower overlooking Apalache Bay.[6]

2. AGI, Santo Domingo, Legajo 840. Carta del gobernador de la Florida al rey, March 25, 1702.

3. AGI, Santo Domingo, Legajo 840. Carta del gobernador de la Florida al rey, Oct. 30, 1701.

4. AGI, Santo Domingo, Legajo 840. Carta del gobernador de la Florida al rey, Dec. 26, 1701.

5. AGI, Santo Domingo, Legajo 840. Carta del gobernador de la Florida al rey, March 3, 1706.

6. AGI, Santo Domingo, Legajo 840. Carta del gobernador de la Florida al rey, March 25, 1702.

[The Siege of Saint Augustine, 1702]

In 1702 Governor Zúñiga had to bring together all the resources of his poorly equipped, undermanned garrison to fight off English invaders, intent on seizing the Florida capital. In 1702 war broke out in Europe over the succession to the Spanish throne, and this conflict quickly spread into the colonies as Queen Anne's War. In Carolina Governor James Moore saw the struggle as an opportunity for mounting a combined land-sea attack on Florida. This, he hoped, would destroy Spanish power in the Southeast once and for all. Organizing a force of six hundred English volunteers and six hundred Yamasee warriors, the English governor personally assumed command of the entire expedition with Colonel Robert Daniel as his chief of staff.[7]

From its rendezvous point in Port Royal, South Carolina, the English force began its invasion in September, 1702. Colonel Daniel led a group of soldiers and Indians up the Saint John's River in canoes after seizing the two tiny Spanish outposts of Santa María and San Juan near the mouth of the river. Proceeding up the Saint John's, Daniel's force moved to a point directly west of Saint Augustine, where he and his men left the river and marched eastward toward the Florida capital.

In the meantime, Zúñiga made plans to meet the impending attack. Assembling all the soldiers, residents, and Indians of the Saint Augustine area in Fort San Marcos, he brought in enough food, supplies, and powder to last four months. He also saw to it that the residents brought their most valuable possessions into the fort to keep them from falling into the hands of the enemy.[8]

Zúñiga had acted wisely. Within a few days after the Spaniards had taken refuge in the fort, Daniel's soldiers and Indians entered Saint Augustine and sacked and looted the town. Falling back with their plunder, they returned to Saint Augustine on November 10 and set up headquarters at the church of San Francisco. The next day Moore, who had forced entrance into Saint Augustine harbor with three brigantines and five sloops, joined Daniel.[9]

7. The best account of the siege of Saint Augustine is Charles W. Arnade, *The Siege of St. Augustine in 1702* (Gainesville, 1959).

8. AGI, Santo Domingo, Legajo 840. Carta del gobernador de la Florida al rey June 6, 1703.

9. There is a conflict in the English and Spanish documents as to the exact date the English vessels entered Saint Augustine harbor and as to the time the Carolinians debarked. English documents state the fleet reached the bar of Saint Augustine on October 21 and entered the harbor on October 27, when Moore's men disembarked

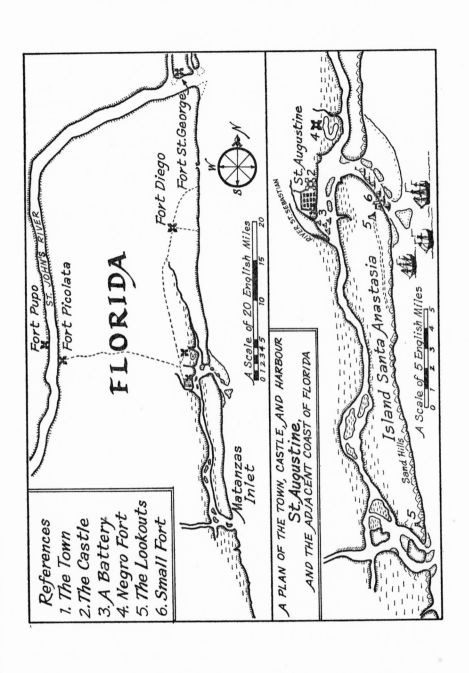

References
1. The Town
2. The Castle
3. A Battery
4. Negro Fort
5. The Lookouts
6. Small Fort

FLORIDA

Fort Pupo
ST. JOHN'S RIVER
Fort Picolata

Fort Diego

Fort St. George

N
W   S

A Scale of 20 English Miles
0 1 2 3 4 5   10   15   20

Matanzas
Inlet

A PLAN OF THE TOWN, CASTLE, AND HARBOUR
St. Augustine,
AND THE ADJACENT COAST OF FLORIDA

RIVER ST. SEBASTIAN

St. Augustine

Island Santa Anastasia

Sand Hills

A Scale of 5 English Miles
0   1   2   3   4   5

The two Carolinians immediately called a council of war. At the meeting Moore and his aides decided that Fort San Marcos was too formidable to be taken by storm. Their force was too small and their equipment inadequate to take the fort. The scaling ladders they carried with them would be of little use because of the deep moat surrounding the land sides of the fort, a surprising development in view of Zúñiga's earlier complaint to the crown concerning the inadequacy of the moat. To the Carolinians Zúñiga's rusty cannon, mounted high on the parapets at San Marcos, presented another difficult obstacle. Both Moore and Daniel thus decided on a siege to starve the Floridians into submission. Immediately they dispatched one of their ships to Jamaica to secure additional mortars and cannon and took the necessary steps to seal off the land sides of the fort. This, they envisioned, would prevent the more than "one thousand Eaters" in San Marcos from obtaining rations and water.[10]

Moore's decision to lay siege to San Marcos was crucial in turning the tide in Zúñiga's favor. Before Moore had surrounded the fort, the governor had dispatched pleas for help to Apalache, Havana, Mobile, and Pensacola. One messenger had reached Cuba, where the governor quickly organized a relief expedition. At the same time the English agent sent to Jamaica to procure mortars and artillery returned to Charleston instead of carrying out his assignment, leaving Moore and Daniel futilely waiting for aid from the English island. Finally, Moore became panicky. With his supplies running low and his bombardment of San Marcos achieving little effect, he sent Daniel to Jamaica to check on the agent and obtain new supplies. Zúñiga and his Floridians remained firmly entrenched in the fort. Their only casualties resulted from the shattering of a sixteen-pound cannon (on November 20) and from losses to patrols sent out to harass Moore's men. For all of its battering, the English cannon had not caused a single casualty.[11]

During the last week of November and the first weeks of December, an uneasy stalemate set in at Saint Augustine, as it became obvious that

---

near the Florida capital. The Spanish documents state that Moore's fleet crossed the bar on November 11. Even with the eleven-day discrepancy between the Julian and Gregorian calendars, the two dates cannot be reconciled. See Verner W. Crane, *The Southern Frontier, 1670-1732* (Ann Arbor, 1956), p. 76.

10. Public Record Office, Colonial Office Records (hereinafter cited as CO), 5: 382, pt. 1. Robert Daniel and James A. Moore to the Board of Trade and Plantations, Saint Augustine, Nov. 9, 1702.

11. AGI, Santo Domingo, Legajo 836. Consulta del Consejo de las Indias, May 22, 1703.

victory would belong to the one whose ships arrived first. Fortunately for Zúñiga the Spanish won the race. The day after Christmas, 1702, four Cuban ships appeared off the bar of Saint Augustine with reinforcements and supplies for the embattled Floridians. Zúñiga immediately dispatched a launch to welcome the vessels, to explain his situation at the fort, and to bring in food.[12]

Arrival of the relief ships forced Moore to raise the siege, and on December 27 he began making preparations to leave Florida. One of his first acts was to set fire to the thatch and board buildings of Saint Augustine, which left all the principal structures except the hospital in ashes. Since he could not retreat by sea because of the galleons blocking the mouth of the harbor, Moore dragged his brigantines and sloops onto the beach near Saint Augustine and set them afire. In their haste to get away, however, the English allowed some of the fires to go out, and Zúñiga managed to salvage three of the boats for use in patrolling Saint Augustine harbor. In any event, on December 30, Moore raised the siege and began retreating north along the tortuous land route to Carolina.[13]

Zúñiga hoped to intercept Moore's retreating force. The governor wanted to embark his Florida regulars aboard the Cuban relief vessels, sail north to the mouth of the Saint John's River, and cut off the Carolinians in a surprise attack. Such an assault on the dispirited English would, he believed, insure a Spanish victory. Esteban de Berroa, the commander of the four ships, however, refused to agree to the plan and would not allow the governor the use of his ships. As a further affront to Zúñiga, Berroa confiscated most of the arms and equipment left behind by Moore's men, leaving the Floridians only three cannon and a few entrenching tools.[14]

Although Zúñiga had thrown back the English, he now faced many new problems. The English had destroyed most of Saint Augustine, leaving many residents homeless and the church and convent in ashes. As an aftermath of the siege, a smallpox epidemic broke out to cause the governor further concern. His defenses had withstood the onslaught,

12. AGI, Santo Domingo, Legajo 840. Carta del gobernador de la Florida al rey, Jan. 6, 1703.

13. AGI, Santo Domingo, Legajo 840. Carta del gobernador de la Florida al rey, Jan. 8, 1703.

14. AGI, Santo Domingo, Legajo 841. Carta del gobernador de la Florida al rey, Nov. 7, 1703.

but the immense task of reconstruction now lay before him. In its present state it was unlikely Saint Augustine could stand another siege.[15]

[*Moore's Revenge: The Massacre at Ayubale*]

While Zúñiga was laying plans to rebuild Saint Augustine, Moore was organizing another campaign against Florida. When he returned to Charleston early in 1703, the English governor found himself exceedingly unpopular. He had failed to take Saint Augustine, had incurred a colonial debt of £26,000 for the costs of the expedition, and had lost valuable ships and supplies in his hurried retreat. Some Carolinians also accused him of organizing the 1702 assault on the Florida capital to avoid an investigation of illegal election practices in which he was involved. In any event, his failure the previous year did not deter Moore, who seemed determined to salvage his reputation as a military leader by launching a new attack on the Spaniards. When he called for volunteers in the summer and fall of 1703, however, only fifty Carolinians agreed to join him, but the addition of 1,500 vengeful Yamasees gave him the force he needed to carry out his plans. Late in 1703 he set out with this unruly horde to ravage Florida anew, this time focusing on the Spanish Indian villages in Apalache near Fort San Luis.[16]

Moore's attack on Apalache proved successful in eliminating almost all Spanish influence in the area. In the villages where the Franciscans had once labored to convert and civilize the Indians, Moore and his Yamasees spread terror and devastation. Either as a deliberate tactic or because the fifty soldiers could not control the Yamasees, the English Indians committed atrocities that cowed and intimidated the Spanish Apalaches into submission. Virtually unchecked, Moore turned Apalache into a land of terror and destruction. His only failure was to destroy Fort San Luis, but this outpost was evacuated only a few months after his sally into western Florida.[17]

Fort San Luis survived because of the events at Ayubale in January,

15. AGI, Santo Domingo, Legajo 864. Carta de Fray Martín de Alcano al rey, June 30, 1703.

16. "To his excellency John Granville, Esqu., Palatine, and to the rest of the true and absolute Lords and Proprietors of the Province of Carolina. The Representations and Address of several of the Members of this present Assembly retinue for Colleton County, and other Inhabitants of this Province, whose names are hereunto subscribed, (150)." In William James Rivers, *A Sketch of the History of South Carolina to the Close of the Proprietary Government by the Revolution of 1719 with an Appendix* (Charleston, 1856), p. 455.

17. AGI, Santo Domingo, Legajo 840. Carta del gobernador de la Florida al rey, March 30, 1704.

1704. Ayubale was a Franciscan mission village and stockade eight leagues northeast of Fort San Luis served by the Franciscan friar, Angel de Miranda. Unlike many of his brethren who left for Saint Augustine when war broke out, Miranda had remained with the Indians. Even in the face of the English-Indian attack, he refused to leave the village, which he effectively organized to meet the invaders. When the Yamasees first assaulted the wooden stockade at Ayubale, they were greeted by a surprising volley of arrows and musket fire that drove them into headlong retreat. Recouping, the Yamasees counterattacked at the mission church. Here they hoped to use their axes to batter down the door, which would give them access to the stockade. But again they were driven back by the friar's Indians, who inflicted heavy losses.[18]

This unexpectedly fierce opposition forced Moore and his Carolinians to work out a new plan of attack. Twice repulsed, they had incurred heavy losses and could ill afford to lose more. It was decided, therefore, to use flaming arrows to set fire to the stockade. In this way they could force the Ayubales into the open, where the Yamasees could overwhelm them. But before the English had an opportunity to carry out this scheme, Miranda emerged from the village carrying a flag of truce. He told Moore that his Indians had no more arrows or powder and were completely spent from continual fighting. Their only alternative, he stated, was to throw themselves on the mercy of their antagonists. The friar and his Indians received no mercy. The Yamasees murdered Miranda on the spot, burned Ayubale, and tortured or killed the Indians who were not able to escape.[19]

Martyred at Ayubale, Miranda had been unable to save his village, but he had saved Fort San Luis. He had temporarily stopped Moore's advance and enabled the Spanish garrison at San Luis to organize an expedition to repulse the invaders. When news of the events at Ayubale reached the Spaniards at the fort, the commandant, Captain Juan Ruiz Mexia, put together a force of 30 Spanish soldiers and 400 Indians, which engaged Moore's force near Miranda's smoking village. In the battle that ensued, the English won another victory. Mexia lost 5 soldiers and 168 Indians; eight of his band were taken prisoner. Moore, on the other hand, lost 6 or 7 militiamen and 100 Yamasees.[20] During the

18. AGI, Santo Domingo, Legajo 836. Despacho del rey al gobernador de la Florida, Aug. 22, 1704.

19. AGI, Santo Domingo, Legajo 840. Carta del gobernador de la Florida al rey, March 30, 1704.

20. AGI, Santo Domingo, Legajo 836. Despacho del rey al virrey de Nueva España, June 30, 1704.

battle a second Franciscan, Juan de Parja, lost his life leading a contingent of Apalaches against the Carolinians, but it was to little avail. The remainder of Mexia's force had to fall back to Fort San Luis, leaving Moore and his Indians free to run wild in the area surrounding the fort.[21] Still resistance by both the Indians of Ayubale and Mexia's force slowed the English attack and prevented the loss of Fort San Luis.

Moore could not control the Yamasees, who pitilessly lanced, burned, or impaled the Apalaches they took prisoner. News of these atrocities spread quickly throughout the Southeast, and many Apalache villages were intimidated into expressing allegiance to the Carolinians by threats of torture, separation of families, or death. At least twelve such villages submitted to the English without a struggle. Moore claimed that by the time he was ready to retire from Apalache only one town of Indians remained under Spanish control, and this village lay under the cannon of Fort San Luis.[22] Zúñiga reported from Saint Augustine that over six hundred Christian Indians had shifted their loyalties to the English late in 1703 and early in 1704.[23] Estimates of the Carolinians claimed at least thirteen hundred new Indian allies and one hundred Indian slaves.[24]

Moore was far more successful in Apalache than in Saint Augustine. He destroyed the vestiges of the once-flourishing Franciscan mission villages in Apalache and won over a great many Indian allies to English allegiance. By defeating Mexia he discredited the Spaniards in western Florida and ultimately forced the evacuation of Fort San Luis. Short of powder, food, and men, and threatened by new Yamasee attacks, the garrison made preparations to evacuate the fort soon after Moore's retirement. On July 16, 1704, the commandant sent his last dispatch to Governor Zúñiga, who ordered the garrison to destroy San Luis and withdraw to Pensacola. In October, 1704, Zúñiga wrote to Philip V: "I have found it to our best interests to retire the garrison and to demolish the fort because of the impossibility of supplying the infantry

21. AGI, Santo Domingo, Legajo 840. Carta de Fray Lucas Álvarez de Toledo al rey, Aug. 22, 1704.
22. Crane, *The Southern Frontier*, p. 80.
23. AGI, Santo Domingo, Legajo 840. Carta del gobernador de la Florida al rey, March 30, 1704.
24. "An Account of What the Army Did Under the Command of Colonel Moore in his Expedition Last Winter, Against the Spaniards and Spanish Indians. In a letter from the Said Col. Moore to the Governor of Carolina." Printed in the Boston *News*, May 1, 1704. In B. R. Carroll, *Historical Collections of South Carolina* (New York, 1836), II, 574-576.

there, eighty leagues away."[25] But without a doubt Moore's attack had been a decisive factor in forcing the withdrawal.

The evacuation of Fort San Luis left Governor Zúñiga with only two defense posts—Fort San Marcos at Saint Augustine and Salamototo, a tiny blockhouse just south of present-day Jacksonville on the banks of the Saint John's River. Florida had once encompassed the territory from the Atlantic Ocean to the mouth of the Río Grande and from the Gulf of Mexico to Nova Scotia. Now the province was reduced to two precarious footholds, liable to fail at any moment if the Carolinians renewed their attacks.

[*Military Policy in Florida during Queen Anne's War*]

Reports of the siege of 1702 distressed Spanish officials, who feared the loss of their strategic outpost at Saint Augustine. Florida was the key to the defenses of the Bahama Channel, the Caribbean, and the Gulf of Mexico, and Spain could ill afford to let the province fall into English hands. In an effort to strengthen the province, a special Junta de Guerra met in June, 1703, suggesting the immediate reinforcement of Saint Augustine and Apalache to make these presidios invulnerable. Once this had been accomplished, the Junta suggested that a counteroffensive be mounted against Carolina.[26] To implement these proposals, the Junta and the Council of the Indies granted Juan de Ayala Escobar men, money, ships, artillery, munitions, and supplies, which proved useful to Zúñiga in bolstering the defenses of Saint Augustine late in 1704 and early in 1705.[27]

The Junta de Guerra also took additional steps toward planning the offensive against Carolina. Hoping to obtain an experienced military officer to lead the attack, its members suggested that Zúñiga be replaced by Andrés de Arriola, widely reputed as a shrewd strategist and tactician. The Junta also ordered the viceroy of New Spain, the Duke of Albuquerque, to remit 50,000 pesos, 150 to 200 soldiers, and arms and powder for use by the expeditionary force. There was also a suggestion— not an order—that the governor in Florida confer with the French

25. AGI, Santo Domingo, Legajo 858. Carta del gobernador de la Florida al rey, Oct. 6, 1704.

26. AGI, Santo Domingo, Legajo 833. Consulta de la Junta de Guerra, June 12, 1703.

27. AGI, Santo Domingo, Legajo 852. Consulta del Consejo de las Indias, July 16, 1703.

governor of Canada on the possibility of mounting a joint offensive on the English simultaneously in both the south and the north.[28]

From the first, plans went awry. The viceroy refused to send the men and money; Arriola refused to accept command in Florida; and there was no collaboration with the French in Quebec. Arriola's refusal of the governorship forced another delay of almost a year before the Council of the Indies found a suitable candidate. Then when the appointment finally went to Francisco de Córcoles y Martínez, additional delays kept the new governor in Spain. Still it was hoped that the attack on Carolina could be carried out, and the king ordered Córcoles to confer with both the governor of Cuba and the viceroy of New Spain on the best way to insure the success of an offensive.[29]

Córcoles himself was eager to undertake an attack on Charleston. Leaving Cádiz on December 5, 1705, he was confident he would succeed, despite the fact that the thirty recruits sailing with him had to be confined to a Cádiz jail to keep them from deserting.[30] When he conferred with Governor Nicolás Chirino Vandevall in Cuba, Córcoles reported that he would surely be victorious, if only the viceroy in Mexico would send him the necessary money, men, and supplies.[31] Once in Saint Augustine, however, he lost his enthusiasm. Of the 389 persons on his military rolls, no more than half were able-bodied men. The others were old, crippled, or the widows of soldiers who had died in Florida. For Córcoles this group could not form the nucleus of an expeditionary force.[32]

Still, Córcoles agreed to support a plan for offensive war fashioned by his predecessor. In August, 1704, Governor Zúñiga had conferred with a French naval officer, Francois Tristán, on the possibility of an attack on Charleston. Together they agreed that Tristán would proceed to Cuba, obtain arms, men, and ships, and return to Florida to solicit aid from Zúñiga before moving on Charleston.[33]

28. AGI, Santo Domingo, Legajo 852. Consulta de la Junta de Guerra, July 18, 1704.

29. AGI, Santo Domingo, Legajo 836. Despacho del rey al virrey de Nueva España, May 22, 1705.

30. AGI, Santo Domingo, Legajo 850. Carta del presidente de la Casa de Contratación al secretaría de Nueva España, Dec. 6, 1705.

31. AGI, Santo Domingo, Legajo 840. Carta del gobernador de la Florida al rey, March 29, 1706.

32. AGI, Santo Domingo, Legajo 840. Carta del gobernador de la Florida al rey, March 3, 1706.

33. AGI, Santo Domingo, Legajo 852. Carta del gobernador de la Florida al rey, Sept. 15, 1704.

Although Tristán himself did not return to Saint Augustine, another French captain, Jacques Lefebvre, entered the harbor in August, 1706, ready to carry out the campaign against Carolina. Lefebvre had secured men and ships in Havana and wanted Córcoles to provide him with dugouts for use in shallow water, a half-galley, and any soldiers he could spare from the defenses of Saint Augustine. With the consent of a special junta, Córcoles granted the French commander two canoes, a half-galley, thirty regular infantrymen, and a few Indian volunteers. On August 31, the expedition weighed anchor and sailed north.[34]

From the very first, misfortune plagued the attackers. No sooner had the fleet left the harbor than a Dutch sloop separated one of Lefebvre's six vessels from the main body of the convoy. The loss proved especially crucial because the ship carried the commander of the land forces of the expedition, General Arbousset. Still, Lefebvre was determined to go through with his plans, and on September 7 his vessels sailed into waters near Charleston. Guards maintaining a vigil at Sullivan's Island at the entrance to Charleston harbor quickly sent up smoke signals to herald the approach of the five enemy ships, and authorities in the city sent out a call for militiamen to assemble in Charleston, suffering at that moment from a yellow fever epidemic. Initially there was some doubt that those living in the surrounding countryside would enter Charleston and risk exposure to the dreaded disease, but for the Carolinians the threat of invasion was evidently greater than the threat of yellow fever and the militia responded to the call. In the meantime Lefebvre's ships moved closer to the harbor entrance. On the evening of September 7 they anchored off Sullivan's Island.

Hoping to take Charleston without a struggle, Lefebvre sent a message to Governor Nathaniel Johnson on the morning of September 8, demanding the surrender of the entire colony. Given an hour to reply, Johnson answered immediately. He needed "not a Quarter of an hour or a minute's time." He would throw back all invaders.[35]

The next morning Lefebvre launched his attack. One Spanish raiding party landed on James Island and set fire to a house, but a counterattack by Carolina militiamen and Indians drove the marauders back to the protection of their half-galley. Another force of 160 Spanish soldiers landed on a narrow stretch of land between the Wando River

34. AGI, Santo Domingo, Legajo 840. Carta del gobernador de la Florida al rey, Sept. 30, 1706.
35. AGI, Santo Domingo, Legajo 840. Auto para llamar a junta para si conveniene dar ayuda a los cabos que van a la Carolina, Sept. 23, 1706.

and the Atlantic Ocean, where they burned two small launches and a storehouse. Supremely confident after their easy victory, the Spanish force decided to remain on land for the night rather than to return to the ships. In celebration of their victory they began roasting chickens they had seized during the day. In the meantime, however, Governor Johnson dispatched a force of 100 militia to engage the invaders. This English force caught the Spaniards completely by surprise and won an overwhelming victory. Of the 160 caught feasting on the chicken, 12 were killed, 60 captured, and 6 or 7 drowned while attempting to swim to safety.[36]

Spanish losses on the Wando River turned the tide in favor of the Carolinians. On September 11 when Governor Johnson ordered six small launches and a fireship[37] to engage the five ships anchored off Sullivan's Island, he delivered the *coup de grace* that drove the attacking force back to Florida. Rather than risk further losses, Lefebvre ordered his five ships to make for the open sea, putting an end to the Spanish-French attempt to take Charleston. Governor Johnson, in the meantime, ended martial law, which he had ordered at the beginning of the attack.[38]

This might have ended the affair, but there was a postscript. Lefebvre had no sooner set sail for Saint Augustine than *La Brilliante*, the ship separated from the rest of the fleet at the outset of the expedition, appeared at the entrance to Charleston harbor. This vessel carried General Arbousset and two hundred soldiers, who were still eager to fight despite the fact that the remainder of their force had departed. With remarkable speed Arbousset debarked his two hundred men east of Charleston and led them directly toward the town. Governor Johnson, however, was again able to throw back the invaders. One body of militia, which he sent to intercept Arbousset's troops, soundly defeated the French and Spaniards in a battle near Holybush Plantation. A smaller group of men, ordered to seize *La Brilliante*, managed to board the vessel during the fighting at Holybush Plantation and to take the ship as a prize. In all, the Carolinians seized 320 Frenchmen,

36. AGI, Santo Domingo, Legajo 840. Auto para llamar a junta para si conveniene dar ayuda a los cabos que van a la Carolina, Sept. 23, 1706.

37. Johnson's fireship was a vessel carrying both explosives and combustibles to be sailed into the midst of the Spanish fleet.

38. CO 5:382, pt. 1. "An Account of the Invasion of South Carolina by the French and Spaniards in the Month of August, 1706, Sir Nathaniell Johnson being our Governour."

Spaniards, and Indians as prisoners[39] and killed over 30 in the fighting.[40]

The governor of Florida believed that the failure of the assault on Charleston could be blamed on the separation of *La Brilliante*. Arbousset's leadership, asserted Córcoles, would have carried the day. Charleston was vulnerable to attack. The governor believed that the English could be driven out of Carolina, and he himself was eager to lead the invasion.[41]

His eagerness for an offensive war was hardly consistent with his dismal reports on the military state of his colony. By the end of 1706 Saint Augustine was the last vestige of Spanish power in Florida, and here conditions were deplorable—the garrison depleted and badly equipped, the city in ashes, and the defenses of Fort San Marcos deteriorating.[42] In addition, the viceroy of New Spain had failed to provide Córcoles with the money, men, and supplies he needed to carry out his military plans. Without help from the viceroy, Córcoles could neither wage an offensive war nor strengthen his defenses against enemy encroachments.[43] In desperation the governor sent Francisco de Florencia as his personal emissary to Mexico City to plead for help, but Florencia's entreaties failed to move the viceroy.[44] Even the remonstrances of the Council of the Indies could not force the viceroy to render military aid to Florida. In New Spain he claimed that fortifications at Charleston were invulnerable and that the large number of English warships infesting the Caribbean Sea and the Bahama Channel would make it impossible to take Carolina. Any aid he might give to Córcoles for an offensive war, stated the viceroy, would be wasted.[45]

Despite the viceroy's adamancy, the governor still contemplated a campaign against Carolina. In March, 1708, Córcoles proposed a plan by which he would lead a Spanish force to Charleston along the pro-

39. CO 5:382, pt. 1. "An Account of the Invasion of South Carolina by the French and Spaniards in the Month of August, 1706, Sir Nathaniell being our Governour." These figures include those taken in the earlier clashes with Lefebvre's force.

40. AGI, Santo Domingo, Legajo 840. Carta del gobernador de la Florida al rey, Sept. 30, 1706.

41. AGI, Santo Domingo, Legajo 840. Carta del gobernador de la Florida al rey, Nov. 30, 1706.

42. AGI, Santo Domingo, Legajo 841. Carta del gobernador de la Florida al rey, Nov. 30, 1706.

43. AGI, Santo Domingo, Legajo 840. Carta del gobernador de la Florida al rey, Feb. 28, 1707.

44. AGI, Santo Domingo, Legajo 841. Carta del gobernador de la Florida al rey, Nov. 12, 1707.

45. AGI, Santo Domingo, Legajo 841. Carta del virrey de Nueva España al gobernador de la Florida, Nov. 12, 1707.

tected channel formed by the coastal islands of Georgia and the mainland. Using Guale Indians as guides, he hoped to transport his force in dugouts and canoes along the coast and avoid the dangers of a land march or travel on the open sea.[46] In an attempt to implement his plan, Córcoles induced the Spanish commandant at Pensacola to ask the viceroy for two thousand men, five frigates, four launches, eight to ten cannon, four mortars, and two hundred grenadiers and lancers. Again the viceroy refused to send military aid to Florida, but this time he took a strong stand in an effort to settle the whole question. After consulting a junta, he stated flatly that he was resolved "to suspend execution of the king's edict" requiring him to aid Córcoles. Although the viceroy was anxious to eliminate the English menace in Carolina, he did not have the means at his disposal to carry out the king's order.[47]

Faced with the viceroy's intransigence, authorities in Spain attempted to get help from other sources. In January, 1709, the Junta de Guerra ordered the governor of Cuba to remit one hundred muskets and one hundred soldiers to bolster the Saint Augustine garrison. The Junta also ordered powder, lead, grenades, muskets, cannon balls, and twenty-five infantrymen sent out from Spain.[48] Five months later in May, 1709, the Junta declared Florida "the first line of defense for New Spain" and censured the viceroy for refusing military assistance to Córcoles.[49] In August Philip V himself stepped in when he issued a general *cédula* calling for the formation of an expeditionary force in Cuba and New Spain to be used against Carolina.[50] He did not specify, however, just how his order should be carried out, and nothing came of it. In Cuba the governor ignored the *cédula*. In Mexico City the viceroy claimed that his treasury gave him no recourse but to request arms, men, and money for the French in Martinique, which he was reluctant to do.[51] Córcoles, of course, could do little without outside help.

Although the governor may have realized the futility of calling for

46. AGI, Santo Domingo, Legajo 841. Carta del gobernador de la Florida al rey, March 20, 1708. Informe del gobernador de la Florida, Feb. 27, 1707.

47. AGI, Santo Domingo, Legajo 841. Carta del virrey de Nueva España al gobernador de la Florida, Nov. 1, 1708.

48. AGI, Santo Domingo, Legajo 833. Consulta de la Junta de Guerra, Jan. 15, 1709.

49. AGI, Santo Domingo, Legajo 833. Consulta de la Junta de Guerra, May 23, 1709.

50. AGI, Santo Domingo, Legajo 836. Real cédula, Buen Retiro. Aug. 27, 1709.

51. AGI, Santo Domingo, Legajo 841. Carta del virrey de Nueva España al rey, Aug. 25, 1709.

an offensive war against Carolina, in 1710 he presented one last plan to his superiors in Spain. Córcoles envisaged the possibility of a Negro slave revolt if he could lead an expedition against the English in Charleston.[52] In fact this time he was so enamored with his scheme that he sent the Franciscan friar, Antonio de Florencia, to appeal personally to the king for help; but Philip V, who was having his own difficulties in Europe, refused to implement the plan.[53] In the end the only aid Córcoles received from the king was a military engineer, who came to Saint Augustine to strengthen the defenses of the colony.[54] By the time the war ended in 1713, little had been done to change the military situation in the colony—either its internal defenses or its external military relationship to Carolina. The most significant changes came after hostilities ended.

[*Refortification of Apalache*]

Queen Anne's War greatly reduced the territory under Spanish control in the Southeast. The English and their Indians destroyed the few remaining Franciscan mission outposts in Apalache and Guale, forced the Spanish to abandon Fort San Luis, and confined the Spanish inhabitants and their Indians to the area surrounding Fort San Marcos at Saint Augustine. Almost all of the governor's military activity centered in this area. Here Zúñiga successfully withstood the English siege of 1702. Here his successor, Francisco de Córcoles y Martínez, organized a new cavalry company, erected new bulwarks at San Pablo (one of the four defense lines for Fort San Marcos), fortified the northern and southern entrances to Saint Augustine Harbor, established regular patrols of the Matanzas River, and placed six cannon in the Indian village of Nombre de Dios near Saint Augustine. He also paid his Indians twenty five pesos for every Carolinian or hostile Indian killed or captured.[55] Although these accomplishments led to no fundamental change in the military or defensive position of the colony, they served their purpose: they prevented the colony from falling into the hands of the English.

52. AGI, Santo Domingo, Legajo 841. Carta del gobernador de la Florida al rey, Feb. 28, 1710.

53. AGI, Santo Domingo, Legajo 841. Carta del gobernador de la Florida al rey, Sept. 6, 1710.

54. AGI, Santo Domingo, Legajo 843. Consulta de la Junta de Guerra, Nov. 29, 1713.

55. AGI, Santo Domingo, Legajo 848. Testimonio en relación sobre la buen obra del Señor Gobernador y Capitán General don Francisco de Córcoles y Martínez, Dec. 20, 1715.

Proposals for fundamental reforms in the colony came soon after the war ended. In February, 1716, the Junta de Guerra submitted a report to the king advocating the removal of the Florida capital to Apalache. Here, stated the report, land was fertile, food plentiful, the climate healthful, and the harbor broad and deep for ships of heavy tonnage, obvious advantages over the old capital. To insure the success of the new venture, the Junta recommended the transferral of all old or crippled soldiers out of the Saint Augustine garrison and their replacement by able-bodied regulars. As further insurance the Junta called for the shipment of 1,000 new muskets and the settlement of two hundred Galician families in Apalache. Properly provided with tools, seed, land, and military protection, these farmers would provide the new capital with a regular supply of food and a sound basis for its economy.[56] Intrigued by the proposal, Philip V ordered the Cuban engineer, Bruno Caballero, to make a preliminary survey of the Apalache Bay area and to delineate a healthful, defensible site for the new capital.[57] Caballero's plans were to include a fort with walls six hundred feet on a side and a town with wide straight streets—"agreeable to the eye," adequately drained, commodious for trade, and convenient for the residents. Upon completion of his survey, the engineer was to submit his plans to the Council of the Indies for final approval.[58]

The question of removing the capital to Apalache remained under discussion for over ten years. Principal hindrance to quick action was the refusal of Caballero to make his survey. He first claimed that his responsibilities in Cuba were too heavy for him to spend his time making a reconaissance of the Apalache area and suggested that another engineer be selected to lay out the site of the new town.[59] When the king refused to name a replacement, Caballero contrived another excuse; he claimed that illness had forced him into a health spa near Havana.[60] In the meantime, Governor Benavides suggested that the Council use *his* recommendations regarding the transfer of the capital to Apalache, but

56. AGI, Santo Domingo, Legajo 833. Consulta de la Junta de Guerra, Feb. 5, 1716.

57. AGI, Santo Domingo, Legajo 837. Real cédula, El Pardo, Feb. 17, 1716.

58. AGI, Santo Domingo, Legajo 843. Memorias de las provincias y precauciones que se han de mandar, observar, y incluir en la instrucción que se diere para el estable-cimiento y conservación de la nueva forteleza que se ha construir en la Provincia de Apalache, Feb. 12, 1716.

59. AGI, Santo Domingo, Legajo 849. Carta de Bruno Caballero al rey, Dec. 28, 1726.

60. AGI, Santo Domingo, Legajo 849. Carta de Bruno Caballero al rey, Sept. 4, 1728.

the Council refused. Its members wanted the opinions of a trained observer, and in July, 1728, ordered two Spanish engineers to delineate the possibilities of locating towns in both the Apalache and Carlos (Charlotte Bay) areas.[61] Like Caballero the two surveyors did not fulfil their obligations, but by this time the king had already decided to give up the plan to remove the Florida capital to Apalache.[62]

The real impetus for resettlement of Apalache came from within Florida long before the matter had been settled in Spain. In 1716 and 1717 many tribes from northern Apalache had come to Saint Augustine expressing their allegiance to the interim governor, Juan de Ayala Escobar. Believing that resettlement of Apalache under royal auspices was imminent, Ayala promised the Indians his protection. Then, after two years passed and Caballero failed to make his survey, Ayala was forced to act on his own initiative. On February 20, 1718, he sent out the cavalry captain, Joseph Primo de Rivera, with fifty men to erect a blockhouse on Apalache Bay. To aid the work party, the governor dispatched supplies and building materials to Apalache by sea, and these awaited Primo's men when they arrived after their land trek to Apalache from Saint Augustine.[63]

Primo's soldiers worked through most of the early spring of 1718. By the end of April they had erected a powder house and a wooden stockade, Fort San Marcos, measuring seventy-two feet on a side. Atop the new structure three cannon proclaimed the re-establishment of Spanish military power in the area. But no sooner had the fort begun to take shape than hordes of friendly Lower Creeks appeared requesting supplies and gifts from the Spaniards. Primo, who barely had enough food and supplies for his own troops, was at first reluctant to aid the Indians but finally decided that he could not risk alienating them and quickly exhausted his meager larder. Short rations, in turn, caused dysentery among Primo's men, who had to slow their work on Fort San Marcos.[64] Still they accomplished enough to re-establish a Spanish outpost in Apalache, the first since 1704. Although it hardly approached the six-hundred-foot structure the Junta had proposed in 1716, it was,

61. AGI, Santo Domingo, Legajo 833. Consulta del Consejo de las Indias, July 13, 1728.

62. AGI, Santo Domingo, Legajo 833. Dictamen del rey, June 23, 1728.

63. AGI, Santo Domingo, Legajo 843. Carta del gobernador interino de la Florida al rey, Feb. 28, 1718. Auto sobre el número de soldados que andar a la guarnación de Apalache, Dec. 10, 1717.

64. AGI, Santo Domingo, Legajo 843. Carta del gobernador de la Florida al rey, Aug. 12, 1718.

nevertheless, strong enough to last until Florida became an English province in 1763.

Not long after the erection of San Marcos, Primo had to undertake a similar mission at Saint Joseph's Bay. In July, 1718, the Spanish governor of Pensacola reported to Governor Benavides in Saint Augustine that the French had established a new outpost on Saint Joseph's Bay, which threatened communications between Pensacola and Apalache.[65] In the meantime the French evacuated the Saint Joseph's area, but to prevent its reoccupation by an enemy force, Benavides ordered Primo to take as many men as he could spare to hold Saint Joseph's until reinforcements arrived. Primo dutifully detached twelve men from his force in Apalache and late in 1718 began fortifying Saint Joseph's.[66] With help from Pensacola and Saint Augustine, the cavalry captain managed to maintain a precarious foothold on Saint Joseph's Bay, but aid was at best sporadic. Lack of supplies and reinforcements, illness, desertion, and Primo's departure for New Spain forced the abandonment of the tiny stockade in 1723, breaking one link in the chain of Gulf Coast fortifications.[67]

[*Governor Benavides and Fort King George: The Brink of War*]

Intercolonial conflicts in the Southeast never followed a consistent pattern. Sometimes the outbreak of war in Europe between England and Spain meant hostilities between Florida and Carolina; at other times events in Europe had little bearing in the colonies. In 1702, for example, the War of the Spanish Succession in Europe had Queen Anne's War as its bloody counterpart in the Southeast. In 1718 when war again broke out in Europe, the Florida frontier remained quiet. Three years later, when Spain joined England and France in a new alliance, relations between Florida and Carolina might have been expected to improve; instead tensions increased almost to the brink of war.

The cause of the conflict between the two colonies was the construction of an English blockhouse, Fort King George, on the banks of the Altamaha River near present-day Darien, Georgia. The Floridians

65. AGI, Santo Domingo, Legajo 837. Consulta del Consejo de las Indias, Jan. 13, 1719.
66. AGI, Santo Domingo, Legajo 837. Consulta del Consejo de las Indias, Jan. 18, 1719.
67. Probably the key to the failure at Saint Joseph's was sending Primo de Rivera to New Spain to stand trial. Without his leadership the tiny garrison simply could not survive.

looked upon the fort as an encroachment on the Spanish domain, a repudiation of the solemn English pledge to respect Georgia as Spanish territory. The Spanish claimed the territory by right of papal donation, prior discovery, prior exploration, effective occupation, and the Treaty of Madrid of 1670 by which England and Spain established boundaries on the southern frontier. The English, however, refused to recognize any of these Spanish claims. During the last three decades of the seventeenth century they drove the Franciscans out of their Guale missions and turned Georgia into a "debatable land."[68]

An English force moved to bring Georgia into the English domain in the summer of 1721, when fifty Carolinians under Colonel John Barnwell fought rain, sickness, hostile Indians, and the sticky heat to erect a rude stockade on the north bank of the Altamaha. This structure consisted of a blockhouse twenty-six feet square with crude earthworks five to six feet high forming a right triangle with the blockhouse and defending the land side of the fort. Within the triangle lay the bark and thatch huts used as living quarters for Barnwell's men.[69] The Carolinians serving at the blockhouse "mocked and reviled" their stockade as a "frontier improvisation," yet this "improvisation" on the desolate Georgia coast almost became the cause for an international conflict.[70]

Governor Benavides was the first to challenge English activities on the Altamaha.[71] In March, 1722, he sent his accountant, Francisco Menéndez Marqués, to Charleston to demand the immediate destruction of the fort. In his representations to the Carolinians Menéndez protested the flagrant disregard of that "sacred document," the Treaty of Madrid of 1670, and demanded that existing agreements between England and Spain guaranteeing colonial territory be respected.[72]

The governor of Carolina, Francis Nicholson, paid little attention to Menéndez's allegations. The governor explained that he had re-

68. See Herbert E. Bolton and Mary Ross, *The Debatable Land* (Berkeley, 1925). See also Herbert E. Bolton, ed., *Arredondo's Historical Proof of Spain's Title to Georgia* (Berkeley, 1925).

69. See Joseph W. Barnwell, "Fort King George, Journal of Colonel John Barnwell (Tuscarora) in the Construction of the Fort on the Altamaha in 1721," *The South Carolina Historical and Genealogical Magazine*, XXVII (Oct., 1926), 189-203.

70. Quoted from Crane, *The Southern Frontier*, p. 237.

71. AGI, Santo Domingo, Legajo 842. Carta del gobernador de la Florida al rey, April 19, 1722. The governor's scouting reports were hardly up-to-date. Evidence points to the fact that Benavides did not learn about Fort King George until February, 1722.

72. AGI, Santo Domingo, Legajo 842. Carta del gobernador de la Florida al rey, April 21, 1722.

ceived no word from England concerning peace between Spain and England. As far as Nicholson was concerned, Spain and England were still at war. As his only concession, the Carolinian agreed that if he received word of a change in Anglo-Spanish relationships he would settle the matter of Fort King George with Benavides. In the meantime his men would continue to occupy the blockhouse on the Altamaha. Unable to sway Nicholson, Menéndez returned to Saint Augustine without obtaining any satisfaction.[73]

In Spain there was also concern over Fort King George. Both Philip V and the Council of the Indies saw the structure as a clear infringement of Spanish rights in Florida territory. Both the king and the Council used the traditional rationale of papal donation, prior discovery, exploration, occupation, and treaty rights, to demand the immediate destruction of the fort.[74] In October, 1722, the Council ordered the Spanish ambassador in London, Jacinto Pozobueno, to request the immediate evacuation of the small English outpost on the Altamaha. If the English seemed reluctant, the ambassador was to threaten forcible action by the governor of Florida. Orders also went out to the viceroy of New Spain and the governor of Cuba to gird for war should the English fail to meet the Spanish ultimatum on Fort King George.[75]

In December, 1722, Pozobueno presented these demands to the English authorities, who at first seemed obliged to bow to them. In their initial reply to the Spanish ambassador, they pointed out that in two dispatches—one on September 6, 1721, and another on November 28, 1722—they had ordered Governor Nicholson to observe friendly relations with the Spaniards in the Southeast.[76] Early in 1723, however, these same officials suddenly became belligerent. In January, Lord Carteret, Earl of Granville and a proprietor of Carolina, wrote to Pozobueno explaining that the Board of Trade and Plantations had taken up the Spanish complaint and concluded that Fort King George was not located in Florida but on the Florida-Carolina frontier. When Pozobueno tried to counter with an argument based on the boundary line set by the Treaty of Madrid (1670), both Carteret and William

73. AGI, Santo Domingo, Legajo 842. Carta del gobernador de la Florida al rey, April 21, 1722.

74. AGI, Santo Domingo, Legajo 842. Dictamen del fiscal, Sept. 11, 1722.

75. AGI, Santo Domingo, Legajo 837. Consulta del Consejo de las Indias, Oct. 7, 1722.

76. AGI, Santo Domingo, Legajo 2541. Real cédula, Seville, June 6, 1723.

Stanhope, British ambassador to Spain, were evasive and refused to order Barnwell's withdrawal from the fort.[77]

Negotiations in both Europe and America thus began moving toward war. On June 6, 1723, Philip V once more ordered Benavides to demand the destruction of Fort King George and an end to English-sponsored Indian raids on Florida. Nicholson was to be given two months to comply with the ultimatum. If he failed to do so within the prescribed period, Benavides was to destroy the fort himself.[78] For some reason, however, the strong policy laid down by the king in June was mitigated by the Council of the Indies. Six months after the king's strong *cédula* to Benavides, the Council recommended the use of diplomacy, not force, to resolve the controversy.[79] Both the *cédula* and the Council's more moderate recommendation reached Florida at the same time, presenting Benavides with two alternatives.

Initially Benavides chose the bolder policy. Early in April, 1724, he dispatched a party of twenty-six men to Charleston to deliver the ultimatum to Nicholson. On their way north the Spaniards called at Barnwell's stockade, where they received a rude reception.[80] Barnwell disarmed the Floridians, seized their longboats, and imprisoned them in the fort. After three days he allowed them to leave for Charleston but under heavy guard and in his own inferior dugouts. Once they reached the Carolina capital, the twenty-six received similar treatment from Governor Nicholson, who confined them to filthy, crowded cells and granted the Floridians barely enough rations to survive. In the diplomatic discussions concerning the destruction of Fort King George, the governor and his advisers were arrogantly adamant. They refused to abandon the fort, and for a time it appeared as if they would hold the diplomatic mission permanently in Charleston as prisoners. Finally, however, the English governor released the Spaniards and allowed them to return to Saint Augustine.[81]

War now seemed inevitable. Benavides' envoys had delivered the

77. AGI, Santo Domingo, Legajo 837. Consulta del Consejo de las Indias, Dec. 13, 1723.

78. AGI, Santo Domingo, Legajo 2541. Real cédula, Seville, June 6, 1723.

79. AGI, Santo Domingo, Legajo 837. Consulta del Consejo de las Indias, Dec. 13, 1723.

80. Just exactly why they stopped at Fort King George is not clear. Perhaps Benavides hoped that the twenty-six men would be a strong enough force to take the fort. Frontier diplomacy hardly demanded the large group of envoys that Benavides sent to Charleston.

81. AGI, Santo Domingo, Legajo 842. Carta del virrey de Nueva España al rey, March 14, 1725.

ultimatum to Charleston, and it appeared certain that Nicholson would not comply with it. But carried to the brink of war, Benavides backed down. Despite the fact that the viceroy of New Spain—for the first time in two decades—had promised him military assistance, the governor refused to take action to destroy Fort King George.[82] Reverting to the more moderate policy recommended by the Council of the Indies, Benavides sent two agents to Charleston in August, 1725, to bargain with Nicholson once again. These negotiators, Francisco Menéndez Marqués and Captain Joseph Primo de Rivera, had instructions to settle all matters under dispute with Carolina. They were to insist on the immediate destruction of Fort King George and the recognition of Spanish claims on Georgia, but in return they were to promise reimbursement to all English slave owners whose Negroes had fled to Saint Augustine. In another step calculated to ease tensions between the two colonies, Menéndez and Primo were instructed to draw up a complete list of boundary disputes with the Carolinians. This would then be sent to Europe for settlement by diplomats there.[83]

The two Floridians accomplished nothing. When they presented their demands in Charleston, Nicholson and his council refused to make any concessions. The Carolinians claimed they had no orders from England to adjust boundaries or to destroy Fort King George, and without orders from the mother country, they could take no action. Nicholson also stated that the price offered for the slaves was too low. Evasive and curt, the Carolinians sent Menéndez and Primo away with no clear statement of English policy on the southern frontier and with no decision on the blockhouse situated on the Altamaha.[84]

Benavides might have avoided at least some of this humiliating treatment if his scouts had kept him abreast of events at Fort King George. In the winter of 1725, unknown to the Floridians, the blockhouse had burned to the ground, and the tiny English garrison there retired—with relief—to more comfortable quarters in Port Royal.[85] Just when Benavides learned of the destruction of Fort King George is not

82. AGI, Santo Domingo, Legajo 842. Carta del virrey de Nueva España al rey, March 14, 1725.

83. AGI, Santo Domingo, Legajo 844. Testimonio de los autos y demás diligencias hechas sobre la división de los terminos de esta jurisdicción y la de Carolina en virtud de las Reales Cédulas que en ellas contienen sus fechas 10 de Junio y 18 de Agosto de 1724, n. d.

84. AGI, Santo Domingo, Legajo 844. Certificación de don Joseph Primo de Rivera y don Francisco Menéndez Marqués, Oct. 2, 1725.

85. Crane, *The Southern Frontier*, p. 245.

clear, but within at least six months after the fire an English work party was back on the original site rebuilding the fort.[86] This time, however, Benavides chose to ignore the existence of the English threat. He neither sent envoys to Charleston to protest nor dispatched panicky letters to his superiors in Spain concerning the infringement on Spanish territory. Evidently he hoped that the issue would resolve itself, and it did. In the fall of 1727 the English withdrew their garrison from Fort King George because of the threat of a war among the Creeks and of a renewal of hostilities with Spain. The evacuation, however, was much against the wishes of the Board of Trade in England, who hoped to maintain their foothold in the "debatable land."[87]

[Palmer's Raid: The End of an Era]

English activity at Fort King George was only one of the governor's military problems in the years following Queen Anne's War. Organizing Indian raids on Carolina was also his responsibility. One offensive tactic that proved effective was to pay Yamasees and Lower Creeks to harass English settlements located in southern Carolina. Ravaging the small farms of English colonists, these Indians kept the frontier continuously in a turbulent state and prevented the extension of English territory through effective occupation. Governor Benavides was especially active in sending Indians into Carolina to counteract the erection of Fort King George. In June, 1727, for example, residents on the Carolina border were so apprehensive about Indian raids that they asked the governor's permission to allow them to remove to Beaufort on the coast. The next month a band of Yamasees and Lower Creeks proved that the fears of the border farmers were well founded: several English traders were scalped near Fort King George.[88] Some of these raids came on the Indians' own initiative, but others were sponsored by Benavides, who found the Indians especially useful in holding back further English extension in Georgia.

That the English took revenge on the Floridians for these Indian raids is not surprising. Late in 1727 irate members of the governor's council in Carolina proposed a retaliatory expedition to repay the Span-

86. In August, 1725, when Primo and Menéndez were in Charleston requesting immediate destruction of Fort King George, it was obvious that they did not know of the fire that had swept through the blockhouse in the winter of 1725. Benavides must have learned of the disaster after the conclusion of this mission, if at all.

87. Crane, *The Southern Frontier*, pp. 246-247.

88. *Ibid.*, pp. 247-248.

iards for the atrocities committed on the border. The council first proposed a two-pronged attack—one on the Lower Creek villages in northern Apalache and the other on the Yamasee villages near Saint Augustine. Later, however, its members decided to concentrate on the Yamasee towns nearer the Florida capital. Colonel John Palmer, a member of the Commons House of Assembly in South Carolina and a veteran Indian fighter, was chosen to head the expedition, consisting of one hundred militia and two hundred Indians. This group set out from Charleston in small boats in February, 1728.[89]

The English dugouts moved southward along the coastal channel without opposition. Early in March Palmer's force reached San Juan Island at the mouth of the Saint John's River, where his men left their boats to make the land trek south to Saint Augustine. Along the way a Spanish scout detected the advancing troop of Englishmen and Indians and sounded the alarm. This enabled the Yamasees to prepare for the attack by concentrating at Nombre de Dios, the best fortified Yamasee village a short distance from Saint Augustine.[90]

Despite the fact Palmer lost the advantage of a surprise attack, he won a decisive victory at Nombre de Dios on March 9. In the battle his Carolinians killed thirty Yamasees, captured fifteen, and wounded many more, while the other Indians fled to Fort San Marcos. They found shelter there but discovered that the governor would not move out to meet Palmer's force, encamped nearby. Refusing to fight a smaller enemy force on familiar terrain, Benavides chose to keep his soldiers under the protective walls of San Marcos, where his only form of resistance was an ineffective barrage of cannon fire on Palmer's positions.

On March 13 Palmer retired from Florida. He had defeated the Indians at Nombre de Dios, but now that they had taken refuge in the fort and refused to come out to engage his men, he had no other choice than to return to Charleston. With only three hundred men and a minimum of supplies, he could not hope to lay siege to San Marcos. As a grim reminder of his visit, Palmer burned Nombre de Dios, destroyed the chapel there, and carried off the few altar ornaments and statues that adorned the church.[91]

Palmer thus avenged the insults suffered by the Carolinians at the hands of the Yamasees. He had struck terror among the Spanish

89. *Ibid.*, p. 249.
90. *Ibid.*, p. 250.
91. AGI, Santo Domingo, Legajo 866. Carta del gobernador de Cuba al rey, Aug. 27, 1728.

Indians and clearly demonstrated the vulnerability of their position. Palmer had shown the Yamasees that their Spanish protectors could not defend the Indian villages lying in the very shadow of the Florida capital. His raid also marked the end of an era. It was the last major clash in the Southeast between the English and Spaniards before the founding of Georgia in 1733, which put the "debatable land" under English control. For the governor of Florida the settlement of Georgia presented even greater defensive problems, as the English moved ever closer to the focus of Spanish power in the Southeast.

Chapter VI

THE GOVERNOR AND DEFENSE, 1733-1763

Between 1670 and 1733 Spanish Guale slowly and relentlessly became English Georgia. With the founding of Charleston in 1670, Spanish influence in Guale began to wane as the English moved to establish their pre-eminence in the area. English pressure forced Spanish missionaries south to labor in less dangerous villages near Saint Augustine or Apalache, leaving their missions and their influence behind them. In the early years of the eighteenth century English Indians ravaged Guale anew, and in 1721 Colonel Barnwell established Fort King George in the heart of Georgia. By 1733 James Oglethorpe's settlement of the area resolved the sixty-year-old struggle over the vast no-man's land. For the governor in Florida this meant a reorientation of military policy. Prior to 1733 the threat to Spanish power in Florida had come from the Carolinians in Charleston, 150 miles away. Now in 1733 the English menace was less than half that distance, forcing the governor to revise his defensive policies to fit the realities of expanding English power in the Southeast.

[*Reaction in Florida to the Founding of Georgia*]

By the summer of 1733 Governor Benavides was thoroughly alarmed over English activity in Georgia. In July he reported to the Council of the Indies that the new Georgia settlement was the first step in an English plot to drive the Spanish out of the Southeast. The Georgians, he stated, were more than simple farmers; they were well-armed military men ready to move first on Saint Augustine and from there on New Spain.[1]

When Moral assumed the governorship in 1734, he became even more concerned over English expansion into Georgia, especially

1. AGI, Santo Domingo, Legajo 2591. Carta del gobernador de la Florida a don Joseph Patiño, July 27, 1733.

[*134*]   THE GOVERNORSHIP OF SPANISH FLORIDA

Oglethorpe's growing prestige among the Lower Creeks in northern Apalache. Moral reported that the Creeks had recently cut the throats of three Spanish Indians. To counter Oglethorpe's activities, Moral suggested the strengthening of Apalache, gateway to the Lower Creek territory. Although he realized the plan was not new, he believed the establishment of English settlements in Georgia gave his proposal a new urgency. His plan called for the agricultural development of Apalache by Canary Islanders, who could farm the rich soil and initiate a fur trade with the Indians, in this "the most beautiful and richest province in all America."[2] He claimed too that Apalache offered fertile fields for further missionary effort. With its silver mines, pearl fisheries, and timber land, the province was certain to become another New Spain or Peru. Repopulation and strengthening of Apalache would also block the advance of the "ambitious and covetous" English on the Gulf Coast.[3]

In the meantime Moral attempted to bolster the defenses of his colony. In August, 1734, he ordered a crew of forced laborers under Francisco Palomino Lasso de la Vega to the banks of Saint John's, seven leagues directly west of Saint Augustine on the Apalache trail, to erect two wooden forts, one on each side of the river. In seventy days this work party constructed Fort San Francisco de Pupo on the west bank and Fort Picolata on the east bank. Each structure consisted of a blockhouse with barracks, storehouses, and batteries of small cannon, all of which cost Moral's treasury 2,036 pesos. Despite the expense, Moral believed the two forts essential to prevent any surprise attack on Saint Augustine from the west similar to Daniel's assault in 1702.[4]

For other projects Moral needed outside aid. He simply did not have the money, men, or supplies to accomplish more. Bemoaning his inadequacy, Moral wrote to the king in March, 1735, requesting funds to replace the wooden blockhouse at Apalache with a more defensible stone structure.[5] He also asked for two new infantry companies to bolster the garrison in Apalache. In all Florida, Moral declared, he had only 228 able-bodied men ready to take arms in case of an English at-

2. AGI, Santo Domingo, Legajo 2541. Carta del gobernador de la Florida al rey, June 24, 1734.
3. AGI, Santo Domingo, Legajo 2541. Carta del gobernador de la Florida al rey, Aug. 21, 1734.
4. AGI, Santo Domingo, Legajo 2541. Carta del gobernador de la Florida al rey, March 7, 1735. Certificación de don Francisco Palomino Lasso de la Vega, n.d.
5. AGI, Santo Domingo, Legajo 2541. Indice de las representaciones que el Gobernador de la Florida remité a su Magistad en la presente cojunto, March 20, 1735. See reference to letter of March 9, 1735.

tack. To fulfil his needs, he asked for at least five hundred troops,[6] but within six months he had doubled this request.[7]

Moral's reports about the inadequate defenses of his colony were verified by the Cuban engineer Antonio de Arredondo, who surveyed the military situation in Florida at the request of the Council of the Indies. Arredondo's report of November, 1736, stated that of the nine bronze cannon available at Fort San Marcos only two—a thirty-six pounder and a six pounder—were in good repair. The other seven were fit only for limited service or were useless. Among the iron cannon nineteen eight pounders were in excellent condition, but there were only eight hundred eight-pound cannon balls in Saint Augustine. Another twenty-eight iron cannon might be pressed into service if absolutely essential, but Arredondo was dubious that they could last through a sustained siege. In all the Cuban engineer counted 6,586 cannon balls at Fort San Marcos, but many of these were suited for cannon either unavailable at the fort or in poor condition.[8]

Arredondo also found that Moral's men were spread thinly throughout the colony. Eighty-nine men garrisoned Fort San Marcos and the fortifications at Saint Augustine. Forty-five soldiers served in Apalache; eighteen manned the twin forts of Pupo and Picolata; four cavalrymen guarded the mouth of the Saint John's River; and three garrisoned Fort Diego, twenty miles north of Saint Augustine on the coast. Five soldiers lived on Santa Anastasia Island, four at Matanzas on the south entrance to Saint Augustine harbor, and one at Peñon just south of the Matanzas lookout. The Indian villages of Chiquito and Pocotalaca each housed two soldiers and San Nicolás one. Of the 297 soldiers available in the regular Florida garrison, Arredondo found eighty too old, sick, or crippled for battlefield service.[9]

[*Governor Moral's Defense Diplomacy*]

Arredondo's report removed all doubts concerning Moral's precarious position. As governor Moral was responsible for the defense of the

6. AGI, Santo Domingo, Legajo 2591. Carta de don Joseph Patiño al gobernador de Cuba, July 25, 1735.

7. AGI, Santo Domingo, Legajo 2541. Carta del gobernador de la Florida al rey, Sept. 8, 1735.

8. AGI, Santo Domingo, Legajo 2591. Relación jurada de Don Francisco Navarro, teniente de artillería, June 16, 1736.

9. AGI, Santo Domingo, Legajo 2591. Relación de Don Antonio de Arredondo, Nov. 27, 1736. See also Don Antonio de Arredondo, Informe al gobernador de la Havana, de todas las puntas que se pusieron a su cuidado, en la comisión que le dió para pasar a la Florida: en que expresá lo que practicó, y observó, Nov. 24, 1736.

colony, but measures he recommended for strengthening the garrison or bolstering the fortifications received little attention. Despite his constant pleas to his superiors in Cuba, Spain, and New Spain, the arrival of one hundred Cuban grenadiers in 1736 was the only help he obtained. Moral therefore resorted to diplomacy to protect his colony. By means of a negotiated settlement with the English, Moral evidently hoped to gain time to strengthen his forces and his defenses enough to throw back impending enemy assaults.

In the negotiations with James Oglethorpe, which opened in the summer of 1736, Moral discussed three principal issues—boundary differences, the status of the Indians, and San Juan Island at the mouth of the Saint John's River, recently occupied by an English patrol. By October the two leaders reached an agreement.[10] Both agreed to restrain Indians in their control and promised that no natives would enter Florida or Georgia without first obtaining a license from their respective governors. Oglethorpe consented to evacuate San Juan Island but in return extracted a promise from Moral that the Spaniards would not refortify it. Both governors agreed to submit all border disputes to Europe for settlement by diplomats there.[11]

This treaty was bitterly denounced in Spain. Moral's superiors objected both to his open admission of English possession of Georgia and to his abandonment of San Juan Island. Moral, however, was a realist. Georgia was already lost to the English. His aim now was to prevent the loss of Florida in the same way, and he needed time to bolster his defenses. In 1736 diplomacy seemed the only convenient stratagem to gain this time.

In the meantime the governor girded for war. Both Moral and Arredondo made desperate efforts to secure more soldiers, arms, and war supplies. Arredondo recommended construction of eighty small boats for use in waters around Saint Augustine and four hundred sailors to man them. The engineer also asked for the addition of eight hundred trained regulars to the Florida garrison and for rum, muskets, tobacco, and cloth to keep the Indians neutral when war broke out. Such measures, Arredondo believed, would not only insure the Florida colony but it would also enable the Spanish to drive the English out of Georgia,

10. These negotiations are described in John Tate Lanning, *The Diplomatic History of Georgia: A Study of the Epoch of Jenkins' Ear* (Chapel Hill, 1936), pp. 34-54, 95-123.

11. See CO 5:656. Some Observations on the Right of the Crown of Great Britain to the N. W. Continent of America, April 1, 1748.

territory properly belonging to Philip V.[12] Moral asked for 1,500 regulars to carry out a surprise attack on Oglethorpe in Georgia, evidence that he was not bargaining with the Georgian in good faith. Moral also wanted a number of gifts to pacify the Indians. He believed the sharp contrast between the gifts offered by the English and those proffered by the Spaniards contributed greatly to the loss of Spanish prestige among those savages, who held the balance of power in the Southeast.[13] Moral made peace as he prepared for war, but on the other side it appears that his protagonist was engaged in the same subterfuge.

[*The Urge to War (1736-1738)*]

While Moral and Oglethorpe were negotiating their differences, Spanish officials forged plans for an offensive war on Georgia. Seeds for the plan had already been planted by Moral and later by Arredondo's *informe* of November, 1736. In this document the Cuban engineer optimistically predicted the ouster of the English from Georgia if the king took the proper military measures. In May, 1737, therefore, Philip V charged the Cuban governor, Francisco Güemes y Horcasitas, with organizing the expedition. From New Spain the king ordered 150,000 pesos, one hundred men, and supplies for four hundred troops.[14] This *cédula* elicited the usual viceregal grumbling, but this time the viceroy obeyed promptly. By late 1737 he had sent all but the one hundred men to Havana.[15] The 150,000 pesos provided Güemes with the money he needed to make the necessary preparations, and he immediately began assembling troops, ships, and supplies. In fact, things went so well for him that he sent word to Philip V that he would be ready to move by the spring of 1738.[16]

Havana became a bustling center of military activity in the winter of 1737-1738. Cuban shipbuilders worked long hours constructing long-

12. AGI, Santo Domingo, Legajo 2591. Don Antonio de Arredondo, Informe al gobernador de la Havana, de todas las puntas que se pusieron a su cuidado, en la comisión que le dió para pasar a la Florida: en que expresá lo que practicó, y observó, Nov. 24, 1736.

13. AGI, Santo Domingo, Legajo 2591. Carta del gobernador de la Florida a don Joseph Patiño, Oct. 2, 1736.

14. AGI, Santo Domingo, Legajo 2592. Carta del rey al gobernador de Cuba, May 8, 1737. Carta del rey al gobernador de Cuba, May 13, 1737.

15. AGI, Santo Domingo, Legajo 2592. Carta del virrey de Nueva España al gobernador de Cuba, Aug. 28, 1737.

16. AGI, Santo Domingo, Legajo 2592. Carta del gobernador de Cuba al Marqués de Torrenueva, Oct. 13, 1737.

boats and canoes for use by the invasion force. Infantry commanders drilled their troops, readying them for the spring offensive. Cuban merchants began assembling large supplies of food, arms, powder, and shot. With the money sent by the viceroy, Güemes was able to fulfil his prediction of a spring sailing date, and on the evening of March 21 he began to embark his troops on the vessels assembled in Havana harbor for departure the next day.

In the meantime, events in Europe caused Philip V to change his plans for an offensive on Georgia. Unexpectedly, the English agreed to negotiate the Florida-Georgia problem and seemed amenable to making a settlement favorable to the Spaniards. Not wishing to endanger these negotiations, the king rescinded his *cédula* ordering the attack on Georgia. In February, therefore, the monarch commanded Güemes in Havana to stop his preparations for the expedition. The Cuban governor, however, had completed his plans and had his fleet ready to sail on the night of March 21, the same evening the king's messenger arrived with the orders to postpone the attack on Georgia. Immediately the agent rushed to the governor's palace with the royal order, and Güemes called off the expedition.[17]

The news went out to the invasion force, anxiously awaiting their departure for Florida the next day. Officers began debarking the more than one thousand men who had been assembled on the waiting ships. Negro slaves took off cargoes of food and war supplies, depositing them in warehouses on the wharves. Wives and sweethearts returned to the docks to greet their husbands and lovers, saved at the last moment from making an uncertain voyage to Florida. For the Spanish force it was both a festive and disappointing occasion.

In the meantime, conditions in Florida had not improved. Governor Montiano reported in November, 1737, that Oglethorpe intended to seize control of the Bahama Channel by taking Saint Augustine and that the defenses of the town could not withstand a sustained attack. One or two English frigates, claimed the governor, could break the lifeline to Cuba and starve out his colony. His description of colonial defenses was dismal. The walls of Fort San Marcos were crumbling; quarters for soldiers were hardly fit for human existence; storehouses and powderhouses leaked. No cannon could last a full day's firing, and there was not one trained artilleryman in all Florida. With six hundred new troops

17. AGI, Santo Domingo, Legajo 2593. Carta del gobernador de Cuba al gobernador de la Florida, March 24, 1738.

and one hundred horses, however, Montiano believed he could avoid disaster.[18]

Well-supplied with men and war goods intended for the attack on Georgia, Güemes took pity on Montiano and dispatched eight companies of pickets (four hundred men) and eighty-two forced laborers to re-build fortifications around Saint Augustine. Güemes also sent Montiano two military engineers, a master bricklayer, six skilled Negro stone-masons, twelve new iron cannon, and 6,000 pesos, which the governor used to build six new barracks and four patrol boats for the Saint Augus-tine harbor area.[19] In the end this aid was decisive in saving the colony. When the War of Jenkins's Ear broke out in 1739, Montiano was at least partially prepared to meet the onslaughts of the English.

[*The War of Jenkins's Ear in Florida: The
Defensive Stage*]

While negotiations were going on in Europe over the Georgia-Florida boundary issue, the southern frontier grew restive. Under Oglethorpe's sponsorship bands of Lower Creeks began making raids on settlements in Florida and harassing Spanish soldiers and Indians west of Saint Augustine. Spurred on by promises of rich rewards for Spanish scalps, the Lower Creeks attacked Fort Pupo in the summer of 1738, damaging the stockade and killing two Spanish soldiers.[20] At the same time Oglethorpe began building up a force of militiamen and Indians at Frederica.[21] Montiano believed they were being trained as an invasion force and sent out Captain Sebastián Sánchez, the nephew of ex-governor Moral, to reconnoiter the Georgia coast. He was dis-covered almost immediately, however, and sent back to Saint Augustine with a report that confirmed what Montiano already knew—that the English had strengthened the fortifications at Frederica and were drill-ing militia there.[22]

18. AGI, Santo Domingo, Legajo 2541. Carta del gobernador de la Florida al rey, Nov. 11, 1737.

19. AGI, Santo Domingo, Legajo 2593. Carta del gobernador de Cuba al gober-nador de la Florida, March 24, 1738. AGI, Santo Domingo, Legajo 844. Carta del gobernador de la Florida al rey, June 12, 1738.

20. AGI, Santo Domingo, Legajo 2541. Carta del gobernador de la Florida al rey, Aug. 31, 1738.

21. AGI, Santo Domingo, Legajo 2541. Testimonio sobre haber arribado a este presidio tres Ingleses fugitivos de las colonias, vecinos de esta nación: año de 1738, Aug. 23, 1738.

22. AGI, Santo Domingo, Legajo 2530. Consulta del Consejo de las Indias, Feb. 14, 1739.

Border raids continued throughout 1738 and 1739, spreading terror among the settlers but inflicting little damage. In October, 1738, a small force of English militia and Indians invested the area fifty miles from the mouth of the Saint John's River and destroyed several Spanish Indian villages. In retaliation an Indian-Spanish patrol raided Amelia Island. Here the Floridians killed two unfortunate English woodcutters and mangled their bodies before being driven off by an English counter-attack.[23]

In 1740 these sporadic border forays yielded to a major war between Florida and Georgia. In January Oglethorpe led a band of two hundred Creek, Chickasaw, and Uchize Indians and a lesser number of Highland Rangers up the Saint John's to Fort Pupo and Picolata, now the favorite target of English raiders. Here the Georgians won a major victory. Oglethorpe's force killed twelve Spanish infantrymen and sent the remainder of the two small garrisons scurrying back to Saint Augustine in headlong retreat. To secure his foothold in the heart of Spanish territory, Oglethorpe left a small force at Pupo and Picolata under a trusted officer, Captain Hugh Mackay.[24]

Not long after, Montiano proposed two plans to dislodge the English interlopers at Pupo and Picolata. After reinforcing Fort San Diego, twenty miles north of Saint Augustine, the Florida governor proposed to send Spanish soldiers and artillery to Majoloa, a point just below the two forts. Here the river was wide, but the navigable channel was so close to the east bank that it was easily vulnerable to musket and cannon fire. In this way Montiano hoped to control the river and to starve out Mackay's small force.[25] When this plan failed to materialize because of the lack of men and artillery for the positions at Majoloa, Montiano proposed a second scheme to cut off Mackay. This time he suggested a timber dam across a narrow portion of the river just below Pupo and Picolata, but again there were no men available to carry out such a task, and Mackay remained entrenched at Pupo. At this juncture, early in 1740, Montiano counted his effective fighting force in Saint Augustine at 613 men—308 Cuban regulars on detached service in Florida, 80 regular

23. CO 5:654, pt. 1. James Oglethorpe to the Duke of Newcastle, Frederica, Nov. 15, 1739.
24. CO 5:654, pt. 1. James Oglethorpe to the Duke of Newcastle, Frederica, Jan. 22, 1739/40.
25. Carta del gobernador de la Florida al gobernador de Cuba, Feb. 23, 1740, in *Collections of the Georgia Historical Society*, Vol. VII, pt. 1 (Savannah, 1909), pp. 44-45. Hereafter cited as *Collections*.

infantrymen, 32 artillerymen, 50 armed Indians, 61 militiamen, 43 free Negroes, and an 80-man garrison in Apalache.[26]

In the spring of 1740, encouraged by his success on the Saint John's, Oglethorpe massed his forces in Georgia for an all-out offensive on Saint Augustine. Careful to insure naval support, he ordered one group of frigates to patrol the waters near the entrances to Saint Augustine harbor, hoping to cut off supply ships arriving from Cuba. Still another fleet of English warships was to harass the tiny half-galleys plying the waters between Havana and Apalache and between Saint Augustine and Apalache and to seize them if at all possible.[27] To control the Bahama Channel, Oglethorpe ordered an English frigate to lay off Cape Canaveral.[28]

The Georgian leader assembled a large expeditionary force. By May 1 he had brought together an estimated 1,620 men, 7 warships, and 40 small dugouts to carry his soldiers to Florida. He also procured the supplies and artillery needed for a prolonged siege. Early in May this force left Frederica in small boats, and on May 9 debarked at the rendezvous point at the mouth of the Saint John's River. The next day the Georgian led a band of his soldiers and Indians southward toward Fort San Diego, and two days later won an easy victory over the fifty-seven Spaniards garrisoning the fort, only twenty miles north of Saint Augustine. Leaving Lieutenant George Dunbar and a small group of militia to hold the stockade, the Georgian returned to the rendezvous point at the mouth of the Saint John's to begin the second stage of his offensive.[29]

Again he lost no time. On May 16 his troops reached Mosa, the fortified Negro village only a mile north of Saint Augustine, and seized thirty horses in the deserted town. Although elated over his successes, Oglethorpe did not wish to extend his lines too close to Fort San Marcos. He retired north of Fort San Diego and from there moved to San Juan to bring the remainder of his troops within striking distance of the center of Spanish power in Florida.

26. Carta del gobernador de la Florida al gobernador de Cuba, March 24, 1740, *Ibid.*, VII, pt. 1, pp. 47-48.

27. Carta del gobernador de la Florida al gobernador de Cuba, March 25, 1740. *Ibid.*, VII, pt. 1, pp. 47-48.

28. Carta del gobernador de la Florida al gobernador de Cuba, April 27, 1740, *Ibid.*, VII, pt. 1, pp. 49-51.

29. See *The St. Augustine Expedition of 1740, A Report to the South Carolina General Assembly Reprinted from the Colonial Records of South Carolina with an Introduction by John Tate Lanning* (Columbia, S. C., 1954), pp. 19-20.

On May 18 when the Georgian reached his headquarters on the Saint John's, his plans went awry. Heavy spring rains had ruined much of his food supply and his powder and had caused considerable discomfort to his men, who were fast losing their morale because of the spread of dysentery. Both the rains and the illness of his troops forced Oglethorpe to postpone any major action, and for eleven days he did nothing but send out small patrols to reconnoiter the area around Saint Augustine. Finally, however, on May 29 the rain stopped long enough and his men became well enough to move their belongings to Fort San Diego, Oglethorpe's new headquarters in Florida.[30]

The transfer of supplies and men to Fort San Diego put Oglethorpe only twenty miles from Saint Augustine, close enough for him to begin laying plans for a sustained siege. On June 1 an English patrol again visited Mosa. With the deserted town as its base, it spent two days carefully scouting the terrain around the Florida capital.[31] On June 6, using the reports of his reconaissance group to good advantage, Oglethorpe began encircling Saint Augustine. He first ordered his principal aide, Colonel Alexander Vanderdussen, to set up artillery emplacements at Point Quartell (Point San Mateo to the Spanish), on the peninsula commanding the north side of the north entrance to Saint Augustine harbor. Here Vanderdussen mounted seven six-pound cannon and many smaller mortars. Oglethorpe himself led two hundred men onto Santa Anastasia Island, where his batteries facing the town and fort consisted of four eighteen pounders, a nine pounder, and smaller mortars with another battery of two eighteen pounders on the extreme northern tip of the island. At the same time a fleet of frigates, schooners, and smaller longboats guarded the entrance to Saint Augustine harbor and gave Oglethorpe control of the sea.[32]

With their cannon in place, the English began their siege in earnest on June 13. Oglethorpe's artillery began laying down a steady barrage of cannon fire on Fort San Marcos, where most of the Floridians had taken refuge. For the most part the incessant pounding had little effect, except to give Montiano and his embattled colonists sleepless nights. The formidable stone fort held up well against the noisy

30. *Ibid.*, pp. 22-23.
31. CO 5: 655, pt. 1. Letter from Lieutenant Colonel Alexander Heron to a friend of his, Frederica, Sept. 24, 1742.
32. Carta del gobernador de la Florida al gobernador de Cuba, July 6, 1740, in *Collections*, VII, pt. 1, pp. 57-58. See also Carta del gobernador de la Florida al gobernador de Cuba, July 13, 1740, in *ibid.*, VII, pt. 1, p. 58.

blasts of the English guns, and casualties were negligible. In fact, after twelve days under siege, Montiano boldly decided upon a counterattack, as much to relieve the monotony for his soldiers as to inflict losses on the Georgians. His plan was to attack the English force encamped at Mosa under the command of Colonel John Palmer, whose soldiers and Indians had ravaged Nombre de Dios in 1728. Headed by Captain Antonio Salgado, a Spanish force of three hundred stealthily crept out of Fort San Marcos at midnight on June 25, and under cover of darkness moved north toward Palmer's encampment. At two Salgado's soldiers reached Mosa, still undetected. An hour-long reconnaissance indicated that the English force was inferior in both arms and numbers, and at three the Spaniards launched their surprise attack, shouting loudly while making their assault. The English were caught completely by surprise and suffered heavy losses. In less than an hour seventy-two of Palmer's crack Highlanders lay dead, together with fifteen infantry-men and thirty-five Lower Creek Indians. Salgado, on the other hand, lost only a few men.[33]

The Spanish victory at Mosa turned the tide against Oglethorpe. Salgado had proved the vulnerability of the English besiegers and had boosted Spanish morale. When Oglethorpe then issued an untimely call for Montiano's surrender, the Florida governor replied haughtily that he would not give up. He would continue to defend Saint Augustine for the honor and glory of Philip V.[34] Salgado's victory had given Montiano new confidence. The moment for Olgethorpe to ask for surrender had vanished.

After Palmer's defeat Oglethorpe lost his penchant for decisive action and inflexibly refused to adopt new strategy, which might have insured his success. Colonel Vanderdussen suggested that the Georgians could easily starve out the garrison at Fort San Marcos by destroying the Spanish half-galleys plying the Matanzas River. These vessels not only managed to keep the narrow southern entrance of the harbor open but also provided at least a little fresh food for the embattled Floridians. Vanderdussen believed that if Oglethorpe would act quickly to seize and destroy these vessels the Spaniards in Fort San Marcos would be forced to surrender. The Georgian, however, refused to take up the suggestion and continued his ineffectual artillery bombardment of the fort.[35]

33. AGI, Santo Domingo, Legajo 845. Carta del gobernador de la Florida al rey, Aug. 9, 1740.
34. AGI, Santo Domingo, Legajo 845. Carta del gobernador de la Florida a Diego Oglethorpe, July 2, 1740.
35. Lanning, *The St. Augustine Expedition of 1740*, passim. See also CO 5:655,

In the meantime relief arrived for the Floridians. Early in July seven heavily armed ships appeared in waters south of Saint Augustine with food, powder, and other supplies from Cuba. Risking heavy losses if they attempted to force entry at the northern entrance to the harbor, the seven ships anchored near the Matanzas entrance twenty miles to the south to await instructions from Montiano. The governor immediately sent Lieutenant Antonio Nieto de Carbajal with two launches and two small dugouts to provide the relief ships with information on the position of Oglethorpe's cannon and to take off some food for the embattled Floridians, now reduced to a half-ration of flour and meat. Under the very shadow of an English packet boat and frigate hovering near the Spanish fleet, Nieto brought back two hundred barrels of flour to Fort San Marcos.[36]

The arrival of the seven relief vessels from Cuba broke the English siege, just as the arrival of Cuban relief ships had broken the siege of 1702. As soon as the ships appeared on July 4, Oglethorpe began evacuating his men. Sixteen days later on July 20 his artillerymen fired their last shot at San Marcos, and his entire force made its way back to Georgia and South Carolina.[37] For the second time in forty years the English had failed to dislodge the Spaniards from their precarious foothold in Saint Augustine. Fort San Marcos had again proved invulnerable.

Montiano indicated that he had suffered few casualties during the thirty-eight day bombardment. In all he claimed that only one of his men was killed and two were wounded. Despite short rations morale had remained high, and no soldier had deserted to the enemy. The rest of the colonists—militia, Indians, free Negroes, slaves, and forced laborers—had also distinguished themselves by their bravery and constancy in the face of extreme danger and privation. Still, stated the governor, he needed aid desperately. Of his regular garrison of 350 and of the 400 Cuban infantrymen on detached service in Florida, only 366 were capable of bearing arms—88 regulars and 278 Cubans. In addition, only 18 cannon remained in service at Fort San Marcos.[38]

pt. 1. Letter from Lieutenant Colonel Alexander Heron to a friend of his, Frederica, Sept. 24, 1742.

36. AGI, Santo Domingo, Legajo 845. Carta del gobernador de la Florida al rey, Aug. 9, 1740.

37. Carta del gobernador de la Florida al gobernador de Cuba, Aug. 2, 1740, in *Collections*, VII, pt. 1, pp. 64-65.

38. Carta del gobernador de la Florida al gobernador de Cuba, Aug. 7, 1740, *ibid.*, VII, pt. 1, pp. 65-67.

Montiano's pleas for aid were prompted by fear of a new attack. Interrogation of three English prisoners indicated that Oglethorpe's army numbered more than two thousand men and that he was planning to sweep south again in the spring of 1741. Without men and arms to meet such an attack, stated Montiano, the colony would surely perish. Yet despite these ominous predictions, Montiano was optimistic about an offensive on Georgia. He had information that the Carolinians, who had fought with Oglethorpe during the siege, had no faith in him and would not aid the Georgian if the Spaniards attacked his colony. An advantage like this, claimed Montiano, should not be wasted.[39]

While preparations were being made for such an offensive, Spanish naval activity increased along the Atlantic Coast. Using Saint Augustine as their base of operations, Spanish privateers from Cuba and New Spain received letters of marque and reprisal from Montiano and preyed on English shipping, especially in waters off Carolina and Georgia. Late in 1740 one of these Spanish corsairs seized an English ship carrying ten thousand bricks to Charleston for use in construction of a school; another intercepted an English schooner carrying nine thousand *arrobas* of rice and flour.[40] Such activity became so profitable that privateering increased, and in 1741 English prizes were a common sight in Saint Augustine harbor. On May 26, for example, Captain Pedro de Estrada entered the Florida capital with three English vessels containing cargoes of corn, pork, pitch, and tar. Two days later a second privateer brought in two more English schooners—one carrying Madeira wine and the other Indian trinkets, beads, and bright-colored cloth. On June 15 Captain Luis Silverio, a Cuban privateer, brought in a small English sloop carrying corn and flour.[41]

These same captains also carried out raids on English coastal settlements. Under Montiano's sponsorship one privateer, Joseph de Estrada, made a daring attack on North Carolina. Debarking a small band of soldiers and sailors at New Brunswick at the mouth of the Albemarle River early in September, 1741, Estrada set fire to a warehouse and two ships under construction on the banks of the river. On his way

39. AGI, Santo Domingo, Legajo 845. Carta del gobernador de la Florida al rey, Aug. 9, 1740.

40. AGI, Santo Domingo, Legajo 2584. Carta del gobernador de la Florida a don Joseph de la Quintana, Jan. 2, 1741. See also AGI, Santo Domingo, Legajo 833. Consulta del Consejo de las Indias, May 27, 1741.

41. AGI, Santo Domingo, Legajo 2584. Carta del gobernador de la Florida al rey, Oct. 1, 1741.

back to Florida, he added further insults by seizing five English ships carrying rice, paper, wood, and glass.[42]

For the Carolinians the activities of Spanish corsairs were particularly vexing. Since the founding of Charleston in 1670, the English had dominated the Southeast. Now Montiano's privateers endangered their position in Carolina and caused severe losses to English merchants. When Governor William Bull wrote from Charleston in October, 1741, that the Spaniards wrought "great damage" in his colony, he was reflecting the feeling of many English colonists in the Southeast who were now suffering at the hands of Spanish privateers.[43]

[*Montiano and the Fiasco at Bloody Marsh*]

While Spanish privateers harassed English shipping on the Atlantic seaboard, plans went ahead for an offensive war on Georgia. In Spain the king was particularly eager to launch such an attack. A large British force commanded by Admiral Edward Vernon had assaulted Cartagena in 1741, and the Council of the Indies believed (without any real basis) that Vernon had drawn many of his soldiers from Georgia and Carolina. With his best fighting men in New Granada, Oglethorpe had become more vulnerable to attack. In the fall of 1741, therefore, Philip V issued orders to Güemes in Havana and to Montiano in Saint Augustine to prepare for a new campaign on Georgia.[44]

Güemes' strategy called for a sea attack on Georgia some time between April and June when storms were least likely to interfere with troop movements. A land offensive, stated the Cuban governor, was too dangerous and too unpredictable. For his invasion Güemes requested at least six frigates of twenty-four to thirty cannon to carry land forces to Georgia and to protect them once they disembarked. He also needed a large number of longboats, canoes, and dugouts to transport his troops. Güemes planned first to seize Port Royal and then move south down the Georgia coast, devastating English settlements on the coastal channel.[45]

Montiano believed the offensive required at least three thousand

42. AGI, Santo Domingo, Legajo 2584. Carta del gobernador de la Florida al rey, Oct. 1, 1741.

43. CO 5:388, pt. 2. William Bull to the Duke of Newcastle, Charleston, Oct. 14, 1741.

44. AGI, Santo Domingo, Legajo 838. Real cédula, Buen Retiro, Nov. 20, 1741.

45. AGI, Santo Domingo, Legajo 2593. Carta del gobernador de Cuba a don José de Campillo, Feb. 24, 1742.

men, four frigates carrying forty to fifty cannon, and a large supply of artillery, pistols, muskets, swords, machetes, scaling ladders, and small boats.[46] The governor also felt that English Negro slaves would prove decisive in insuring a Spanish victory. He predicted that slaves in Carolina would rise up to join the Spaniards and set the entire Southeast aflame. Once a Spanish victory had been won, Montiano planned to use the Negroes to build a great new presidio at Saint Augustine.[47] Evidently, there was a real basis for the governor's view. Oglethorpe himself reported that forty thousand Carolina Negroes "would be either an assistance to the Invader or a Prize worth near Eight Hunderd Thousand pounds Sterling to them."[48]

In Cuba, however, preparations for the offensive did not go well. Güemes encountered problems, both in enlisting an army and in obtaining supplies. He was also concerned about leaving Cuba undefended. Havana alone, he stated, demanded 4,000 men to protect it adequately.[49] In Cuba Güemes could only raise 1,300 men—600 regulars and 700 militiamen, many of them mulattoes or freed Negroes. For his part Montiano was to provide 300 regulars, 100 Cuban pickets already on detached service in Saint Augustine, 100 mulattoes and Negroes, and enough launches and half-galleys to transport a force of 500. Despite the fact that the army was 1,200 short of the 3,000 originally estimated as the number of men needed to insure the success of the expedition, the Cuban governor was still hopeful the offensive would succeed. Appointing Montiano as commander in chief, Güemes gave the Florida governor two experienced strategists and military engineers as advisers— Lieutenant Colonel Francisco Rubiani and Antonio de Arredondo.[50]

Late in the spring, 1742, Güemes, Rubiani, and Arredondo made feverish, last-minute preparations for the assault on Georgia. A few days before the main body of the expedition left Havana on June 5, the Cuban governor dispatched a small vanguard of soldiers and supplies to Saint Augustine along with his final instructions to Montiano. Güemes

46. AGI, Santo Domingo, Legajo 2593. Carta del gobernador de Florida al gobernador de Cuba, March 13, 1742.
47. AGI, Santo Domingo, Legajo 2593. Carta del gobernador de la Florida a don José de Campillo, March 12, 1742.
48. CO 5:655, pt. 1. Copy of a letter from General Oglethorpe to Sir Robert Walpole, Frederica, Dec. 7, 1742. See also James Oglethorpe to the Duke of Newcastle, Frederica, June 7, 1742.
49. AGI, Santo Domingo, Legajo 2593. Carta del gobernador de Cuba a don José de Campillo, April 6, 1742.
50. AGI, Santo Domingo, Legajo 2593. Carta del gobernador de Cuba al gobernador de la Florida, May 14, 1742.

now regarded the seizure of Saint Simon's Island, not Port Royal, as indispensable for the success of the Spanish enterprise. Once Saint Simon's fell, Montiano was ordered to lead his army northward along the channel between the coastal islands and the mainland, destroying all the English plantations and settlements he passed along the way. When the Spaniards had conquered the Georgia coast to Port Royal, Montiano was to send out Spanish Negroes into the Carolina countryside, promising land and freedom to any English slaves who would join the Spaniards against the English. Güemes also instructed Montiano to keep strict accounts of booty seized and to treat all prisoners humanely.[51]

The main body of the expedition under Rubiani and Arredondo left Havana on June 5 in a steady rain. Although it took the fleet of twenty-four vessels ten days to make a voyage that normally took no more than five, all the ships reached Saint Augustine safely, despite a violent storm that separated them. Once in Florida Rubiani and Arredondo received bad news from Montiano. The vessels sailing to Saint Augustine earlier in June had engaged several English men-of-war as they neared the Florida coast. In the battle that followed, the Spanish fleet easily drove off the enemy ships, but word had already reached Saint Augustine that these English vessels had sailed to Frederica and Charleston to spread the word of the Spanish military buildup in Florida.[52]

Montiano was, nevertheless, hopeful that the offensive would succeed. He had assembled approximately 1,900 men, including militia and a large number of armed Negroes. He had 5 large men-of-war to support these troops and 49 small boats to transport his soldiers and militia along the coast. His ordnance consisted of 18 cannon, 34 falconets, 22 mortars, and a large supply of various small arms.[53] This, he realized, was the largest, best equipped force ever assembled in Florida, and hopes ran high among his officers and men that they would drive the English out of Georgia once and for all.

Montiano and his two Cuban aides agreed to adhere closely to

51. Carta del gobernador de Cuba al gobernador de la Florida, June 2, 1742, in *Collections of the Georgia Historical Society*, Vol. VII, pt. 3 (Savannah, 1913), pp. 32-35.

52. Journal kept by Don Antonio de Arredondo, Chief Engineer of the Present Expedition, in *Collections*, VII, pt. 3, pp. 52-57.

53. "Return which gives Ships of War, Transports, Staff Officers, Troops, Militia, Rations, Ammunition, Arms, and Tools for the River Service and to leave in reserve in Florida, destined for the Expedition which is directed from the port of Havana for operations in the Royal Service in the Provinces of Florida; as follows: . . .," in *Collections*, VII, pt. 3, p. 108. See also AGI, Santo Domingo, Legajo 2593. Carta del gobernador de Cuba a don José de Campillo, June 8, 1742.

Güemes' second set of instructions. Rather than point their assault at Port Royal as initially suggested, they chose to strike first at Saint Simon's Island. Frederica, the capital of Georgia lying at the northern end of the island, was the key city in the colony, and the three strategists hoped to break Oglethorpe's resistance there. In his plan to take the island, Montiano proposed to surround Saint Simon's, cutting off Oglethorpe's supply lines and preventing the landing of rein- forcements. Scouting reports had already indicated that once Spanish men-of-war and half-galleys had sealed off the island, the sandy beaches on the southern tip of Saint Simon's would make safe, easily accessible landing points for the main body of his troops. Not long after this strategy had been agreed upon, on June 20, each member of the invasion force received his assignment to a ship or small boat. On June 23 the expedition was ready to sail.[54]

Bad weather plagued the Spaniards from the outset. First, a savage northeastern storm broke just as the fleet was about to weigh anchor and delayed final departure of the expedition for a full week. Then, when the squadron finally put to sea on July 1, westerly squalls caused the separation of many of the smaller boats from the main body of the fleet. In good weather these vessels could have negotiated the voyage from Saint Augustine to Saint Simon's in no more than two days, but ultimately it took sixteen days before all the launches, pirogues, galleys, and half-galleys assembled at the entrance to Jekyl Sound at the southern tip of Saint Simon's Island.[55]

When his entire force finally reached the rendezvous point, Montiano did not delay. On July 16 he sent fourteen of his larger ships into Jekyl Sound under the guns of the English batteries located on both sides of the narrow inlet to the sound. After a four-hour battle against Oglethorpe's artillery and a small fleet of naval vessels, the Spaniards emerged victorious. It had cost them a galley and two dugouts, but they had succeeded in routing the Georgians from their gun emplacements and had gained control of the southern end of Saint Simon's.[56] Here Montiano disembarked his troops, who immediately

54. Journal Kept by Don Antonio de Arredondo, Chief Engineer of the Present Expedition, in *Collections*, VII, pt. 3, pp. 60-64.

55. "Details of what occurred in the Present Expedition entrusted to the care of Brigadier Don Manuel de Montiano from the 15th day of June, on which the convoy arrived from Havana at St. Augustine, the whole being contained in a journal kept by the Marquess of Casinas," etc., *ibid.*, VII, pt. 3, pp. 65-68.

56. CO 5:655, pt. 1. James Oglethorpe to the Duke of Newcastle, Frederica, July 30, 1742.

made for the English positions and inexplicably destroyed a number of supplies they found nearby—beer, cheeses, butter, flour, meat, and hard tack.[57]

Montiano was heartened by his easy victory and began preparing for the attack on Frederica. He immediately sent out patrols to reconnoiter the terrain on the northward path to the Georgia capital and small boats up the Frederica River to ascertain whether or not the English stronghold could be taken by a sea attack.

This patrol activity led to the debacle at Bloody Marsh. On the morning of July 18, two days after the victory in Jekyl Sound, Montiano ordered fifty men under Captain Sebastián Sánchez to make a reconnaissance of the terrain north of the Spanish encampment and to pick out a suitable landing place near Frederica for his cannon still on board his ships in the sound. At the same time the governor sent out a patrol of twenty-five soldiers and forty Indians under Captain Nicolás Hernández to report on the various approaches to the Georgia capital.[58] A cautious tactician, Montiano evidently wanted to examine all possible alternatives before committing himself to a specific course of action. Somehow, however, Sánchez and his men lost their way in the marshes on the eastern edge of Saint Simon's and fell in with the sixty-five soldiers and Indians under Hernández, who were also lost. Together the two infantry captains tried to find their way out of the swamp, but instead they became even more befuddled as their men moved single file through the marshland on narrow strips of dry land which wound through the dense underbrush.[59]

In the meantime English Indian scouts had observed the confusion among the two Spanish patrols and reported this to Oglethorpe, who quickly saw the advantage of fighting a disorganized enemy on familiar terrain. Without delay he ordered all the regulars, militia, and Indians he could spare out to engage the Spanish force. In the fighting which followed, Oglethorpe's men won an easy victory, killing many of the Spaniards and sending others into full retreat through the swamps. When Montiano finally heard the news of what had occurred, he sent out three companies of grenadiers to aid the embattled patrols, but it was too late. Taking good advantage of the trees and underbrush, Oglethorpe's men ambushed the relief force as it made its way through

57. "Journal from the day when the Port of Gualquini, otherwise known as St. Simon, was forced," in *Collections*, VII, pt. 3, p. 70.
58. *Ibid.*, pp. 72-73.
59. *Ibid.*, p. 73.

the marsh.[60] In all the Spaniards lost an estimated two hundred men killed and sixteen captured.[61]

The English victory at Bloody Marsh was as decisive as the Spanish victory at Mosa, two years earlier. It destroyed Montiano's confidence and boosted the morale of Oglethorpe's force at Frederica. After Bloody Marsh Montiano was reluctant to continue his assault, despite the fact he still had 1,500 men ready to fight and his artillery in good condition. Not wishing to risk further losses, Montiano and his aides decided to avoid a major engagement with Oglethorpe's troops, and they leisurely began making preparations to leave Georgia.[62]

Still under no pressure from Oglethorpe, Montiano's men remained on Saint Simon's for over a week following the disaster at Bloody Marsh. They might have stayed even longer had it not been for a piece of alarming news gleaned from a French prisoner-of-war. This Frenchman informed Montiano that Oglethorpe, who had assembled a force of a thousand, was planning a major attack on the Spanish positions on the southern tip of Saint Simon's as soon as he received aid from Boston, which was expected momentarily. The Spaniards might have ignored these statements, but when five English sail appeared on the horizon at noon on July 24, Montiano became panicky and immediately convoked a junta of his chief officers. They voted to leave Saint Simon's at once, recommending a retreat along the coastal channel in order to destroy the English outposts of San Pedro and Saint Andrews on Cumberland Island.[63] On July 25 these officers began embarking their 1,500 troops on the waiting ships, a process which was not finally completed until July 26. On their way south the fleet paused long enough to destroy the two English blockhouses on Cumberland Island, and by August 1, 1742, most of Montiano's force was back in Saint Augustine. The remainder of the fleet under Arredondo and Rubiani chose to ride a favorable wind back to Cuba.[64]

In his report to the king Montiano found many excuses for his failure to take Frederica. He declared that he did not have enough

60. Carta del gobernador de la Florida al rey, Aug. 3, 1742, in *Collections*, VII, pt. 3, pp. 91-92.

61. CO 5:655, pt. 1. Duplicate of a letter, James Oglethorpe to the Duke of Newcastle, Frederica, July 30, 1742.

62. Carta del gobernador de la Florida al rey, August 3, 1742, in *Collections*, VII, pt. 3, p. 93.

63. *Ibid.*, pp. 93-94. See also "Journal from the Day when the Port of Gualquini, otherwise known as St. Simon, was forced," in *Collections*, VII, pt. 3, pp. 78-79.

64. "Journal from the Day when the Port of Gualquini, otherwise known as St. Simon, was forced," in *Collections*, VII, pt. 3, pp. 84-87.

supplies to sustain his troops during a prolonged campaign and that the failure of thirteen vessels carrying men and supplies to reach Florida had greatly hindered his efforts. Montiano also feared the onset of the hurricane season, which he felt might cause serious losses to his men. The Florida governor pointed out, too, that Güemes had enjoined him not to jeopardize the welfare and safety of his men. In Montiano's judgment destruction of his expeditionary force would have left both Saint Augustine and Havana completely defenseless. Besides, he had devastated the forts and fields surrounding Frederica and inflicted damage on Georgia estimated at 300,000 pesos. Montiano had also managed to keep his entire force intact, except for the losses at Bloody Marsh.[65]

The king's secretary, José de Campillo, refused to accept Montiano's excuses and blamed the failure entirely on the governor. Campillo wrote Güemes that he was completely satisfied with the measures taken by the Cuban governor to insure the success of the expedition, but Montiano's "poor leadership, lack of diligence, and inefficiency" were deplorable. The Florida governor had the most to gain from the offensive, yet he was the principal cause of its failure.[66] Campillo was probably right; extreme timidity had cost Montiano a victory. He had refused to take advantage of his superiority and had allowed the disaster at Bloody Marsh to cast an enervating spell over his expedition.

[*Oglethorpe's Counterattack*]

Not long after he had returned to Saint Augustine, Montiano faced the prospects of a new English siege. Early in September, 1742, twelve English ships anchored off the entrance to Saint Augustine harbor in what the governor believed to be a new invasion attempt. On September 6, surprised and worried, Montiano sent two launches to Cuba with frantic requests for help.[67]

At high tide on the morning of September 8, the English fleet made its first move. Eight heavily armed British men-of-war under full sail, protecting a number of small landing craft, headed directly for the narrow entrance to Saint Augustine harbor. Using all his ingenuity as a

65. Carta del gobernador de la Florida al rey, Aug. 3, 1742, *ibid.*, VII, pt. 3, pp. 92-95.
66. Carta de don José de Campillo al gobernador de Cuba, San Ildefonso, Oct. 28, 1742, *ibid.*, VII, pt. 3, pp. 51-52.
67. AGI, Santo Domingo, Legajo 2593. Carta del gobernador de la Florida al gobernador de Cuba, Sept. 6, 1742.

defensive strategist, Montiano had his batteries at the harbor entrance and his six half-galleys in the bay lay down a blistering fire on the British vessels as they approached the narrow channel. This barrage forced the English back, but the British captains regrouped and attacked again. Montiano threw back one attempt after another until nightfall, when the invasion force finally returned to the main body of the fleet.[68]

The next day the English fleet sailed southward and anchored off the Bar of Matanzas, where they evidently hoped to force an entrance to Saint Augustine harbor at the Matanzas Channel. On September 10 two English dugouts began taking soundings along the bar. Immediately, the Spanish blockhouse at Matanzas Point laid down a withering cannon fire on the two craft, one of which suffered a direct hit and barely reached the larger men-of-war before sinking. Finally, bad weather, which had conspired so often against the Spaniards, ruined whatever plans the English entertained for taking Saint Augustine. On September 11 a northeastern storm scattered the British fleet, ending the threat to the Florida capital.[69]

Incidents like these kept the Floridians continually tense and anxious and particularly susceptible to rumors. Any word of an English military activity in Boston, Jamaica, Antigua, Charleston, or any other part of English America was interpreted in Florida as a buildup against Saint Augustine.[70] For the most part such fears were groundless, but they prompted considerable defensive activity in Saint Augustine. Late in 1742 and early in 1743, for example, Montiano became convinced that the English were preparing a new assault on his colony and made fever-ish preparations to meet it. He bolstered the fortifications at Fort San Marcos, mounted six cannon along the San Sebastián River, and erected a stone fort at Matanzas Point.[71] This was typical of Montiano's strategy. After Bloody Marsh he contented himself with strengthening the defenses of his colony. Since 1687 Fort San Marcos had served the Spaniards well, and Montiano knew it. In 1743 an English officer observed that the Indians serving under Montiano had great contempt

68. AGI, Santo Domingo, Legajo 2541. Carta del gobernador de la Florida al rey, Sept. 15, 1742.

69. AGI, Santo Domingo, Legajo 2541. Carta del gobernador de la Florida al rey, Sept. 15, 1742.

70. AGI, Santo Domingo, Legajo 2541. Carta del gobernador de la Florida al rey, March 23, 1742.

71. CO 5: 384. Deposition of Captain Edmond Gale, February 16, 1742/43. AGI, Santo Domingo, Legajo 2584. Carta del gobernador y los oficiales reales de la Florida al virrey de Nueva España, March 26, 1743.

for him because he refused to move out of Saint Augustine to fight the English and their Indians. The officer, however, had more respect for the Florida governor. He believed that Montiano, a shrewd tactician, was slyly waiting for Oglethorpe to put himself in an untenable position. Once the Georgian made a mistake, Montiano would strike decisively against the English.[72] Apparently, though, the governor had had enough of offensive war at Bloody Marsh.

In Georgia Oglethorpe feared more Spanish attacks on his colony, but he used more aggressive tactics than his counterpart in Florida. Oglethorpe believed he could best defend Georgia by carrying the war to the enemy. Indian raids proved an especially effective tactic and caused much anxiety among the Floridians, especially when these assaults assumed major proportions.[73] Early in the spring of 1743, for example, a detachment of two hundred Indians, joined this time by a number of English militiamen, marched into Florida and destroyed the newly restored Fort San Diego, killing forty Spaniards.[74] Other raids were less significant and only harassed the Floridians, but they were exceedingly effective in keeping Montiano on the defensive and off balance militarily.

[*The Quiet Border, 1743-1763*]

The English raid on Fort San Diego in the spring of 1743 marked the end of an era on the Georgia-Florida frontier. For the first time in seventy-three years, the border became quiet. Except for occasional raids on English and Spanish settlements by Indians from both sides, a relative peace pervaded the Southeast, which contrasted sharply with the constant fighting which had kept the frontier aflame since 1670. Two factors seem to explain the change. First, Saint Augustine had proved impregnable, able to resist all English efforts to take it. Two major assaults on the Florida capital—one in 1702 and another in 1740—failed, and evidently the English gave up hope of seizing this Spanish stronghold in the Southeast. As one English officer observed: the Spaniards "make the greatest Jest, Burlesque, and ridicule of all our Expeditions from Cartagena to Augustine."[75]

72. CO 5:655, pt. 2. Copy of a letter from one of General Oglethorpe's officers to a friend in Charles Town, South Carolina, March 25, 1743.
73. AGI, Santo Domingo, Legajo 2593. Carta del gobernador de la Florida a don José de Campillo, Feb. 16, 1743.
74. CO 5:655, pt. 2. James Oglethorpe to the Duke of Newcastle, Florida, on the River San Matheo, March 21, 1743. Copy of a letter from Andrew Rutledge, Esq. to Mr. Herman Verelst, Charleston, April 27, 1743.
75. CO 5:388, pt. 2. Extract of a letter dated 15 October 1742 from Benjamin

The second reason for this relative peace on the border was the shift in the balance of power in the Southeast. After 1743 the French replaced the Spaniards as the most serious menace to the English in Georgia and Carolina. French traders, working out of settlements along the Gulf Coast, effectively extended their influence over many Lower Creek tribes and became a real threat to English hegemony. The Floridians, on the other hand, were less of a factor in the power struggle in the Southeast and were seemingly content to maintain their defensive position within the confines of the Florida peninsula. The English, therefore, turned their attention to the French at Mobile and Natchez.

In Florida the governor used this reprieve to good advantage. Between 1743 and 1763 Montiano and his successors strengthened the defenses of the colony to such a degree that by the time the English took over Saint Augustine in 1763 it was never stronger. Near the end of his tenure Montiano rebuilt and refitted the six half-galleys that had driven off the English landing force in September, 1742, and mounted new cannon at the mouth of the Saint John's River.[76] Later governors continued this work. Forced laborers erected new storehouses for powder and food, raised the walls of the fort, and built new counterscarps and covered walks. In Apalache a Cuban engineer laid plans to replace Primo's wooden fort with a stronger, more defensible stone structure, and during the 1750's forced laborers undertook a building program that bolstered Apalache's makeshift defenses.[77] The usual problems—lack of labor, materials, and money—caused delays in the work of refortification, but after 1743 the governors of Florida did not have to expend their efforts in repairing damage inflicted by the English and their Indians. They were able to make real progress toward improving Florida's defense lines in order to make the colony less vulnerable to outside attack.

Whitaker, Esq., Chief Justice of the Provinces of South Carolina to Colonel Vanderdussen in London, Charles Town.

76. AGI, Papeles Procedentes de Cuba, Legajo 2263. Carta del Marqués de la Ensenada al gobernador de Cuba, San Ildefonso, Aug. 6, 1745.

77. AGI, Papeles Procedentes de Cuba, Legajo 2263. Carta del Marqués de la Ensenada al gobernador de Cuba, Jan. 2, 1753. AGI, Santo Domingo, Legajo 2534. Carta del gobernador de la Florida al Marqués de la Ensenada, June 18, 1753. AGI, Santo Domingo, Legajo 2542. Carta del gobernador de la Florida al rey, Aug. 26, 1756. See also Chatelain, *The Defenses of Spanish Florida*. AGI, Santo Domingo, Legajo 846. Carta del gobernador de la Florida al rey, April 20, 1759.

[*Military Reorganization: The New Law of 1753*]

While work went ahead in Florida to strengthen the defenses of the colony, plans were being formulated outside the colony for its military reorganization. In May, 1748, Ferdinand VI ordered the viceroy of New Spain, formerly the governor of Cuba (Güemes) and now the Conde de Revillagigedo, to recommend measures that would reduce the expense of maintaining garrisons in Florida, Cuba, Puerto Rico, and Santo Domingo. These garrisons, all supported by *situados,* were a drain on the royal treasury, and the king evidently hoped to eliminate some of the high costs of maintaining his troops in the Caribbean without sacrificing their efficiency.[78]

The viceroy submitted his recommendations in 1753. For Florida he advocated a basic complement of 400 men—310 in six infantry companies, 40 for an artillery company, and 50 for a cavalry company. In no case would a soldier be allowed to hold two posts or enjoy two salaries, a common practice in the past. When a soldier died or was transferred, his commanding officer was ordered to pick three men as possible replacements and submit their names to the governor, who would choose one and send on the nomination to the king for final approval. All old and crippled soldiers were ordered to Cuba, leaving only able-bodied men in the garrisons at Saint Augustine and Apalache. Revillagigedo also suggested new red-and-blue uniforms for Florida infantrymen and new swords for cavalrymen. Golden epaulets were to adorn the shoulders of each officer serving in Florida. To eliminate the morale problem of those forced to serve in Saint Augustine, the viceroy proposed a yearly interchange of half the Florida garrison with a comparable number of men from the garrison at Santiago de Cuba. All soldiers being transferred were to use the gear and equipment of the soldiers with whom they exchanged places, removing the high costs of transporting baggage between Cuba and Florida. Each soldier would, however, carry one item to his new assignment—his own sword, rifle, or pistol, depending upon his rank and company affiliation. The viceroy also proposed that the garrisons be exchanged in April or May when storms were less likely to interfere with the voyage between Santiago and Saint Augustine.[79]

78. AGI, Audiencia de Mexico, Legajo 1506. Real cédula, Aranjuez, May 19, 1748.

79. "Reglamento para las peculiares obligaciones de el Presidio de San Augustín [*sic*] de la Florida y reglas que en el se deben observar, mediante a lo dispuesto, para

Other recommendations bore directly or indirectly on military policy in the colony. Forced laborers and slaves working on the fortifications in Florida received a daily ration of two meals of bread and meat, one blanket a year, and a crude suit of unbleached linen. Revillagigedo also allocated 9,864 pesos 2 reales a year for payments to widows and orphans, many of whom had formerly received their livelihood from the military payroll and held places allocated for effective infantrymen.[80]

The New Law remedied a great many ills in the colony. It provided Florida with an able-bodied complement of artillerymen, infantrymen, and cavalrymen for the first time in almost two hundred years. The New Law relieved the governor of the burden of providing for forced laborers and slaves working on the fortifications at Saint Augustine and Apalache, and eliminated the old abuse of allowing widows and orphans to assume places on the military rolls held by their husbands and fathers. By providing a two-year term for soldiers serving in Florida, the viceroy solved a major morale problem. Troops in Saint Augustine knew now that they were not destined to serve indefinitely in the desolate Florida province and could look forward to returning to Santiago once their two-year term was completed. Undoubtedly the red-and-blue uniforms for the infantry, the epaulets for the officers, and the swords for the cavalry also improved morale and provided more *esprit de corps*. Combined with the strengthening of the defenses that had proceeded apace since 1743, the New Law was a significant step toward improving Spain's military position in the Southeast. Unfortunately the reforms had just taken hold when the governor had to turn the province over to the English.

[*The Governor as a Military Tactician: A Critique*]

Within the Spanish Empire Florida was a vitally strategic outpost that protected the Bahama Channel and the north coast of the Gulf of Mexico. Called by some Spaniards "the first line of defense for New Spain," Florida was significant for the king militarily. In the first two decades of the eighteenth century, it appeared as if he would lose the province. Apalache was abandoned in the early years of Queen Anne's

la Tropa, que en le ha de guarnecer en el reglamento formado para la Habana. Año de 1753." Microfilm copy, Manuscript Division, John Carter Brown Library, Brown University, Providence, Rhode Island.

80. "Reglamento para la guarnación de la Habana, Castillos y Fuertes de su juris-dicción, Santiago de Cuba, San Augustín [*sic*] de la Florida, y su Anexo San Marcos de Apalache, Añó de 1753." Microfilm copy, Manuscript Division, John Carter Brown Library, Brown University, Providence, Rhode Island.

War, and by 1706 all Spain could claim in Florida was the area immediately surrounding the indestructible Fort San Marcos. Saint Augustine was in ashes as a result of the English siege of 1702, and hostile Indians made continuous raids on Spanish settlements. But somehow the governor managed to hold the colony for the king, and once Queen Anne's War was over, he effectively re-established Spanish power in Apalache, built new fortifications at Saint Augustine, and deployed his troops in critical points throughout the Florida peninsula. Strong enough to withstand another major assault in 1740, Florida stood defiantly as a symbol of Spanish power in the Southeast until 1763, when England assumed control of the province.

Skilled as defensive strategists, the governors of Florida were less successful when they waged offensive war. Lack of supplies, insufficient troops, bad weather, bad luck, indecisive leadership, and the shrewd defensive tactics of their English opponents thwarted all Spanish attempts to recover Carolina and Georgia. It appears, however, that the failure to bring these two colonies again under Spanish control could hardly be blamed solely on the governor. By the opening of the eighteenth century Spain had had its day in the Southeast. If the governor kept the Spanish flag flying over Fort San Marcos in Saint Augustine and Fort San Marcos in Apalache, he was fulfilling the expectations of his superiors in Spain. Hopes for great offensive victories were surely chimerical.

Chapter VII

THE GOVERNOR AND
THE CHURCH

A mong the governor's many titles was royal vice-patron of the church. It was his obligation as the most important civil official in Florida to attend to the religious welfare of his province—to aid the regular clergy in their missionary activities and to support the secular clergy in the performance of their duties in Saint Augustine, Apalache, and Fort San Marcos. In most areas of the Spanish Empire the vice-patron was a significant figure, for he controlled both clerical appointments and the tithe. In Florida the governor had no such duties. He made no clerical appointments and collected few tithes. Appointive power rested with civil and religious officials outside of Florida, and the Saint Augustine populace was too impoverished to contribute more than a few mites to the church. Like the military, the religious were dependent upon the subsidy and outside contributions for their sustenance. As vice-patron the governor's chief duties were to administer this aid and to resolve religious controversies.

The eighteenth century was a difficult period in the religious life of the Floridians. After 1670 the Franciscans laboring in the missions along the Georgia coast and in Apalache had to give up their work and retreat to the safety of the Convent of the Immaculate Conception in Saint Augustine.[1] Raids of English frontiersmen and their Indians made it impossible for the dedicated brown-robed friars to continue their work among the Indians and restricted the Franciscans to the areas under the guns of Fort San Marcos. The shrinking of the missionary frontier had serious repercussions in Florida. It reduced the territory under Spanish control in the Southeast and was at least partially responsible for a general loss of religious fervor in the colony.

1. See Lanning, *Spanish Missions, passim.*

[*Organization of the Regular and Secular Clergy*]

The regular clergy in Florida were organized according to the Franciscan pattern and had close ties with the order in Cuba. In the eighteenth century Florida was a part of the larger Franciscan province of Santa Elena, which included all missions and convents in Florida and those in Cuba at Havana, Santiago, Bayamo, Puerto Principe, Guanabacoa, Sancti Spiritus, and Trinidad.[2] A provincial, elected every three years in chapters *(capítulos)*, directed the activities of the friars in the province. Elected advisers *(definadores)* and the guardians of the convents counseled and assisted him. A *procurador* acted as a kind of recruiting and supply officer for the entire province. Over all Franciscan provinces in the Indies sat a commissary general residing in Madrid. He, in turn, was responsible to the minister general of the order in Rome.

In Florida Franciscan activity centered at the Convent of the Immaculate Conception. Here lived a *comisario provincial*, the guardian of the convent, a quartermaster *(síndico)*, an evangelical preacher *(predicador)*, three interpreters *(atiquis)* of Indian languages, a primary teacher *(maestro de gramática)* for the children of Saint Augustine, a lay brother, and a few ailing and elderly friars.[3] In the seventeenth century many Franciscans worked among the Indians of Apalache, Georgia, and the area around Saint Augustine,[4] but as the English and French extended their influence in the Southeast, the number of friars laboring in native villages diminished sharply, and by 1706 the only Franciscans in the field were those working with tribes located near Saint Augustine.[5]

The secular clergy had a small establishment in Florida. As part of the diocese of Cuba, the province fell under the jurisdiction of the bishop of Cuba, who was charged with making periodic visitations to Saint Augustine to make confirmations and to give the Floridians the benefit of his spiritual counsel. At the parochial church of San Francisco in Saint Augustine the curate *(cura vicar)* administered the sacraments and directed the religious life of the colonists. Assisting him were a

2. The convents and missions of the Province of Santa Elena are listed in Maynard Geiger, *Biographical Dictionary of the Franciscans in Spanish Florida and Cuba (1528-1841)* (Paterson, N. J., 1940).

3. AGI, Santo Domingo, Legajo 836. Despacho del rey al obispo de la ciudad de Valladolid de Michoacán, Sept. 5, 1703.

4. In 1655, for example, fifty friars operated in thirty-nine missions and had purportedly converted 26,000 Indians. Lanning, *Spanish Missions*, p. 169.

5. AGI, Santo Domingo, Legajo 840. Carta del provincial Fray Simón de Salas del orden de San Francisco al rey, June 14, 1705.

sacristan (*sacristan mayor*), an organist, and later in the eighteenth century two altar boys. A chaplain served in the small Saint Mark's chapel of the *castillo* and later at San Marcos de Apalache.[6]

[*Creation of a Bishopric in Florida*]

It was difficult for both the regular and secular clergy to maintain close ties with their superiors in Cuba. The distance and the dangers of the voyage from Havana to Saint Augustine prevented the two provinces from establishing strong religious bonds. In the seventeenth century, for example, only two bishops visited Florida—Bishop Juan de las Cabezas Altamirano in 1606 and Bishop Varas Díaz Calderón in 1674.[7] Other prelates either ignored the royal prescription that they make periodic visitations to Florida or sent their representatives to Saint Augustine. Sickness and the risks of travel served as convenient excuses for evasion of this obligation. For the Floridians, however, the bishop's neglect of their spiritual welfare was a serious matter; without a visitation the newly baptized could not be confirmed.

In 1670 the king responded to complaints about the infrequent visitations by demanding recommendations from the bishop of Cuba, the dean of the cathedral chapter in Havana, and the Audiencia of Santo Domingo on the suitability of setting up an auxiliary bishopric of Cuba expressly for Florida. The replies were not enthusiastic. The bishop and the dean both argued that the costs of supporting an auxiliary bishop would not be worth the beneficial effect he might have on the colony. Then in 1674 to quell the agitation for a new diocese, Varas Díaz Calderón, the bishop of Cuba, made a visit to Saint Augustine, and the matter lay dormant for the next quarter of a century.[8]

In 1701 when the new bishop of Cuba, Diego Evelino de Compostela, revived the issue, roles were completely reversed. The bishop this time proposed a separate diocese for Florida, claiming that it was impossible for him to make the dangerous voyage to Saint Augustine. A resident

6. In San Marcos de Apalache the Franciscan friar serving among the Indians sometimes doubled as chaplain for the garrison stationed there.

7. John Gilmary Shea, *The Catholic Church in Colonial Days* (New York, 1883), I, 160, 168. For an account of Altamirano's visitation, see Lanning, *Spanish Missions*, pp. 136-163.

8. AGI, Santo Domingo, Legajo 865. Resumen de lo que ha ocurrido para la erección de obispo auxiliar a proprietario de las provincias de la Florida y estado en que esta, año de 1724. See also, Extracto de todo lo que ha ocurrido desde un origen en el punto de obispo para la Florida el qual se ha executado para dar curso al expediente que en el año de 1724 se vió en la cámara sobre que respondido el Señor Fiscal.

bishop in Florida, he believed, would be beneficial for the colony.[9]

Governor Zúñiga opposed the proposal. He stated that the voyage from Havana took eight days at most, and there was absolutely no need for a new diocese. He gave no other reasons for his opposition, but apparently the governor either did not want to pay the costs of maintaining a new prelate or was fearful that a bishop might challenge his own gubernatorial pre-eminence in Saint Augustine.[10]

In October, 1701, the Council of the Indies acted to implement the bishop's proposal. The Council believed that the bishop had too many responsibilities in Cuba to be burdened with the troublesome Florida visitation. Its members also agreed that many "pernicious spiritual consequences" had resulted from the bishop's neglect of Florida, but with an auxiliary bishop resident in Saint Augustine, these old abuses would be swept away. Including the provinces of Apalache, Carlos, and Catalina (Guale), Florida encompassed an area large enough to warrant creation of an auxiliary bishopric. The auxiliary could supervise mission work, advise the Spaniards and Indians on religious matters, and make confirmations. The Council also suggested six assistants for the new bishop.[11] Philip V acted quickly on the recommendation, and on December 1, 1701, ordered his ambassador in Rome to seek papal sanction for the new auxiliary bishopric.[12] Within six months the pope gave his approval, making the new auxiliary suffragan to the bishop of Cuba, who received the power to appoint the new secular clergyman.[13]

Finding a suitable candidate for the new post was only one of the difficulties encountered in creating the auxiliary bishopric. Bishop Diego Evelino de Compostela first chose his assistant, Father Andrés de Olmos, who refused the office. Eighty years old and infirm, he stated that he was incapable of making the trip to Florida. The bishop then delayed almost a full year before naming Dionisio Resino, eldest priest in Cuba, whose appointment was finally confirmed by the king on September 18,

9. AGI, Santo Domingo, Legajo 840. Carta del gobernador de la Florida al rey, March 10, 1701.

10. AGI, Santo Domingo, Legajo 840. Carta del gobernador de la Florida al rey, March 10, 1701. The document circulating in Spain stated that no bishop of Cuba had visited Florida since 1595, ignoring the two visitations of 1606 and 1674.

11. AGI, Santo Domingo, Legajo 836. Consulta del Consejo de las Indias, Oct. 12, 1701.

12. AGI, Santo Domingo, Legajo 836. Despacho del rey al Duque de Uzeda (Embajador de España en Roma), Dec. 1, 1701.

13. AGI, Santo Domingo, Legajo 836. Consulta del Consejo de las Indias, July 23, 1704.

1704.[14] This immediately created a new problem over who would pay for the papal bulls creating the new office and for the maintenance of the auxiliary bishop. Evelino de Compostela adamantly refused to pay either. Meanwhile the bishop died. His successor, Gerónimo de Valdes, proved more co-operative and willingly consented to pay for the bulls and to grant Resino an income from Cuban tithes.[15]

In the meantime officials in Spain had wrestled with the problem of Resino's maintenance and arrived at their own solution. On October 29, 1706, Philip V awarded the new auxiliary 1,000 pesos a year from the Florida tithe.[16] In Saint Augustine the governor and his treasury officials immediately protested. Between 1703 and 1707 revenue from the tithe had produced a total of 1,413 pesos, an average of only 283 pesos a year.[17] In December, 1708, therefore, the Council of the Indies proposed another solution. Its members decided to award Resino an income of 3,000 pesos—1,000 from the Florida tithe, which they probably realized could not be collected; 1,000 from the vacant bishoprics of New Spain, always a convenient source to tap; and 1,000 from Cuban tithes.[18] Resino's six assistants were each to receive two hundred pesos a year from the Cuban import and export tax (almojarifazgo).[19]

This satisfied the governor and the new auxiliary, but a new obstacle arose. The bishop could not take his post in Florida without being consecrated. Canon law required three bishops to invest him with his office. Since three such dignitaries could not be found in Cuba, Resino had to sail to Mérida, Yucatán, for the formal rites, which took place early in 1709.[20] After the ceremony Resino returned to Cuba, packed his few belongings, and sailed for Florida on the *Nuestra Señora del Rosario*. Harried by eleven English men-of-war, the Spanish vessel, nevertheless,

14. AGI, Santo Domingo, Legajo 836. Consulta del Consejo de las Indias, Sept. 18, 1704.
15. AGI, Santo Domingo, Legajo 875. Resumen de lo que ha ocurrido para la erección de obispo auxiliar a proprietario de las provincias de la Florida y estado en que esta, año de 1724.
16. AGI, Santo Domingo, Legajo 836. Despacho del rey al gobernador de la Florida, Oct. 29, 1706.
17. AGI, Santo Domingo, Legajo 847. Carta de los oficiales reales de la Florida al rey, March 5, 1708.
18. AGI, Santo Domingo, Legajo 833. Consulta del Consejo de las Indias, Dec. 30, 1708.
19. AGI, Santo Domingo, Legajo 836. Despacho del rey al gobernador de Cuba, July 20, 1709.
20. Shea, *Catholic Church*, I, 464.

managed to escape capture.[21] On June 23, 1709, Resino disembarked at the Florida capital.[22]

Despite their earlier opposition to an auxiliary bishopric, Governor Córcoles and his colonists gave Resino a warm welcome. For the first time in thirty-five years a bishop had come to Saint Augustine to make confirmations. The Floridians were also impressed by Resino's humble manner and appreciated his interest in their spiritual welfare. The auxiliary, however, was wretched in his new charge. All the principal religious buildings were in ashes, and there was no suitable episcopal residence in the colony. Because of the war raging with England, the Franciscans had given up their mission work, and there was no longer any need for episcopal visitations of the three provinces of Apalache, Carlos, and Guale. All he could hope to accomplish was to confirm the newly baptized Spaniards and the few Indians who still remained under Spanish control.[23] Disheartened by conditions in his new charge, Resino departed for Havana only three weeks after his arrival. A short time later on September 12, 1711, he died, leaving the auxiliary bishopric open once again.[24]

[*A Replacement for Resino*]

For the bishop of Cuba finding a successor for Resino was a vexing task, and initially he chose to ignore the problem by neglecting to report Resino's death to his superiors in Spain.[25] He also subverted the issue by renewing his request for a separate bishopric in Florida, completely independent of his own episcopate.[26] In November, 1715, therefore, Philip V again put the question before the pope.[27] A short time later when the king learned that 50,000 Indians inhabiting 161 villages in the

21. Resino had a premonition that he might encounter difficulties in making the voyage to Florida and told the king in a letter that he had prayed fervently to God to insure him a safe passage to Saint Augustine. AGI, Santo Domingo, Legajo 864. Carta del obispo auxiliar de Cuba al rey, June 10, 1709.

22. AGI, Santo Domingo, Legajo 864. Carta del obispo auxiliar de Cuba al rey, July 5, 1709.

23. AGI, Santo Domingo, Legajo 841. Carta del Fray Claudio de Florencia al rey, July 10, 1709. Carta del gobernador de la Florida al rey, July 20, 1709.

24. AGI, Santo Domingo, Legajo 836. Despacho del rey al obispo de Cuba, Feb. 10, 1714.

25. The date of the bishop's letter informing the king of Resino's death was February 15, 1713.

26. AGI, Santo Domingo, Legajo 865. Resumen de lo que ha ocurrido para la erección de obispo auxiliar a proprietario de las provincias de la Florida y estado en que esta, año de 1724.

27. AGI, Santo Domingo, Legajo 833. Consulta del Consejo de las Indias, Feb. 11, 1716.

Southeast had expressed allegiance to Spain, he believed a separate
bishopric even more vital. Philip V thus ordered the governor to
delineate the territorial boundaries of the proposed new diocese and requested reports from Cuba and Florida on the feasibility of erecting a
new bishopric.[28]

Opinions differed widely on whether to establish the new diocese.
Religious leaders in Cuba seemingly wanted to rid themselves of
Florida and strongly advocated its establishment. The Cubans realized
no tithe from the poverty-stricken colony and spent 1,000 pesos a year in
support of the auxiliary bishop. A separate diocese would put the
financial burden on the governor of Florida and relieve the Cubans of
onerous obligations.[29] On the other side, the Florida governor strongly
opposed separation of his colony from the Cuban diocese and assailed
the Cuban arguments on economic grounds. Not only were his Floridians too poor to support a new bishop but the great number of Indians
now being maintained by the Spanish had put a severe strain on his
treasury. Both reasons made it untenable to set up a separate diocese.
The governor had all the financial burdens he could bear without
assuming a new one.[30]

Arguments over a separate diocese continued until 1723, when
Cuban religious leaders finally gave up their struggle to rid themselves
of Florida. It appears that Bishop Varas and his advisers in Cuba
had become alarmed over Governor Benavides' attempts to dominate
the secular clergy in Florida. Since assuming the governorship in
1718, he had purged the curate of the parochial church, brought charges
against his temporary replacement, and in every way tried to assert his
influence over the clerics serving in Saint Augustine. The bishop gave
up his fight for a separate diocese and appointed Father Diego Rubi de
Celis as auxiliary bishop, a move evidently calculated to challenge the
Florida governor's growing power over religious affairs.[31] In the meantime, however, Bishop Varas died, and his replacement, Gaspar Molina,
took a leaf from Compostela's book. The new prelate refused either

28. AGI, Santo Domingo, Legajo 837. Despacho del rey al obispo de Cuba, Feb.
17, 1716.
29. AGI, Santo Domingo, Legajo 837. Despacho del rey a Cardenal Aquaviva,
Jan. 18, 1717.
30. AGI, Santo Domingo, Legajo 865. Resumen de lo que ha ocurrido para la
erección de obispo auxiliar a proprietario de las provincias de la Florida y estado en
que esta, año de 1724.
31. AGI, Santo Domingo, Legajo 865. Resumen de lo que ha ocurrido para la
erección de obispo auxiliar a proprietario de las provincias de la Florida y estado en
que esta, año de 1724.

to pay for the papal bulls authorizing the appointment or to provide the 1,000 pesos for the auxiliary's maintenance, and once again Florida was without an auxiliary bishop.[32]

In Florida Governor Benavides was undoubtedly pleased over the course of events, for he opposed a religious supernumerary in any form as a threat to his own pre-eminence in the colony. He stated in a report to the Council of the Indies that any bishop or auxiliary bishop should concern himself solely with religious affairs and stay out of political matters, which were his province. The Council, however, sensed the governor's hostility and were sharply critical of his stand. Its caustic reply maintained that the bishop could not hope to advance the spiritual welfare of the colony without the support of the governor. Both officials had to recognize the close ties binding church and state and do their best to promote the religious interests of the colony. The Council also believed that an auxiliary bishop would make a valuable adviser for the governor and provide the impetus needed to rebuild the church and the convent.[33]

In the end Benavides had little to fear. Until his death in 1729 Bishop Molina adamantly refused to release the money necessary to establish the auxiliary bishopric in Saint Augustine. His two successors, however, the short-lived Francisco de Sarregui, formerly dean of the cathedral chapter at Segovia, and in 1731, Juan Loso de la Vega, proved willing to bear the financial burden of the office. Late in 1731 Loso de la Vega appointed Francisco de San Buenaventura y Tejada, master of arts in theology and guardian of a Franciscan convent in Seville, as auxiliary bishop.[34] In February, 1732, Buenaventura accepted the post and left Spain for the Indies.[35]

By the time Buenaventura arrived in Cuba, the only problem remaining to be resolved was his consecration. Eager to get the new auxiliary bishop to Florida quickly, Philip V ordered the rites to be performed in Cuba. He dispensed with the law requiring three bishops to be present at the ceremony and ordered the bishop of Cuba to secure two prebendaries or canons to substitute for the two prelates.[36] These

32. AGI, Santo Domingo, Legajo 837. Consulta de la Cámara, Aug. 22, 1729.
33. AGI, Santo Domingo, Legajo 865. El acuerdo del Consejo de las Indias, n.d., 1724.
34. AGI, Santo Domingo, Legajo 865. Consulta de la Cámara, Dec. 6, 1731.
35. AGI, Santo Domingo, Legajo 865. Despacho del rey al obispo de Cuba, Nov. 12, 1732.
36. AGI, Santo Domingo, Legajo 865. Despacho del rey al obispo de Cuba, Nov. 29, 1733.

orders arrived too late, for Buenaventura had already departed for Vera Cruz. Here in the summer of 1734 he underwent the solemnities that consecrated him as auxiliary bishop of Cuba.[37] A year later in July, 1735, he arrived in Florida to assume his duties.[38]

[*Buenaventura in Florida*]

Conditions in Florida had apparently not improved since Resino's visitation twenty-six years earlier. Like Resino, Buenaventura was appalled at the spiritual decadence within the colony—the scandals, the lack of moral standards, the desecration of holy law. The tiny hermitage that served as the parochial church profaned the Mass. Chalices and other church ornaments were hardly fit for use. The curate was old and sick, and no suitable residence could be found for Buenaventura.[39] The dedicated auxiliary was also distressed about the languishing mission program and the apathy of his Franciscan brethren, who were rent by factionalism and had allowed drunken Indians to roam the streets of Saint Augustine.[40] Worst of all, heretical English traders, posing as Roman Catholics, preached Protestant doctrines in the Florida capital, undermining the religious beliefs of the colonists.[41]

For a short time Buenaventura maintained friendly relations with Governor Moral. Moral gave the auxiliary a warm welcome and initially pressed his superiors in Spain to send out the six assistants allotted to the bishop. The governor also complained that Buenaventura lacked sufficient funds to maintain himself in the style befitting his office.[42] In fact during the summer of 1735 it seems as if gubernatorial co-operation with the bishop, preached so strongly by the Council of the Indies in 1727, had become a reality.

It was not long before the two quarreled openly. Early in the fall they took opposite sides in a scandal that split the Franciscan

37. AGI, Santo Domingo, Legajo 837. Despacho del rey al obispo de Cuba, Oct. 30, 1735. Buenaventura's letter of July 8, 1734, recounted the events of his consecration in Vera Cruz.

38. AGI, Santo Domingo, Legajo 844. Carta del gobernador de la Florida al rey, Aug. 27, 1737.

39. AGI, Santo Domingo, Legajo 844. Carta del obispo auxiliar de Cuba al rey, Aug. 27, 1735.

40. AGI, Santo Domingo, Legajo 2584. Carta del obispo auxiliar de Cuba a Fray Guillermo Clarke, Oct. 1, 1735.

41. AGI, Santo Domingo, Legajo 864. Carta del obispo auxiliar de Cuba al rey, April 29, 1736.

42. AGI, Santo Domingo, Legajo 844. Carta del gobernador de la Florida al rey, Aug. 27, 1735.

order in Florida.[43] Then, when Moral ordered all Floridians to obtain his permission before they conferred with the auxiliary bishop, tension increased, as Buenaventura became convinced that the governor meant to separate him from the soldiers, colonists, and Indians he was trying to serve.[44] At the same time the two men clashed personally. Both were ambitious, jealous of their authority, and determined to protect their positions in Florida. Given their strong wills, a clash was inevitable.

Moral's ouster in 1737 gave Buenaventura the opportunity he needed to carry out many religious reforms in Florida. With alms contributed by the residents of Saint Augustine, he rebuilt the parochial church of San Francisco and secured new ornaments for the edifice. He also persuaded several small boys from the more pious families of the town to study Latin in order that they might assist him in the church choir during daily Mass, vespers, and festival-day communions.[45] As a stimulus to the mission program, he proposed teaching Castilian to the Indians. The multiplicity of Indian tongues, the scarcity of interpreters, and the penchant of the Indians for learning Spanish quickly had convinced Buenaventura that this was the only feasible program. For Spanish-speaking friars to learn the countless Indian dialects was, to him, an unrewarding and unnecessary task.[46] To refurbish the hospital, the auxiliary revived an old assessment of six reales a year on the salaries of each of the soldiers of the military payroll.[47] Buenaventura also gathered the children of Saint Augustine in the church three days a week to teach them long-neglected catechism. Children of the poor, who could not contribute to the bishop's instruction, received similar lessons free from a Franciscan resident of the convent. In an attempt to improve the moral standards of the colony Buenaventura prohibited lewd dancing and gambling in local taverns. He also confirmed newly baptized Spaniards, Indians, Negro slaves, and free Negroes.[48]

43. AGI, Santo Domingo, Legajo 867. Carta del obispo auxiliar de Cuba al rey, Oct. 15, 1735. See also pp. 184-192.

44. AGI, Santo Domingo, Legajo 2584. Carta del obispo auxiliar de Cuba a Fray Guillermo Clarke, Oct. 1, 1735.

45. AGI, Santo Domingo, Legajo 864. Carta del obispo auxiliar de Cuba al rey, April 29, 1736. In a series of letters of this date, Buenaventura recounted what he had accomplished in Florida.

46. AGI, Santo Domingo, Legajo 864. Carta del obispo auxiliar de Cuba al rey, April 29, 1736.

47. AGI, Santo Domingo, Legajo 864. Carta del obispo auxiliar de Cuba al rey, April 29, 1736.

48. AGI, Santo Domingo, Legajo 864. Carta del obispo auxiliar de Cuba al rey, April 29, 1736.

In his ten years as resident auxiliary bishop, Buenaventura brought
the colony out of its religious apathy. Through his efforts the church
and the convent were rebuilt. By comparison his minor innovations,
such as the choir boys in the church or saying the rosary in the streets of
Saint Augustine on the afternoons of festival days, seem inconsequential;
yet taken all together, his efforts added civilized amenities to the religious life of this rude frontier town. The auxiliary's only failures
were his inability to resolve the factional struggle among the Franciscans and to revive the mission program, but these were virtually impossible tasks. Able and diligent, Buenaventura proved willing to face
poverty, apathy, and opposition from the governor in order to bring
about a religious regeneration in Florida. Ultimately, his good record
won him the bishopric of Yucatán, to which he was appointed in 1745.[49]

Buenaventura's departure in 1745 initiated efforts to find a successor.
At first it appeared as if the process would take only a short time, for
Pedro Ponce y Carrasco immediately accepted the appointment.[50]
But once again familiar obstacles arose to keep him from Florida—lack
of money to pay for the papal bulls, difficulties in consecration, and inadequate provision for the auxiliary's maintenance.[51] In fact, it was almost
ten years before Ponce y Carrasco reached Florida.

When the new auxiliary bishop arrived in Saint Augustine in April,
1754, he showed none of Buenaventura's militancy or enthusiasm for
reform. Although he was reported to be a model prelate, conforming
in every way to royal and ecclesiastical law and to the orders of the
bishop of Cuba, he had none of the vitality of his predecessor and
showed no predilection for disturbing the life of the colony.[52] The
only real problem he encountered was finding a suitable place to live.
Since the governor's residence was not habitable, Interim Governor
Fulgencio García de Solís had agreed to contribute sixty-four pesos a
year to the work of the secular clergy and moved into the episcopal
palace, but upon the arrival of Ponce y Carrasco, García de Solís gra-
ciously consented to turn the residence over to the new prelate while
he found other quarters.[53] In the end the governor did not have to give

49. AGI, Santo Domingo, Legajo 838. Carta del obispo de Cuba al rey, May
14, 1745.
50. AGI, Santo Domingo, Legajo 854. Consulta de la Cámara, Dec. 15, 1745.
51. AGI, Santo Domingo, Legajo 833. Consulta del Consejo de las Indias, Nov.
6, 1747.
52. AGI, Santo Domingo, Legajo 2542. Carta del gobernador interino de la
Florida al rey, Feb. 11, 1755.
53. AGI, Santo Domingo, Legajo 2542. Carta del gobernador interino de la
Florida al rey, April 20, 1754.

up the episcopal palace for long. Within ten months after his arrival in February, 1755, Ponce y Carrasco departed for Cuba.

[*The Auxiliary Bishop: A Check on the Governor?*]

As an institution the auxiliary bishopric had little lasting influence in Florida, despite Buenaventura's personal triumph in Saint Augustine. Three factors kept the auxiliary bishop from contributing more to the religious life of the colony. First, only one of three prelates remained in Saint Augustine long enough to exercise real authority, inspire any real respect, or gain a large following. Dionsio Resino remained in the colony for only three weeks and Ponce y Carrasco for ten months. Buenaventura resided in Saint Augustine for a decade and brought about significant changes, but not all of these lasted. Moreover, he served during an unfortunate period. He had to deal both with the difficult Moral Sánchez and with the factionalism that split the Franciscan order. Then in 1739 war broke out and continued as long as the dedicated Buenaventura remained in Florida, limiting his religious activities in the colony.

A second factor reducing the auxiliary's effectiveness was the interminable delays encountered in filling the office. Unlike the governorship there was no continuity in the auxiliary bishopric. Years, even decades, passed between the time an auxiliary left Saint Augustine and the time a successor assumed the post. Resino left Florida in 1709; his replacement did not arrive in Saint Augustine until 1735, twenty-seven years later. Buenaventura departed for Yucatán in 1745; Ponce y Carrasco did not assume the auxiliary bishopric until nine years later, in 1754. Both Resino and Ponce y Carrasco also desired to administer the religious affairs of Florida from Havana rather than from Saint Augustine where they might have been more effective.

The decline in the number and the influence of the Franciscans was a third factor that contributed to the ineffectiveness of the auxiliary bishop. Working with a nucleus of dedicated friars, he might have been able to revive religious work among the Indians and to revitalize the spiritual life of the colonists, but the Franciscans had found it impossible to labor effectively in Florida in the face of English and Indian attacks. Many friars chose either to leave for Cuba or to retire to the convent in Saint Augustine. Those who remained in Florida became involved in bitter factional disputes for control of the order and failed to unite under the auxiliary bishop—Buenaventura in particular—to promote the religious life of the colony. Without the support of the Franciscans, the bishop could not wield great influence or challenge the governor's pre-eminence in Florida.

[*The Governor and the Secular Clergy*]

The secular clergy in Florida always remained within the shadow of the regular clergy and the governor. Except for Buenaventura there was no effective resident auxiliary bishop, and there were very few seculars in the colony—only a curate, sacristan, organist, and chaplain of Fort San Marcos. This small group could hardly constitute a threat to the governor, who usually maintained amicable relations with the curate and his aides at the parochial church. During the eighteenth century only two governors—Antonio de Benavides and Francisco del Moral Sánchez—engaged in feuds with the secular clergy.

When Benavides assumed the governorship in 1718, he tolerated no interference with his rule and believed that his success as governor depended upon his ability to rid the colony of all those who had even the remotest possibility of challenging him. In his first years as governor he indicted his sergeant major, treasurer, and several experienced military officers on vague, unsubstantiated charges and sent them away to Spain, New Spain, and Cuba for trial.[54] Also included in Benavides' purge were two successive curates of the parochial church, whom the governor saw as a threat to his authority in Florida.

The curate Pedro Lorenzo de Acebedo was the first secular clergyman to clash with Benavides. In 1719 the governor accused the priest of drunkenness and summarily sent him to Havana for trial by an ecclesiastical court.[55] Determined to protect the privileges and station of those in his diocese, the bishop of Cuba made a quick investigation of the case, exonerated Acebedo, and ordered him back to Saint Augustine.[56] In the meantime Benavides submitted new charges against the curate, hoping to prevent his return to the colony. This time the governor accused Acebedo of adultery with three women of Saint Augustine. One of them, the housemaid, Juana de la Cruz, had supposedly become pregnant by the curate, but because she had aborted early in pregnancy, the governor stated that he could not absolutely substantiate this charge.[57]

54. See pp. 64-71.
55. AGI, Santo Domingo, Legajo 833. Dictamen del fiscal, Jan. 8, 1721.
56. AGI, Santo Domingo, Legajo 833. Consulta del Consejo de las Indias, Feb. 5, 1721.
57. AGI, Santo Domingo, Legajo 842. Carta del gobernador de la Florida al rey,

These new charges were successful in keeping Acebedo in Cuba until December, 1722, when the bishop exonerated him once again. Incensed over Benavides' attack on the clergy, the bishop claimed to the king that he wanted to visit Florida to investigate the governor's charges personally but that his age prevented him from making the exhausting voyage. The prelate insisted also that Acebedo be restored to his curacy.[58]

In the meantime, Benavides had proceeded against the curate's temporary replacement, Father Pedro Alonso Lodares Cota, close associate of the bishop of Cuba, who apparently won the appointment because of his friendship with the Cuban prelate. Almost as soon as he arrived in September, 1722, Lodares Cota clashed with the governor. When Benavides transferred four small ships from Spanish to English control, the interim curate objected. He told the governor that the four vessels should have remained under Spanish jurisdiction and threatened excommunication to all those involved in the transaction, including the governor.[59] Two months later Benavides accused his curate of adultery with a married woman of Saint Augustine, a charge supported by many residents of the town.[60] For the bishop of Cuba these new charges were particularly unsettling. Lodares Cota was a close friend, whose morals had always been impeccable. Benavides, in the opinion of the Cuban prelate, had contrived the charges against the curate.[61]

Throughout 1723 the governor and the bishop exchanged bitter words over the Acebedo-Lodares affair. In March, 1723, the governor pointed out in a letter to the king that Lodares Cota had been involved in many scandals in Saint Augustine but that lack of legal jurisdiction over the clergy made him powerless to prevent them. His only recourse was to forward his findings to the bishop of Cuba for his disposition.[62]

Dec. 6, 1721. Testimonios de los autos fechos de oficio contra el beneficiado Don Pedro Lorenzo de Acebedo, siendo juez el Senor Don Juan Esteban Romero Montañes, Visitador General Eclesiastico de esta dicha ciudad, sus doctrinas y provincias, secretario notario de dicho Don Francisco Gabriel de Pueyo, Presbyterio, año de 1721.

58. AGI, Santo Domingo, Legajo 842. Carta del obispo de Cuba al rey, Dec. 22, 1722.

59. AGI, Santo Domingo, Legajo 842. Carta del gobernador de la Florida al rey, Sept. 30, 1722.

60. AGI, Santo Domingo, Legajo 842. Carta del gobernador de la Florida al rey, Nov. 10, 1722. Carta de los vecinos de la ciudad de San Agustín de la Florida al rey, Nov. 23, 1722.

61. AGI, Santo Domingo, Legajo 837. Despacho del rey al obispo de Cuba, Dec. 23, 1724. This dispatch cites the bishop's letter of December 22, 1722, defending Lodares.

62. AGI, Santo Domingo, Legajo 842. Carta del gobernador de la Florida al rey, March 17, 1723.

For his part the bishop took his case to the Council of the Indies. Here in July, 1724, a *fiscal* observed that Benavides seemed anxious to rid Florida of all clerics favored by the bishop. The governor had first banished Acebedo and then brought charges against Lodares Cota. A new curate, he stated, would apparently get the same treatment and serve no useful end. Therefore the *fiscal* advised the recall of Lodares and the restoration of Acebedo to his post in Saint Augustine. This, he believed, would demonstrate to the governor that he could not proceed arbitrarily against the clergy.[63] In December the king approved this action, and Acebedo returned to his curacy.[64]

This by no means ended the struggle between the governor and the curate, who remained bitter enemies. Still determined to get rid of Acebedo, Benavides settled on a new plan of attack. In March, 1729, the governor declared the curate too old to carry out his duties in the parochial church. Seventy-four years old with twenty-two years of service in Saint Augustine, the curate should retire. To provide for him, Benavides recommended a three-peso-a-day pension.[65] This new stratagem at first appeared successful. A royal *cédula* of July 11, 1731, awarded the curate the pension suggested by the governor and seemingly opened the way for Acebedo's retirement.[66] The curate, however, had no intention of retiring. Gratefully accepting the pension but continuing in his post at the church, he thwarted Benavides once again. In the meantime, the governor departed Florida for Vera Cruz, leaving the Acebedo problem to Moral.

The new governor was no more successful than his predecessor in dealing with the curate. In 1735 Moral described Acebedo as having an "unmistakable weakness of mind," unable to administer the sacraments properly or to resolve religious questions in the colony. Even more significant, he was unable to control the scandalous conduct of his sacristan, Juan de Paredes.[67] Unlike Acebedo, the sacristan had won the favor of Governor Benavides. In fact the sacristan was so deeply in the former governor's good graces that he received a long gubernatorial

63. AGI, Santo Domingo, Legajo 842. Dictamen del fiscal, July 18, 1724.
64. AGI, Santo Domingo, Legajo 837. Despacho del rey al gobernador de Cuba, Dec. 23, 1724.
65. AGI, Santo Domingo, Legajo 844. Memorial del gobernador don Antonio de Benavides, March 10, 1729. Carta del gobernador de la Florida al rey, July 7, 1730.
66. AGI, Santo Domingo, Legajo 844. Real cédula, San Ildefonso, July 11, 1731.
67. AGI, Santo Domingo, Legajo 2584. Carta del gobernador de la Florida al rey, March 1, 1735.

testimonial to his good works. In his eulogy Benavides praised Paredes as pious, dedicated, and faithful. When an epidemic swept through the colony in 1732, the sacristan had ministered untiringly to the sick for four long months.⁶⁸ In this praise the governor also got the support of several civil, military, and religious functionaries in the colony.⁶⁹

Moral did not hold the same opinion of Paredes. Not long after he assumed his office, the governor accused the sacristan of adultery with Gerónima de Argüelles, a married woman of Saint Augustine. In a heart-rending testimony, seemingly calculated to appeal to the king and the Council of the Indies, her husband, the illiterate infantryman Onafre de Argüelles, explained that he had been happily married for six years and that during this time his wife had faithfully performed all her wifely duties. Suddenly, however, all this had changed. His wife now left the house at eight or nine each evening without explanation and did not return until after midnight, if at all. She now neglected to prepare his supper and failed to leave him even a few cold scraps in the cupboard. Continual remonstrances and entreaties had accomplished nothing. The sacristan had seduced his wife and she now spent her evening hours with him.⁷⁰ Other testimony garnered by Moral accused Paredes of adultery with other Saint Augustine women and reinforced Argüelles' charge against the sacristan.⁷¹ The curate, claimed Moral, admitted knowledge of Paredes' lechery but refused to intervene to prevent it, still another mark against the aging curate.⁷²

The evidence against Paredes was by no means conclusive. In his own defense he claimed that Moral had fabricated the testimony against him and implied that Moral had paid Argüelles to accuse him. The governor also refused to admit defense testimony, which the sacristan believed would have cleared him completely. In addition, charged Paredes, the governor had perverted both royal and ecclesiastical law and failed to maintain peace in the colony.⁷³ In September, 1735, in the

68. AGI, Santo Domingo, Legajo 844. Testimonio de don Antonio de Benavides, May 10, 1734.

69. AGI, Santo Domingo, Legajo 844. Certificaciones de los vecinos de la Florida, 1734.

70. AGI, Santo Domingo, Legajo 844. Testimonio de don Onafre de Argüelles, March 14, 1735.

71. AGI, Santo Domingo, Legajo 844. Testimonio de don Francisco Nuñez Pernada, n.d., 1735.

72. AGI, Santo Domingo, Legajo 844. Carta del gobernador de la Florida al rey, March 1, 1735.

73. AGI, Santo Domingo, Legajo 844. Carta del sacristan mayor de la santa iglesia de la ciudad de San Agustín de la Florida al rey, March, 1735.

face of these charges and countercharges, Philip V ordered the bishop to Cuba to investigate the sacristan's affairs,[74] but evidently this command was never carried out, for in April, 1737, the king ordered the cleric to Spain.[75] Final disposition of the Paredes case is not clear, but probably he was exonerated.[76] The curate, however, once again escaped the net the governor had spread for him. Acebedo remained in Saint Augustine until his death, enjoying the pension obtained for him by Benavides and most likely relishing the victories he had won over the highest civil authority in the colony.

Benavides and Moral were both unsuccessful in dominating the secular clergy serving in the parochial church. In their battles with various clerics, they could not overcome the power and influence of the bishop of Cuba, the constant defender of the Florida clergy. The bishop opposed all attempts to discredit the seculars in Saint Augustine and prevented their domination by the governor there. Most governors, however, maintained, a semblance of good relations with the clergy. Benavides and Moral were exceptions and did not reflect the normally peaceful ties binding the governor with church leaders.

[*The Governor as Arbiter of Religious Controversies*]

As royal vice patron of the church, the governor occasionally stepped in to settle clerical disputes in Florida. Generally these quarrels did not erupt into major colonial issues and were crucial only to the officials involved. In the period 1700-1763 two such controversies arose. One involved the right to administer sacraments to Christian Indians, the other the use of two choir boys assigned to the parochial church.

The quarrel over the administration of the sacraments to the Indians broke out in 1701 between the regular and secular clergy. In November the guardian of the Franciscan convent complained to the king that the curate had usurped his right to say Mass, hear confessions, and render other religious services to the Indians, *mestizos*,[77] and mulattoes residing in Saint Augustine. On the other side the curate objected violently to

74. AGI, Santo Domingo, Legajo 837. Despacho del rey al obispo de Cuba, Sept. 11, 1735.

75. AGI, Santo Domingo, Legajo 838. Real cédula, Aranjuez, April 28, 1737.

76. See, for example, the case of the friar, Silvestre Ruiz, accused of deserting his post in Florida. Returned to Spain for trial, he was found guilty by an ecclesiastical court. Ultimately, he appealed to Rome, where the pope absolved him completely. AGI, Santo Domingo, Legajo 849. Carta de Joseph Manuel Rodríguez al rey, n.d., 1748.

77. In Florida an individual of mixed Indian and Spanish blood, usually born of a Spanish father and an Indian mother.

the charge, claiming that he had ecclesiastical jurisdiction over *all* Christians residing in Saint Augustine—Spaniards, Creoles, Indians, *mestizos*, mulattoes, and Negroes.[78] Called in as arbiter, Governor Zúñiga refused to take sides and run the risk of incurring the hostility of one of the clergymen. Instead of deciding the matter himself, he referred it to the king, who decided in favor of the Franciscans.[79]

For the next five years there was no trouble over this question, but when Pedro Lorenzo de Acebedo assumed his curacy in 1707, the dispute erupted once again. Although the entire story is not clear, it appears that Acebedo hoped to obtain jurisdiction over the Indians who had taken refuge at Saint Augustine during Queen Anne's War and secure rights over what little the Indians could pay in tithes. Apparently he also hoped to raise his personal prestige in Florida. In this case Governor Córcoles acted more boldly than his predecessor. With a precedent already established, Córcoles sided with the Franciscan guardian, Martín de Molina, and refused Acebedo's request.[80] This may well have been the event that turned the curate against the governor; at any rate for the next three decades Acebedo consistently opposed him.

In 1745 the outgoing auxiliary bishop revived the issue for the last time. In this case it appears that the bishop was attempting to save the prestige of the secular clergy and prevent its domination by the regulars. Especially after the decline in their mission program, the conventual church had become a busy center of religious activity for the residents of Saint Augustine. Most of the more prestigious citizens heard Mass there and requested burial in the conventual plot. Apparently, too, Buenaventura hoped to strengthen the secular clergy by getting a reversal of the king's decisions of 1702 and 1707. When the matter first came before Governor Montiano, he followed Zúñiga's course by referring the question to the king. Montiano knew he would alienate either the curate or the guardian and lose the support of one or the other. He reasoned that any decision he made would be appealed to the king, and he could save time by submitting the question to the crown immediately. In any event, in this case the king reversed his decisions of 1702 and

78. AGI, Santo Domingo, Legajo 840. Carta del gobernador de la Florida al rey, Nov. 15, 1701.

79. AGI, Santo Domingo, Legajo 840. Despacho del rey al obispo de Cuba, July 21, 1702.

80. AGI, Santo Domingo, Legajo 841. Carta del gobernador de la Florida al rey, Nov. 12, 1707.

1707 and awarded the curate sacramental jurisdiction over *all* residents of Saint Augustine.[81]

Although the decision of 1746 closed the matter, the pattern of the controversy was surprising. In the first decade of the century the king twice sided with the regular clergy in a reversal of the pattern developing throughout the Indies. In most cases in America the crown was secularizing towns controlled by the regular clergy, taking power out of the hands of the friars and awarding it to the priests, who could more rigidly be brought under royal control through the royal patronage. In Florida the trend toward secularization did not occur until 1746. Evidently, it made little difference whether the secular clergy dominated the out-of-the-way province.

The controversy over the choir boys had its origins in 1698 when the king awarded rations and vestments for two acolytes for the parochial church. Under the terms of the *cédula* these boys were to assist the curate at the Mass, to sing in the sacristan's choir on holy days, and to aid church officials in other ways.[82] Although the *cédula* filled a real need, the two acolytes were not adequate. They could not assist the curate at the altar and the sacristan in the choir simultaneously, and under Acebedo the boys were used solely at the altar. In 1709, therefore, the sacristan complained to Governor Córcoles that the curate monopolized both acolytes, disobeying the *cédula* of 1698 specifically calling for the two boys to assist him in the choir as well.[83] Córcoles refused to be involved in the dispute and submitted the problem to his superiors in Spain for their resolution. Five years later, after obtaining the opinions of both a royal *fiscal* and the Council of the Indies, Philip V ordered the curate to let the acolytes serve in the choir as well as at the altar.[84] The curate, however, ignored the order and kept both boys at his side during the Mass.

For the next fifteen years the sacristan had no choir boys but registered no complaints. Then in 1730 the accountant, Francisco Menéndez Marqués, revived the issue by reporting that the two acolytes assisted Acebedo at the altar of the parochial church and had not yet

81. AGI, Santo Domingo, Legajo 849. Carta del obispo auxiliar de Cuba al rey, March 28, 1745.

82. The *cédula* was dated August 1, 1698.

83. AGI, Santo Domingo, Legajo 847. Carta de los oficiales reales de la Florida al rey, Dec. 18, 1709.

84. AGI, Santo Domingo, Legajo 849. Despacho del rey a los oficiales reales de la Florida, Sept. 7, 1741.

sung one amen in the sacristan's choir.[85] But if the accountant hoped to get action from the king or the Council of the Indies, he was disappointed. They ignored the accountant's report and refused to act in the matter. A short time later in 1735 Auxiliary Bishop Buenaventura quickly resolved the problem by instituting a course in Latin for the boys of the pious families of Saint Augustine and later installed them in the sacristan's choir.

Ostensibly the controversy over the acolytes was inconsequential, yet it was indicative of several trends in the colony. It showed the extreme sensitivity of the seculars to clerical protocol, even in remote Florida. The incident demonstrated also that the secular clergy, like the regular clergy, could engage in petty quarrels. Moreover, the dispute indicated the governor's unwillingness to mix in clerical quarrels, even in such a minor matter as the use of two choir boys. They thus became problems for the king and the Council of the Indies, who were already overburdened by other more important colonial questions.

[*The Governor and the Regular Clergy: Support for the Franciscans*]

Like the rest of the Floridians the Franciscans were almost completely dependent upon outside aid for their existence. Since tithes produced such a meager sum, the king had awarded a 158-peso (115-ducat) stipend to each of the forty-three missionaries serving in Florida at the opening of the eighteenth century.[86] Like the garrison, they received aid from the subsidy allocated annually to Florida from New Spain and special annual grants of flour, wine, oil, salt, and other necessities. In the seventeenth century this appropriation for the regular clergy went to the provincial of Santa Elena, residing in either Cuba or Saint Augustine, who then distributed the money and supplies among his brethren in Florida.[87] In 1698 this system underwent a slight change when the king gave civil authorities in Saint Augustine partial control over the religious subsidy. Under a new order Charles II ruled that only those friars certified by the treasurer and accountant as bona fide

85. AGI, Santo Domingo, Legajo 847. Carta del contador de la Florida (Francisco Menéndez Marqués) al rey, Feb. 16, 1730.

86. AGI, Santo Domingo, Legajo 836. Despacho del rey a los oficiales reales de la Florida, Oct. 27, 1700.

87. AGI, Santo Domingo, Legajo 836. Consulta del Consejo de las Indias, Jan. 29, 1706.

missionaries or as conventual officials would receive the 158 pesos. All others would get no stipend.[88]

According to the Franciscans, the 158 pesos were inadequate to fulfil their needs. Their Indians were destitute and were continously looking to the friars for help. Without money for food and clothing they were helpless to prevent the Indians from shifting their allegiance to the English or from fleeing to the mountains. In their petitions to the Council of the Indies, the Franciscans pointed out that missionaries in the Mexican province of Michoacán received three hundred pesos a year. With the miserable conditions existing in Florida, the friars believed they deserved an equal amount. Flatly rejecting the request, the Council only sent a short dispatch to the viceroy of New Spain, ordering him to speed delivery of the special subsidy to the friars.[89]

After the English siege of Saint Augustine in 1702, the friars enlisted the aid of their commissary general in Spain, Lucás Álvarez de Toledo, to present their case to the crown. Not only did he request an increase in the annual stipend for the Franciscans and funds for rebuilding the convent, but he also asked for a revival of two royal *cédulas*, one of 1641 and another of 1663. These had awarded the regular clergy in Florida annual supplies of flour, wine, oil, vinegar, salt, blankets, robes, dishes, candles, paper, and other commodities. At first these articles had arrived regularly, then sporadically, and finally by the end of the seventeenth century there was no delivery at all. Álvarez insisted that the bishop of Puebla, charged with remitting the military *situado* to Saint Augustine, enforce the provisions of these royal orders and aid the friars.[90]

The commissary's pleas seemed to get immediate results. After a conference with Álvarez, two members of the Council of the Indies, the Duke of Atrisco and Manuel García Bustamante, returned to their compatriots stating that it was impossible to maintain the friars in Florida on 158 pesos in a province "so poor and full of dangers." Moreover, Jesuits in some areas of the Indies received as much as 500 pesos a year. The Florida Franciscans, stated the two Councilors, deserved equal treatment. The full Council, however, was not like-minded and

88. AGI, Santo Domingo, Legajo 836. Despacho del rey al virrey interino de Nueva España, Jan. 29, 1702.

89. AGI, Santo Domingo, Legajo 833. Consulta del Consejo de las Indias, Jan. 29, 1702.

90. AGI, Santo Domingo, Legajo 864. Carta del comisario general del orden de San Francisco al rey, Sept 4, 1705.

refused to grant the increases requested by the commissary. Its only action was to revive the *cédulas* of 1641 and 1663, and even then the king and Council limited the amount or supplies allocated to each friar to 200 pesos annually.[91] Three years later the king took steps to strengthen civil control over the regular clergy in Florida. In order to receive their yearly allotment of supplies, the friars had to be certified by the governor and his two treasury officials.[92] This, he believed, would insure efficient, economical administration of the clerical subsidy and would give civil authorities at least partial control over the regular clergy.

In 1715 an opportunity arose for the Franciscans to revive their mission program in Florida. In that year chiefs representing an estimated 50,000 Indians (probably an exaggeration) from 161 villages entered Saint Augustine requesting the friendship and protection of the governor. Lower Creeks, Yamasees, and Apalaches, many of whom had opposed Spain during Queen Anne's War, were now seeking a Spanish alliance. In 1715 it appeared as if the Spaniards would be able to re-establish their pre-eminence in the Southeast, especially if the Franciscans increased their numbers and received plentiful supplies of food, clothing, and trinkets to complement their spiritual ministrations.

During Queen Anne's War and after there were feeble attempts to bring new friars to Saint Augustine. In 1709 the king ordered thirteen Franciscans to join their brethren in Saint Augustine, but lack of funds and the risks of a wartime voyage kept the thirteen from fulfilling the royal order. Then in 1718—three years too late—the king requested fifty Franciscan volunteers to work among the Indians who had recently sworn their allegiance to the Florida governor. Again the response was hardly enthusiastic. By the end of 1719 only nine friars had reached Florida. Ten more sailed in 1722 to bring the total to nineteen, but this number was far less than the fifty originally requested by the king.[93] Further evidence that recruitment had failed came from Governor Benavides in 1724 when he reported that only 11 of the 161 villages enjoyed the services of a Franciscan.[94]

91. AGI, Santo Domingo, Legajo 833. Consulta del Consejo de las Indias, Jan. 29, 1706. Real cédula, Madrid, Feb. 20, 1706.

92. AGI, Santo Domingo, Legajo 833. Real cédula, Madrid, Feb. 25, 1709.

93. AGI, Santo Domingo, Legajo 833. Consulta del Consejo de las Indias, June 25, 1720. AGI, Santo Domingo, Legajo 844. Carta del gobernador de la Florida al rey, Sept. 10, 1727.

94. AGI, Santo Domingo, Legajo 866. Carta del gobernador de la Florida al rey, Nov. 4, 1724.

For the most part inadequate financial assistance and lack of military support held back the Franciscans. Although some were willing to go to Florida and serve in the missions, they could not hope to succeed without soldier-protectors and supplies for their Indian congregations. Most of the friars were willing to undergo severe hardships and extreme privation, but not senselessly, and in Florida there was little chance that the civil authorities would aid them. Still another factor preventing a religious revival among the Indians was the bitter struggle that broke out in the 1720's between the Creoles and the Spaniards for control of the Franciscan order. As tensions grew among the Franciscans, chapter and conventual politics became more vital to them than mission work. Morale broke down completely.

[*Early Signs of a Split within the Order*]

During the first two decades of the eighteenth century there were few signs of a split within the order. During Queen Anne's War the destruction of the missions by the Carolinians and the Indians and the martyrdom of Franciscans in Guale and Apalache bound the friars together and kept them from engaging in petty disputes. In addition some friars—mostly Spaniards without strong ties in the colony—left for more profitable fields elsewhere in the Indies, leaving religious work in Florida principally to the Creoles, whose roots were deeper in the province.

Initially there was no opposition in Florida to the Creole orientation within the order. During the early years of the eighteenth century neither the Spanish governor, the Spanish residents, nor the remaining Spanish friars challenged the new Creole focus. In fact, Creole domination of chapter and conventual affairs fitted the Creole emphasis in the military and economic spheres in Florida. In 1719, however, the factional quarrel broke into the open for the first time when the nine friars arriving from Spain found the order completely dominated by Creoles, with Spanish friars being relegated to secondary positions. Creoles, declared three of the nine soon after disembarking in Saint Augustine, held all choice posts in the chapter and in the more opulent Indian communities. Colonial-born, colonial-trained Franciscans, complained the trio, had assumed powers that properly belonged to peninsulars and were abusing their new-found authority to the detriment of the order and the spiritual well-being of the colony.[95]

95. AGI, Santo Domingo, Legajo 842. Carta de tres doctrineros del orden de San Francisco de la Florida al rey, Feb. 25, 1720.

In Spain Philip V and Franciscan officials became immediately aroused. In the seventeenth century the Hapsburgs had worked out compromises in such cases,[96] but the Bourbon monarch was more rigid and determined to assert peninsular superiority. Rather than attend to the complaints of the three friars by the usual methods—remonstrance and admonition—the king immediately arranged to send ten more Spanish friars to Saint Augustine. With the nine who had arrived in 1719, Philip V and the Franciscan Commissary General, José Sanz, created a block of peninsulars, which they undoubtedly hoped would be powerful enough to challenge the Creole majority and break their grip on the chapter.[97]

This strategy was not successful. In the end only two of the nineteen Spaniards stayed to face the hardships of life in Florida. By 1727 seventeen Spanish friars had returned to Cuba, much to the distress of Governor Benavides, who accused the Spaniards of feigning illness in order to get passage back to Cuba. Then once safely in Havana, they had not returned to Florida. Outraged by the conduct of the seventeen friars, the governor lashed out against them. He contrasted their indifference, complacency, and lack of dedication with the devotion, energy, and piety of the Creoles. The Spaniards, stated the governor, whose sympathies might naturally have lain with the peninsulars, were wholly unfit for service in Florida.[98]

In Madrid the new Franciscan Commissary General, Domingo Losada, came to the defense of the Spanish Franciscans. He pointed out to the king that Florida had never lacked dedicated, selfless missionaries. Those who had departed from Havana had served the required ten-year term and were justified in leaving. Moreover, there were enough missionaries in Florida to perform the necessary religious tasks. Four friars labored in Indian towns near Saint Augustine, nine lived in the convent, and two served in Pensacola and Apalache.[99]

96. See the study of the *alternativa* in seventeenth-century Peru by Antonine S. Tibesar, O. F. M., "The *Alternativa*: A Study in Spanish-Creole Relationships in Seventeenth-Century Peru," *The Americas*, XI (Jan., 1955), 229-283. Under this agreement Creoles alternated with Spaniards in the various significant provincial offices in Peru.

97. AGI, Santo Domingo, Legajo 833. Consulta del Consejo de las Indias, June 25, 1720. See also Geiger, *Biographical Dictionary, passim.* In 1722 Father Blas Pulido led a contingent of eighteen Spanish friars to Cuba and Florida. Eight of these stayed in Cuba; ten went on to Florida.

98. AGI, Santo Domingo, Legajo 866. Carta del gobernador de la Florida al rey, Sept. 10, 1727.

99. AGI, Santo Domingo, Legajo 866. Carta del comisario general del orden de San Francisco al rey, April 18, 1730.

This was enough to convince Philip V of the innocence of the Spaniards. Determined to stifle anti-peninsular attitudes in Florida, he declared the nineteen friars "indispensable" for the instruction and conversion of the Indians. Statements concerning their misconduct—whether justified or not—insulted both the Franciscan commissary and his enlistment officer, who were responsible for sending the nineteen to Florida in the first place. The king also admonished Creole Franciscans to welcome all Spanish friars with affection and to attend to their needs.[100] Benavides received royal orders to prevent any further recurrence of this "natural antipathy" between Spaniard and Creole and to see to it that all regular clergymen received instruction in the Indian languages in order to increase their effectiveness once they took their place among the natives.[101] In 1732 the monarch also took steps to send nine additional Spanish friars to Florida.

By 1732 sides were clearly drawn. On the one hand stood the Creoles, supported by the governor, who saw them as a virtuous, consecrated band, meriting the conventual authority they held in the colony. On the other side stood the Spanish friars and the king, who saw the Creoles as a devious band of conspirators, constantly intriguing to maintain their supremacy within the order at the expense of their Spanish brethren and the mission program. In essence, however, the problem had many dimensions. Creoles in Florida and throughout the Spanish Indies were acutely aware of their inferior political and social status. Members of their class could not hold high positions in colonial government and remained politically and socially within the shadow of their Spanish superiors. Careers within the church or the army were open to Creoles, but the stigma of being born in the Indies impeded their quest for prestigious office. Creoles, for example, rarely became viceroys, archbishops, generals, or even governors. In Florida, however, the Creoles had taken control of the Franciscan order by default. During Queen Anne's War the departure of a number of Spanish friars enabled colonial-born Franciscans to take over conventual affairs and control the order. Once they had secured this power, they were determined not to relinquish it. Deliberately exploiting Spanish friars who would not join their faction, the Creoles made life so miserable for the peninsulars that they were virtually forced to leave the colony. Creole conventual

100. AGI, Escribanía de Cámara, Legajo 157C. Real cédula al padre provincial del orden de San Agustín de la Florida, Sevilla, May 14, 1732.
101. AGI, Santo Domingo, Legajo 837. Real cédula, Sevilla, May 14, 1732.

leaders assigned new Spanish arrivals to the most abject Indian villages, failed to train them in the native dialects, and neglected to alert them to the dangers and problems to be encountered in their missions. The governor's statements about the Spaniards' lack of devotion were undoubtedly true; certainly the friars coming from Spain were not the most dedicated representatives of the order. Still, relentless persecution at the hands of the Creoles, intent or retaining power in Florida, was surely the principal reason for their inadequacy.

In 1732 the arrival of nine Spanish friars demonstrated just how far the Creoles were prepared to go to retain control of the order. They assigned the nine new friars to hostile or difficult villages, gave the peninsulars no training in Indian languages, and prepared no briefing for them on the difficulties to be encountered among the natives. Heaping one abuse upon another, the Creoles shifted the Spaniards from one mission post to another every few months. This maneuver gave the Spanish friars no time to learn more than just a few simple phrases of the Indian dialects and subjected them to the rigors and dangers of travel in Florida. Between 1732 and 1735 one of the nine new missionaries served in Pocotalaca, Chiquito, Iororo, Apalache, Costa, Rosas, and Costa a second time. A compatriot served in Pocotalaca, Chiquito, Rosas, Costa, and Pensacola within the same period. The story of the seven others was much the same.[102]

In such circumstances it is not surprising that the Spanish clergy made such a poor showing among the natives. Treatment like this at the hands of Creole conventual leaders compounded their difficulties and made success among the Indians impossible. Yet the nine had more tenacity than their predecessors in the 1720's. They managed to withstand this abuse and remained in Florida, girding for a struggle against their Creole tormentors. In 1735 the crisis came.

[*The Crisis of 1735*]

Reports coming out of Florida in the spring of 1735 warned of the impending break within the order. In March seven Spanish Franciscans reported to Philip V that Creole chapter officials, in collusion with Governor Francisco del Moral Sánchez, had created intolerable conditions for them. They had received no language training and had been given

102. AGI, Santo Domingo, Legajo 864. Carta del contador de la Florida al rey, Feb. 25, 1735. Nine arrived in Saint Augustine out of a group of fourteen leaving Spain for service in Santa Elena. See Geiger, *Biographical Dictionary, passim.*

difficult villages in which to work. In addition, the Creoles had put colonial-born friars alongside the Spaniards in Indian villages. With greater facility in the Indian tongues and armed with a greater number of supplies and gifts to distribute among the natives, the Creoles pointed up the inadequacies of the Spaniards and turned the Indians against them. When the peninsulars went before Governor Moral in an attempt to put an end to this practice, the governor scoffed at their pleas and told them to return to their missions. He also continued to award supplies for the Indians to the Creoles and in this way further weakened the position of the Spaniards among the natives.[103]

Moral's alliance with the Creoles is not surprising. Assuming the governorship in 1734, he seemed at first to be a model administrator. He eagerly put forward schemes to remedy the chronic problems afflicting Florida—poverty and low morale—and helped to strengthen the tottering defenses of the colony. He fortified Forts Pupo and Picolata, established new lookout posts north and south of the Florida capital, and proposed plans for the revival of Apalache. But it was not long before he alienated many Floridians. He tolerated illicit trade with merchants from Charleston and seems to have taken bribes for allowing the commerce. In his administration of the annual subsidy he distributed money and supplies only to his friends and discriminated against those in the colony whom, he believed, constituted a threat to his authority. His rigid censorship of communications leaving Florida and arbitrary imprisonment of a number of influential Floridians also helped turn the colony against him.[104]

By 1735 he needed allies in his struggle to retain the governorship, and the Creole Franciscans made convenient and powerful friends. He could use the friars as his defenders in representations to the court in Spain, while the Creoles could use him in their fight to maintain control over the order. On their side the Creole friars wrote idyllic letters to Philip V praising Moral's administration. In return the governor refused to listen to the complaints of the peninsulars and stoutly defended the Creoles in his dispatches to the king. He also placed supplies for the succor of the Indians at the disposal of the colonial-born clergymen, giving them a great advantage with the natives. All the poor

103. AGI, Santo Domingo, Legajo 864. Carta de los frailes españoles (7) de la Florida al rey, March 6, 1735.
104. See pp. 45-50.

Spanish friars could offer the natives were promises of eternal life, which they had to preach in a language completely alien to the Indians.[105]

The alliance between the Creoles and the governor was more than the Spanish faction could bear. In the fall of 1735 the peninsulars completely broke with their Creole oppressors when they held their own separate chapter election. In a combined meeting on September 17 the Creole majority clearly outmaneuvered the Spaniards. By negating the votes of certain Spanish friars, they insured themselves continued ascendancy in the order by elevating Creoles or Spaniards sympathetic to their cause to conventual offices. To head the order in Florida, they chose Joseph Ramos de Escudero.[106] Bitter and resentful, the Spanish faction met surreptitiously four days later on September 21 at Pocotalaca for its own chapter election. Here they annulled the earlier election and voted for a new conventual leader, Antonio Navarro.[107]

News of this second chapter, held without Moral's knowledge, drove the governor into a fury. When he discovered what had occurred at Pocotalaca, he angrily ordered the seizure of all those who had participated in the meeting there. With a real crisis threatening, Auxiliary Bishop Buenaventura intervened to prevent it. Learning of Moral's plan through an informer, Buenaventura rushed to the governor's residence to intercede on behalf of the Spanish faction. In the discussion that followed, the bishop pointed out that seizure of the Spanish friars would do irreparable harm to the floundering mission program, create a permanent rift in the order, and demoralize both the Indians and the colonists. What else was said is not clear, but the governor finally yielded to the bishop and did not molest the Spanish friars.[108]

After the disputed chapters of September, 1735, tension did not immediately give way to a spirit of compromise. Each faction continued to recognize its own set of officials and refused to move toward a rapproche-

105. AGI, Santo Domingo, Legajo 864. Carta de los frailes españoles (7) de la Florida al rey, March 6, 1735.

106. To insure a Creole majority, the Creoles had nullified the vote of Pedro de Morales, a Spanish friar, who was accused of living in sin with an Indian woman, a charge that was not substantiated. AGI, Santo Domingo, Legajo 867. Carta de los frailes españoles (7) de la Florida al rey, Sept. 30, 1735.

107. AGI, Santo Domingo, Legajo 867. Resumen punctual de todos las cartas que ultimamente se han recibido de la Florida y la Habana para despacjarse en el Consejo el expediente sobre la celebración del Capítulo Provincial del orden de San Francisco que se ejecutó la 17 de Setiembre de 1735 en la Florida. See also carta del gobernador de la Florida al rey, Oct. 8, 1738.

108. AGI, Santo Domingo, Legajo 865. Consulta de la Cámara, Dec. 6, 1731. AGI, Santo Domingo, Legajo 867. Carta del obispo auxiliar de Cuba al rey, Oct. 15, 1735.

ment. Moral and the Creoles remained close allies. He continued to support Creole claims to leadership of the order, while the friars praised the governor for his devotion, impartiality, and Christian zeal.[109] On the other side Auxiliary Bishop Buenaventura, formerly superior of a Franciscan convent near Seville, aligned himself with his Spanish brethren. He refuted Creole contentions concerning Moral's benevolent and enlightened administration and labeled their statements as lies. He also condemned the governor for his partiality, tyranny, and flagrant disobedience of royal law.[110]

The rift in the order seemed to move toward a solution in December, 1735, when representatives from both factions appeared in Havana to present their cases before the bishop of Cuba. Deciding tentatively in favor of the Creoles, he refused to take any action to settle the problem and asked Franciscan officials in New Spain for their determination. In Mexico, therefore, the commissary general for New Spain voided both chapters and appointed a new provincial, Juan Romero, to lead the order in Florida.[111]

Meanwhile news of the split reached Spain. Here Philip V had no question where right and justice lay. He angrily criticized Governor Moral, the bishop of Cuba, and the Franciscan commissary general of New Spain for supporting the Creoles and deriding the Spaniards. He demanded that the Creoles in Florida stop buffeting Spanish missionaries from village to village, that the peninsulars be given instruction in the Indian languages, and that the governor stop showing partiality in distributing money and supplies to the Creole friars.[112] Ultimately, this dispatch, the appointment of Romero, and Moral's dramatic ouster in the spring of 1737 worked together to relieve tension among the friars and mend the rift. By the time Governor Montiano took office, the atmosphere was more favorable to reform and reconciliation.

[*Remedies for the Religious Ills of Florida*]

Suggestions for changes within the Franciscan order and in the conduct of missionary work had already come from former Governor Benavides in Vera Cruz. He proposed that all loyal Spanish Indians be

109. AGI, Escribanía de Cámara, Legajo 157B. Carta de los religiosos (18) de la Florida a la Audiencia de Santo Domingo, Dec. 20, 1736.

110. AGI, Santo Domingo, Legajo 864. Carta de don Miguel de Villanueva al rey, Nov. 9, 1736.

111. Geiger, *Biographical Dictionary*, p. 99.

112. AGI, Santo Domingo, Legajo 866. Real cédula, San Ildefonso, July 20, 1737.

consolidated into one or two towns, where they would be taught Castilian. This measure, he stated, would greatly increase the effectiveness of those friars still laboring in Florida. During his sixteen years in the governorship, Franciscans had always taught Christian doctrine in Indian languages, which they learned from old vocabularies compiled in the seventeenth century. But continuation of this policy, Benavides believed, was not feasible in present circumstances. Only a few Indians still remained under Spanish control, and among these few Apalaches, Timucuas, Yamasees, and Lower Creeks there was no common language. With only a handful of Indians from each tribe being served by the Franciscans, it would be far easier for the Indians to learn Castilian than for the friars to waste their time learning a multitude of Indian dialects. Reduced to one or two villages, the natives could easily be instructed in Spanish. This consolidation, he believed, would also insure more efficiency in the functioning of the mission program. Unable to resist the opportunity to praise his own administration—the penchant of most Spanish administrators—Benavides smugly pointed out that during his tenure as governor the friars had eaten, worked, and slept among the natives. They had not retired to the town each night, the current practice in Saint Augustine.[113]

Montiano also made proposals for reform, but he took issue with Benavides on the language problem. Montiano advocated that interpreters in the convent teach the Indian languages to the missionaries. To aid their learning, the governor asked for the compilation of an up-to-date dictionary of the Indian language to be distributed to those taking instruction. To stimulate those who showed no aptitude for learning the various native dialects, the governor suggested compulsory daily reading periods over and above the time spent by the more able students. Once the friars mastered the Indian tongues, stated Montiano, they could carry out their mission work effectively.[114]

After further investigation Montiano made other recommendations which he considered necessary to improve the state of religious affairs in the colony. In a vigorous, forthright letter of October, 1738, the governor described the "deep abyss of enmity and disunion" into which the Franciscans had fallen. Riddled by factional strife and dissension, the order was at a low ebb. Franciscan leaders in Spain, explained the

113. AGI, Santo Domingo, Legajo 866. Informe del gobernador de Vera Cruz, Antonio de Benavides, April 28, 1738.

114. AGI, Santo Domingo, Legajo 844. Carta del gobernador de la Florida al rey, July 11, 1738.

governor, were partially responsible for this degeneration. They had sent friars from Spain to Florida who lacked "maturity, judgment, and stamina," men who were least likely to make good in his colony. These and the two chapters of the friars had discredited both the Spanish faction and the entire order. The Jesuits, the governor suggested, should replace the brown-robed followers of Saint Francis. Zealous men, the Jesuits would bring the colony out of the religious doldrums and revive the floundering mission program. Montiano also proposed a new religious official for his colony, a commissary of missions, to direct religious work among the Indians and to educate the children of Saint Augustine. It would be advisable, stated Montiano, to choose a Spaniard for the post—mature, virtuous, intelligent, and prudent. Under him twenty-four friars were adequate for the religious needs of the colony. Nine would serve actively as missionaries among the Indians, eight as interpreters and teachers, and seven as conventual residents. Montiano wished to reserve four additional places for sick or disabled friars in order to insure a full complement of clergymen at all times. Repeating his recommendation concerning language training, Montiano advocated instruction in Indian dialects one-half hour each morning and one-half hour each afternoon. Those showing no progress would be kept over-time for additional instruction until they could demonstrate their proficiency. With language training, a new commissary, a new conventual organization, and replacement of the Franciscans by Jesuits, Montiano believed he could strengthen the mission program and remedy the ills which had grown up in the religious life of the colony.[115]

Suggestions for reform also came from Auxiliary Bishop Buenaventura. He agreed to all but one of the governor's proposals and added some of his own. The bishop proposed that the governor distribute the annual quota of money and supplies allocated to the Franciscans from the Florida subsidy. In the past this power had rested with officials of the order, who administered the grant with only token civil control. Since chapter leaders tended to favor the Creoles, supplies and money had gone to Creole friars to the detriment of the Spanish faction. The governor, asserted Buenaventura, would be more dispassionate and distribute the subsidy impartially without prejudice to either faction.[116]

115. AGI, Santo Domingo, Legajo 866. Carta del gobernador de la Florida al rey, Oct. 26, 1738.

116. In 1737 the king had ordered the two treasury officials in Florida to supervise the annual stipends awarded to the regular clergy in Saint Augustine. Buenaventura, however, was unaware of the king's action when he made his suggestion.

Buenaventura also suggested that a high Franciscan dignitary from New Spain visit Florida once every three years. A Franciscan himself, Buenaventura was not inclined to accept Montiano's view concerning the replacement of the Franciscans by Jesuits; he ignored this proposal.[117]

These suggestions were received coldly in Spain. Philip V and the Council of the Indies rejected all recommendations submitted by Montiano and Buenaventura, and Spanish officials continued to hold the view that peninsular friars should dominate in Florida. No amount of evidence, even that put forward by trusted religious or civil officials, could persuade authorities in Madrid that Spanish Franciscans might not be as useful or as dedicated as the Creoles. Philip V, therefore, blamed the chapter split on the Creoles and ordered Montiano to give first preference in mission assignments to Spanish friars.[118] A short time later the Council of the Indies repeated the king's views. Its report asserted that Spanish Franciscans were not to blame for the lack of conversions in Florida and that Creole conventual leaders were the real culprits.[119]

The disputed chapter and the unsavory factional struggle within the order was undoubtedly more the effect than the cause of the decline of the Franciscans. The dispute between Creoles and Spaniards was the culmination of the gradual decline of the order which set in after 1670. After the founding of Charleston the friars had fought in vain against the encroachments of English traders and frontiersmen on their missions in the Southeast. With little help from Spanish civil authorities—either in military support or in supplies—the missionaries could not meet English competition for the loyalties of the natives and had to abandon their mission villages. At the same time, the number of friars serving in Florida began to decrease. In 1650 there were fifty-five, in 1702 forty-three.[120] By 1738 this number had reached twenty-five, and by 1759 only ten regular clergymen remained.[121] Those departing claimed, like one Franciscan, that they did so with deep regret, "sadly and tearfully," but most likely these were "crocodile tears."[122] Life and

117. AGI, Santo Domingo, Legajo 866. Carta del obispo auxiliar de Cuba al rey, Oct. 26, 1738.

118. AGI, Santo Domingo, Legajo 866. Real cédula, San Ildefonso, May 5, 1739.

119. AGI, Santo Domingo, Legajo 866. Consulta del Consejo de las Indias, n.d., 1740.

120. Lanning, *Spanish Missions*, p. 159. AGI, Santo Domingo, Legajo 864. Informe del provincial de Santa Elena, March 13, 1702.

121. AGI, Santo Domingo, Legajo 866. Carta del gobernador de la Florida al rey, Oct. 26, 1738. AGI, Santo Domingo, Legajo 2584. Informe de Joseph Solana, April 22, 1759.

122. AGI, Santo Domingo, Legajo 849. Carta de Fray Pedro Ximénez, ministro provincial de Santa Elena, al rey, Nov. 3, 1749.

work in Florida were unrewarding. For those who remained in the colony, conventual politics came to substitute for missionary endeavors, formerly carried on to such a wide extent throughout the Southeast. That the factional struggle erupted was symptomatic of the decline, not really its cause.

Perhaps the best indication of how the Franciscans suffered during the first half of the eighteenth century was the recommendation for reorganization of the order submitted by the viceroy of New Spain in 1753. In his report he proposed eleven friars to fill the religious needs of the colony—one superior and five friars in the convent, three lay brothers to teach the children of Saint Augustine, and two friars to labor among the Indians. With only the four tiny Indian villages of Tolomato, Palica, Pocotalaca, and Punta still enjoying religious instruction, the viceroy suggested consolidation of these missions into two Franciscan centers at Tolomato and Punta, lying west of Fort San Marcos on the San Sebastián River.[123] Contrasted with the Franciscan report one hundred years earlier claiming twenty-six thousand Indian converts in thirty-nine mission villages, this recommendation indicates all too clearly that the day of the Franciscans in Florida had come and gone.

[*The Factional Struggle, the Governor, and the Colony: An Assessment*]

At first glance the dispute between the Creole and Spanish friars hardly deserves more than passing notice. In an isolated corner of the Empire colonial-born Franciscans—after a bitter fight with the peninsulars—had come to dominate conventual affairs. In the process the order had split and lost much of its influence in Florida. But the Spanish-Creole rift had wider implications. It is significant that the fight within the order did not spread to the rest of the colony to pit Spaniard against Creole. The quarrel was confined almost solely to the friars with only minor repercussions in the social and political life of the colony. Creole residents or soldiers did not join Creole friars in their drive to maintain their ascendancy in the order, nor did Spanish colonists join Spanish Franciscans in their attempt to break the Creole hold on the chapter. Among the residents of Florida, there was ap-

123. Reglamento para la guarnación de la Habana, Castillos y Fuertes de su jurisdicción, Santiago de Cuba, San Augustín [*sic*] de la Florida, y su Anexo San Marcos de Apalache, Año de 1753. Microfilm copy, Manuscript Division, John Carter Brown Library, Brown University, Providence, Rhode Island.

parently no division based on class or birth except within the order. Three Spanish governors—Benavides, Moral, and Montiano—showed no peninsular bias; in fact, they supported the Creole faction, the group they believed best served the interests of the colony.

In the mother country, however, the attitudes of the king and his advisers in the Council of the Indies were rigid and uncompromising. The superiority of the peninsular over the colonial was explicit in all royal edicts, in those of the Council of the Indies, and in the opinion of the Franciscan commissary general. The king and his advisers never strayed once from the principle that Spanish ascendancy must be maintained. For them this was more important than the religious welfare of the colony. The era of compromise, like the *alternativa*, had apparently ended, at least in Florida. Bourbon policy dictated a firmer, more arbitrary course.

Chapter VIII

THE GOVERNOR AND
INDIAN POLICY

Spanish influence over the Indians steadily waned after 1670. Christian Indians and tribes friendly to the Floridians slowly succumbed to the temptations of shrewd English traders, who offered the Indians rum and muskets in return for alliances against the Spaniards. After the settlement of Charleston Yamasees, Lower Creeks, Apalaches, Guales, and other tribes began turning on their Spanish friends, ravaged Franciscan villages, and reduced Spanish control over their territory in the Southeast. For the governor the Indians posed an especially vexing problem, and he found it difficult to formulate a workable, consistent Indian policy.

The governor was responsible for the three Indian provinces of Guale, Timucua, and Apalache. By 1700 the few Indians remaining under Spanish control in Guale lived on the coastal islands just north of the mouth of the Saint John's River. Most Gualean activity centered at the mission of San Felipe on Cumberland Island. Timucua included villages near Saint Augustine and those lying to the west on the Apalache trail. The largest of the three provinces, Apalache, included villages in and around present-day Tallahassee and those lying to the north on the banks of the Chattahoochee and Apalachicola rivers. Other Indian provinces included Ais and Carlos in the southern half of the Florida peninsula, but they received more attention from Cubans than from the governor and his friars in Saint Augustine.

[Governor Zúñiga and Spanish Indian Policy]

In general the Spaniards pursued a benevolent, altruistic Indian policy in Florida. The colony had no *encomiendas*, mines, or textile workshops (*obrajes*) in which natives might be exploited by Spanish taskmasters, and the Florida Indians were saved from the evils usually accompanying such enterprises in other parts of the Spanish Empire.

Occasionally the governor called upon the Indians to labor on the fortifications at Saint Augustine, but usually he used white forced laborers or Negro slaves for such tasks. On the frontier the friars labored to consolidate scattered tribes into villages, to teach the Indians the methods of sedentary agriculture, and to convert them to Christianity. Rather than using force or coercion, the Franciscans bound the Indians to them by exemplary personal conduct, gifts, instruction in farming, and promises of eternal life.

Allegiance to the Franciscans imposed certain obligations upon the Indians. In February, 1701, for example, Governor Zúñiga declared that all converted Indians must live as Christians with crucifixes and images of saints adorning the walls of their rude huts. The governor ordered them to obey the commands of the friars and attend to their needs. No Indian could marry unless he first pledged to support his prospective bride. No Indians could take part in war dances or possess firearms, although they were ordered to hold their canoes and native weapons in readiness for defense of their villages. Indians might seed only that land designated by the friars and could not enter Saint Augustine without first obtaining a license from the senior military officer residing in their village. In return for obedience to these commands, the governor agreed to provide for Indian widows and orphans, to pay for all labor done by the Indians in Saint Augustine, and to give all Indians a full hearing before punishing them for any crime.[1]

Unfortunately official promises were not always kept, nor were individuals—Spaniards or Indians—always careful to observe rules of conduct laid down by their leaders. Incidents arose that caused bitterness and misunderstanding and sometimes led to open revolt. Such was the case with the Iororos, a small tribe living at Mayacá on the Saint John's River near present-day Sanford. Governor Zúñiga's predecessor, Laureano de Torres y Ayala, had set off the revolt in 1699 when he seized an Iororo and brought him to Saint Augustine without giving him a fair hearing. In 1701, after failing to obtain justice, the Iororos fled their village to take refuge in the mountains to the north.[2]

Governor Zúñiga immediately took steps to intercept the Indians. After securing the approval of his junta, he dispatched twenty-six infantrymen and thirty armed Indians under Captain Joaquin de Florencia

1. AGI, Santo Domingo, Legajo 858. Junta general de los tres lugares de esta provincia de Guale, San Juan del Puerto, Feb. 7-14, 1701.
2. AGI, Santo Domingo, Legajo 840. Carta del gobernador de la Florida al rey, March 10, 1701.

to bring the Iororos back to Mayacá. In a few days the armed band overtook the Indians. After a short battle in which three of the Iororos were killed, the infantrymen took the Indians captive and returned them to their village on the banks of the Saint John's.[3] Governor Zúñiga ultimately granted a full pardon to the rebels, but to insure their continued loyalty, he placed Lieutenant Juan Alonso de Esquibel in Mayacá.[4] In a postscript to the affair, charges were brought against several of the armed Indians accompanying Florencia for brutally murdering three of the Iororos. The infantry captain denied that any atrocities had occurred, but the governor secured enough evidence to convict one of Florencia's Indians of manslaughter and condemned him to six years' hard labor in Cuba.[5]

Zúñiga also encountered problems in Apalache. Here trouble came as a surprise, for in February, 1701, an important Apalache chief (Nanhuluchuba) reported that Spaniards in the province treated his people kindly. His tribe was suffering because the Floridians could not provide large supplies of food and other necessities, but was in no way being abused or exploited by the military or religious in Apalache.[6] Within a few months, however, the situation changed. The same chief complained bitterly that the commandant at Fort San Luis, Jacinto Roque Pérez, had abused his Indians and treated them as slaves. Alarmed that the Iororo incident might be repeated in Apalache, Zúñiga rushed his troubleshooter, Juan de Ayala Escobar, to the province to relieve Don Jacinto of his command and to re-establish friendly relations with the natives.[7] Ayala carried out his orders, but Roque Pérez had bred discontent among the Apalaches. Enticed by English gifts of muskets, rum, food, and cloth, some Vitachuco tribes forsook their Spanish ties even before Moore swept through the province in 1704.

In Guale the governor faced still another problem. Here the issue concerned the request of the Guale Indians living on San Juan Island

3. AGI, Santo Domingo, Legajo 840. Carta del gobernador de la Florida al rey, Oct. 30, 1701.

4. AGI, Santo Domingo, Legajo 840. Carta del gobernador de la Florida al rey, Nov. 15, 1701.

5. AGI, Santo Domingo, Legajo 840. Carta del gobernador de la Florida al rey, Nov. 15, 1701.

6. AGI, Santo Domingo, Legajo 840. Carta del cacique principal de las provincias de Apalache, Nanhuluchuba (Don Patricio), al rey, Feb. 28, 1701. He signed the letter in the name of all the *caciques* in his province, called Vitachuco.

7. AGI, Santo Domingo, Legajo 840. Carta del gobernador de la Florida al rey, June 22, 1701.

to move inland to a new village. Unhappily situated on their island setting, the Guales wanted to make a new life for themselves in a town in the interior nearer Saint Augustine. Zúñiga was reluctant to grant this request. San Juan commanded the mouth of the Saint John's River, and removal of the Indians would weaken colonial defenses. Yet he still made an attempt at a compromise. He agreed to allow a majority of the natives to move into the hinterland if a few would remain on the island.[8] The Guales were unreceptive to the plan. They did not wish to divide their village and refused to acquiesce to the governor's proposal. But because of the English invasion, a showdown never occurred. In 1702 the English force swooping down from Carolina drove the Indians off the island and into villages near Saint Augustine.

Incidents like those at Mayacá, Apalache, and Guale were seemingly minor episodes of little consequence in the life of the colony, yet taken all together, they are highly significant. They reveal the type of problem with which the governor had to deal and the extreme sensitivity of the Indians to the treatment they received at the hands of the Spaniards. These incidents also demonstrated that it was difficult for the governor to control the actions of individuals like Roque Pérez or the armed Indians. Acting on personal whim or at their own discretion, they could undo at one stroke the efforts of the governor to build strong ties with the Indians. Moreover, Indian problems put the governor in a continual dilemma. Wishing to pursue a benevolent policy towards the natives, he found that he could not always look to the best interests of the Indians when their welfare conflicted with the total welfare of the colony.

[*Queen Anne's War and the Florida Indians*]

Queen Anne's War seemed to deal the final blow to Spanish influence over the Indians of the Southeast. When Governor James Moore led his force of militia and Indians down the coast in 1702, he devastated all but the two villages of Santa Fé and San Francisco in the provinces of Timucua and Guale. Those few Indians who were not killed or captured or who did not express their allegiance to the Carolinians fell back to Saint Augustine. Here they huddled together in seven new villages established within a cannon shot of the town.[9]

8. AGI, Santo Domingo, Legajo 840. Carta del gobernador de la Florida al rey, June 22, 1701.
9. See pp. 110-113.

In January, 1704, Moore beat an equally destructive path through Apalache. His force of one thousand Carolinians and Indians ran wild through the province, plundering, raping, and murdering at will. According to Spanish reports, English Indians (Yamasees and Chiscas) devised "exquisite methods of torture" for those who challenged them. They tore some Apalaches limb from limb and plunged white-hot knives into the trembling bodies of others. "Like hungry wolves," stated one observer, they impaled and murdered the Spanish Indians until "the grass turned scarlet with the blood of these poor people."[10]

Moore's two attacks seemingly delivered the *coup de grace* to 130 years of Franciscan missionary work in Apalache, Timucua, and Guale. By 1705 the Carolinians had leveled thirty-two Indian towns, leaving only a few Indians in the Saint Augustine area still loyal to the governor.[11] As the war continued, more Indians deserted the Spaniards. In 1710 one Englishman boasted that no Spanish Indian town in Florida contained over ten houses and that only the Indians who had sought refuge in the Florida capital remained under Spanish influence.[12] Governor Córcoles indicated that this was not an idle boast when he reported in 1711 that only 401 Indians still remained under his wing, certainly a sharp contrast to the 26,000 converts reported in the mid-seventeenth century. Córcoles had gathered the faithful 401 into six towns near Fort San Marcos—Nuestra Señora de Rosario (displaced Apalaches), Nombre de Dios, Tolomato, Santa María, San Francisco Potano, and Costa (an infidel town). Here he and his Franciscans protected the Indians from attack and ministered to their physical and spiritual needs.[13]

[*Resurgence of an Indian Program, 1715-1718*]

At no time between 1700 and 1763 was Spanish influence over the Indians at a lower ebb than during Queen Anne's War. Driven from their villages, intimidated, captured, tortured, and murdered, the Indians found the poverty-stricken Spaniards poor allies, and in the end only four hundred natives withstood English pressure and deprivation to

10. AGI, Santo Domingo, Legajo 840. Carta del provincial Fr. Claudio de Florencia del orden de San Francisco al rey, June 9, 1707.

11. AGI, Santo Domingo, Legajo 847. Carta de los oficiales reales de la Florida al rey, April 18, 1708.

12. AGI, Santo Domingo, Legajo 841. Carta del gobernador de la Florida al rey, Jan. 22, 1710.

13. AGI, Santo Domingo, Legajo 843. Carta del gobernador de la Florida al rey, April 9, 1711.

remain with the governor in Saint Augustine. By the end of the war it appeared that the Floridians had lost all hope of re-establishing their pre-eminent place among the Indians of the Southeast.

But in 1715 hope suddenly revived that the Spanish could regain their Indian alliances. On the evening of May 27, 1715, four Yamasee chiefs, representing 161 villages, appeared in Saint Augustine asking aid and protection of Governor Córcoles. Bitter enemies of the Spaniards during the war and perpetrators of many atrocities in Apalache, the Yamasees had recently defected from their English allies because of demands now being made upon them. During the war Carolina traders had furnished the Yamasees with muskets, powder, shot, and rum on easy terms, allowing the Indians to pay for these items gradually in kind—in corn, beans, furs, and other commodities. Then in 1713 when the war ended and the English no longer needed Yamasee military aid, the Carolinians demanded immediate payment for what they had sold to the Yamasees. When the Indians could not pay, these traders seized Yamasee wives and children as slaves and murdered the heir of the principal chief. In desperation the Indians rebelled against their English masters. Some made their way into Florida to seek a reconciliation with the Spanish governor.[14]

Governor Córcoles received the Yamasees warmly. He believed that an alliance with the 161 villages would lay the way open for a revival of the Franciscan mission program and would create a formidable band of Indian allies, who could help defend Florida's northern frontier. In effect, Córcoles hoped to use the Indians as the English had used them so effectively in Queen Anne's War—as military allies.[15] As proof of his good will, the governor gave gifts to the Indians and promised them firearms and foodstuffs from Spain and Mexico. He also sought and obtained an increase in the annual allowance set aside for the Indians in the subsidy, a rise from 2,063 pesos (1,500 ducats) to 6,000 pesos.[16]

English officials in Carolina were greatly alarmed over the Yamasee exodus into Florida. The Yamasee War had turned into a life-and-death struggle for the Carolinians, and that the Indians could now go to the governor in Saint Augustine to obtain war supplies for use

14. AGI, Santo Domingo, Legajo 833. Consulta del Consejo de las Indias, Jan. 8, 1716.

15. AGI, Santo Domingo, Legajo 843. Carta del gobernador de la Florida al rey, July 5, 1716.

16. AGI, Santo Domingo, Legajo 843. Carta del gobernador de la Florida al rey, Jan. 25, 1716.

against settlements in Carolina was a grim prospect. Then, when the Indians began stealing English cattle and trading them for Spanish muskets, powder, and shot, the Carolinians protested violently to the governor in Saint Augustine. The war had ended in 1713, they stated; now the Spaniards seemed eager to renew hostilities.[17] In Saint Augustine interim governor Juan de Ayala Escobar saw a certain irony in the English protest. The war supplies he furnished to the Yamasees had been purchased from Charleston merchants in the first place.[18]

Besides the Yamasee, other tribes sought preferment in Saint Augustine after Queen Anne's War. This was principally the result of a shift in English Indian policy. The Carolinians were masters at the game of power politics on the frontier. During wartime they sought out Indian allies and insured their friendship with lavish gifts of rum, muskets, and foodstuffs. Then, when hostilities ended, the English reduced or eliminated their aid to the Indians, although their traders stood ready with more gifts and more rum and muskets should another conflict threaten with the French or Spanish. For the English it was too costly to maintain the Indians during peacetime. In Florida the Spaniards had always been more idealistic in their dealings with the natives. The Floridians were eager to proselyte and convert the Indians but were not at first eager to use them as military pawns. In fact in the seventeenth century the governor refused to provide the Indians with either rum or muskets, items that the English found such effective inducements. In the eighteenth century the governor of Florida became more practical, but it was always difficult for him to find the money and supplies to meet English and French competition.

In 1715 bands of Lower Creeks joined the Yamasees in seeking aid and protection from the Florida governor. Chiscalachisle, *cacique* of the Uchizes, one of the first to lead a group into Saint Augustine, received a warm welcome from Governor Córcoles. Both Córcoles and Chiscalachisle made professions of friendship and smoked the peace pipe. Córcoles gave the chief many gifts and requested him to spread the word among other tribes concerning the warm reception accorded him in Saint Augustine. The next year Chiscalachisle returned, again seeking

17. AGI, Santo Domingo, Legajo 843. Autos sobre la venida del emperador de Caveta y traducción de una carta que quitarón a los Ingleses que deja vuelta de foxas, Dec. 15, 1717.

18. AGI, Santo Domingo, Legajo 843. Carta del gobernador interino de la Florida al rey, Nov. 22, 1717.

aid, but bringing the optimistic report that other bands of Lower Creeks would soon seek alliances with the Spaniards.[19]

The new governor, Pedro de Olivera y Fullana, was also anxious to secure new Indian allies but was not willing to wait for them to appear in Saint Augustine. When Chiscalachisle departed, the governor ordered Lieutenant Diego Peña and three soldiers to accompany the chief to his territory on the banks of the Chattahoochee. Olivera laid down rigid instructions for Peña and his men. They were to list all chiefs and villages desiring Spanish aid and protection and to urge the *caciques* to select new sites for villages in the Apalache area near old Fort San Luis. All chiefs agreeing to a Spanish alliance would be given muskets and powder but would be required first to make the trek to Saint Augustine with their lesser chiefs (*principales*) to express their loyalty to Philip V and the Spanish governor in a formal ceremony. Peña had orders to keep a diary, obtain cattle and horses for the Florida garrison, report all unusual events, and prevent his men from trading with the Indians.[20]

Armed with these orders, Peña left Saint Augustine in August, 1716. Moving west along the Apalache trail, he visited many Lower Creek villages on the Chattahoochee and Apalachicola rivers. On September 28 he met with a council of the important Lower Creek chiefs. Distributing muskets and powder among them as a token of his friendship, Peña explained the governor's desire for eternal friendship with the Lower Creeks and his willingness to give them aid and succor in return for permanent alliances. Peña also stated that his gifts of muskets and powder and the good treatment already accorded Chiscalachisle were evidence that the Spaniards meant to keep their promises. The speech and the arms proved effective. Chiefs from the villages of Chiscalachisle, Savacola, Apalachicola, Achito, Ocmulgee, Uchi, Tasquique, Casista, Caveta, and Chavagali agreed to become vassals of Philip V and the governor in Florida. Some of the *caciques* also agreed to return to Saint Augustine with Peña.[21]

19. AGI, Santo Domingo, Legajo 843. Autos y demas diligencias sobre la remisión de los Indios a dar la obedencia: año de 1716.

20. Mark F. Boyd, ed., "Diego Peña's Expedition to Apalache and Apalachicolo in 1716," *Florida Historical Quarterly*, XXVIII (July, 1949), 6-7. See also AGI, Santo Domingo, Legajo 843. Autos y demas diligencias sobre la remisión de los Indios a dar la obedencia: año de 1716.

21. AGI, Santo Domingo, Legajo 843. Junta para dar la obedencia a S.M. a Apalachicola, Sept. 28, 1716. Indian tribe names are oftentimes difficult to determine. In the documents the tribes are often referred to by the name of their chiefs, sometimes by the name of their village, and sometimes by the name of the confederation

Although torrential rains and heavy winds slowed their progress, Peña and the Indian chiefs arrived in Saint Augustine on November 9, 1716. Here the new interim governor, Juan de Ayala Escobar, feted the Lower Creeks with a large festival—parades, cannon salutes, toasts, gifts, dancing, and more toasts. Ayala conferred the title of *general-issimo* on the chief of the Apalachicolas and promised to establish an infantry garrison among the Lower Creeks within a few months. Pleased with this treatment, the Indians returned to their own country, 160 leagues to the northwest.[22]

This policy of regaling and feting the Indians appeared eminently successful. Tribes formerly hostile to the Floridians now seemed willing to form alliances and to aid the Spaniards in their attempt to maintain their foothold in the Southeast. Spanish prestige and influence over the natives, which had diminished so sharply during Queen Anne's War, had seemingly been regained. In April, 1717, for example, 157 Lower Creeks, including 25 *caciques*, entered Saint Augustine to pledge their loyalty to Philip V and to receive as many tokens of the governor's good will as they could obtain. Included in the delegation were most of the important Lower Creek leaders—Tsipacaya (Chipicasi or Seepey-coffee), nephew and heir to the grand emperor Brims; the ubiquitous Chiscalichisle, brother of Brims and Uchize chief; Tactipique of the truculent Talapuses; and Adrian, Christianized leader of the Apalach-inos. Again Governor Ayala gave his visitors a reception worthy of their high positions. He plied the twenty-five chiefs with gifts and smoked the peace pipe with them. In an effort to awe the Indians and introduce them to the Christian religion, the governor led the Lower Creeks to the makeshift hermitage church to hear the most impressive Mass the curate could devise. Wine and rum flowed freely during the Indian visit, and in the end the chiefs promised everlasting allegiance to Spain. In return the governor promised the Lower Creeks military aid and pledged to educate the sons and heirs of their chiefs.[23]

These festivals in the Florida capital had become an essential part of the governor's program to strengthen his bonds with the Indians,

---

of which they were a member. Wherever possible I have remained faithful to the documents. The difficulties in nomenclature are outlined in John R. Swanton, *The Indians of the Southeastern United States*, Smithsonian Institution Bureau of American Ethnology. Bulletin 137 (Washington, 1946).

22. Boyd, ed., "Diego Peña's Expedition to Apalache and Apalachicolo in 1716," p. 12.

23. AGI, Santo Domingo, Legajo 843. Carta del gobernador interino de la Florida al rey, April 18, 1717.

who seemed to hold the balance of power in the Southeast. Through liberal gifts, lavish banquets, rum, and promises of military aid, Córcoles, Olivera, and Ayala obtained professions of friendship from a large number of Indian tribes. Included among them were the Talapuses and Uchizes, two tribes noted for their savagery and brutality. The Indians enjoyed themselves in Saint Augustine. They liked the feasting, the drinking, the attention, and the presents which Chiscalichisle had discovered in 1715. Soon many of his fellow chiefs joined him in Saint Augustine, and visits became more frequent. In July, 1717, less than three months after their April sojourn at the presidio, Tsipacaya, Chiscalichisle, and Adrian again re-entered Saint Augustine seeking aid from Governor Ayala. Once again he welcomed the Indians with cannon salutes, drinking, feasting, and dancing, which followed the usual manifestations of good will. Ayala also awarded the three chiefs a few muskets and powder, which sent them away contented.[24]

Ayala, however, was not completely satisfied with the progress of his Indian program. Despite vows of friendship from most of the lesser chiefs of the Lower Creeks, he had not received a pledge of loyalty from the grand emperor, old Brims. Without the support of Brims the professions of friendship made so freely by his lesser chiefs in drinking bouts at Saint Augustine meant little. To woo the emperor, therefore, Ayala sent Diego Peña back to the banks of the Chattahoochee with the Lower Creek delegation that visited Saint Augustine in July, 1717.

Peña was a logical choice. He had traveled widely among the Indians northwest of Apalache and had bargained with them successfully in 1716. Inured to the rigors of life among the natives and acquainted with their attitudes, Peña was the most likely one to persuade Brims to side with the Floridians. Ayala also considered gifts a requisite for success, and he armed Peña with silver, fine hats, muskets, pistols, powder, shot and an elegant gold-braided uniform especially for Brims. Peña had strict instructions to treat the emperor kindly, patiently, and gently and to refrain from any disputes with the Lower Creek tribes. No Spanish soldier accompanying the lieutenant could trade with the Indians for personal gain. Ayala also instructed Peña to press the Indians for removal of their villages to sites closer to the new fort he intended to establish on Apalache Bay.[25]

24. AGI, Santo Domingo, Legajo 848. Carta del gobernador interino de la Florida al rey, Nov. 19, 1717.
25. Mark F. Boyd, trans. and ed., "Documents Describing the Second and Third Expeditions of Lieutenant Diego Peña to Apalache and Apalachicolo in 1717 and 1718," *Florida Historical Quarterly*, XXXI (Oct. 1952), 111-113.

Peña's second sally into Lower Creek country was not as successful as his first. When the Spanish Indian agent reached the Chattahoochee late in August, 1717, Brims was unreceptive. Although he agreed to assemble his chiefs and military leaders at Tasquique to give Peña a hearing, he seemed unenthusiastic about a Spanish alliance. At Tasquique where Peña had the opportunity to present Brims with the gifts from Ayala, the Indian agent made his plea for an alliance. Brims accepted the gifts but was reluctant to agree to a treaty and put off Peña when the Spaniard pressed the emperor for a decision. In the meantime, the lieutenant learned that the Lower Creek country had become the center of a three-cornered struggle among the French, English, and Spanish for the friendship of the Indians. Just before Peña's arrival, three English traders with a Negro lackey had been plying Brims and his chieftains with gifts, hoping to win the Indians over to the English side. The French in Mobile had also become active in Caveta country when they sent 150 men into the Ayabamo territory to secure an alliance with Tactipique's Talapuses. Ultimately, Peña went so far as to ask Brims to oust his French and English competitors, but the emperor refused. At this the Spanish lieutenant retired to his camp site and drank an entire bottle of rum, which, he claimed, gave him at least temporary solace.[26]

Despite this discouraging turn of events, Peña remained among the Lower Creeks and at his next meeting with Brims and his fellow chiefs was more successful. After presenting the Indians with more presents, this time including rum, Peña set off an argument between Brims and his heir Tsipacaya, who disagreed over whether the Lower Creeks (Cavetas) should accept Peña's overtures of friendship. Brims wanted to pursue a policy of "splendid isolation" and saw many advantages in remaining aloof from ties with the European powers competing for Lower Creek allegiance. Tsipacaya, on the other hand, was convinced that a Spanish alliance fitted the best interests of the Lower Creeks. In the end the two Indian leaders could not reconcile their differences. Brims remained noncommital, while his nephew informed Peña that the Tasquiques, Savacolas, Apalachicolas, Uchizes, Bucuquas, and Chiscalachisles were ready to join the Spaniards and move their villages to Apalache.[27]

26. AGI, Santo Domingo, Legajo 848. Carta del gobernador interino de la Florida al rey, Nov. 19, 1717.

27. AGI, Santo Domingo, Legajo 843. Autos sobre el viaje de que hizo el teniente Diego Peña a Apalachicola, Dec. 15, 1717.

Peña was elated over Tsipacaya's declaration, but he believed strongly that the governor must take immediate steps to erect the new fort on Apalache Bay. With a presidio situated nearer the Lower Creek villages, the Spaniards could give the Indians more adequate protection and regulate their activities more closely. Since English traders had already proclaimed that the fort would never be built, erection of a blockhouse would strengthen Spanish prestige. More specifically, the Spanish lieutenant recommended that materials and men to build the fort be sent by sea because of the hardships and dangers of land travel across Florida.[28]

[New Problems, 1718-1726]

The Spaniards in Florida needed a fort in Apalache. Without it the governor could not hope to keep the Lower Creeks faithful allies. In 1717 Ayala had requested funds to rebuild the fort,[29] but the interim governor had lived in Florida long enough to realize that he could not count on quick action on such requests. In February, 1718, therefore, he took matters into his own hands and sent a party of soldiers and laborers under Captain Joseph Primo de Rivera to the northern tip of Apalache Bay to build a blockhouse. Ayala instructed Primo to erect a fort with quarters for one hundred soldiers, a storehouse for supplies, and a powder house. Primo also had orders to treat the Indians benevolently, to supply their needs if he could, and to aid the Franciscans in their missionary endeavors. The Lower Creeks were not to receive muskets, however, until their loyalty was assured. In addition the Spanish cavalry captain was commanded to place a cross and the banner of Philip V high atop the new blockhouse and to construct a launch for communicating with Pensacola. When he completed his assignment, Primo was to send word immediately to Saint Augustine.[30]

Primo's sixty-man expedition reached Apalache on March 15, 1718, and began work immediately. Almost as soon as they broke ground, twenty Indians appeared from Chiscalachisle's tribe, and on March 20, 150 more Lower Creeks joined them seeking food and muskets. With barely enough supplies on hand to sustain his own force, the Spanish commander could do little more than offer the Indians a little food.

28. Boyd, trans. and ed., "Documents Describing the Second and Third Expeditions of Lieutenant Diego Peña," pp. 115-139.

29. AGI, Santo Domingo, Legajo 843. Carta del gobernador interino de la Florida al rey, April 21, 1717.

30. AGI, Santo Domingo, Legajo 843. Orden al capitán de cavallos en la nueva guarnación de Apalache, Feb. 17, 1718.

Remembering Peña's glowing promises in the fall of 1717, the natives left for their villages to the north, disillusioned and disgruntled. They had not obtained the rum, flour, muskets, powder, shot, bright-colored cloth, beads, and hats that had in the past been the tangible tokens of friendship.[31]

In the end events in Apalache took a curious turn. From hours of continuous work and without adequate supplies of food, Primo's men grew weaker and contracted dysentery. In desperation Primo sent the experienced agent Diego Peña, who was working with the Spanish force in Apalache, into the Lower Creek country for fresh supplies.[32] Ironically, it was this same Peña who in the fall of 1717, had promised the Indians a golden age once a presidio was erected in Northwest Florida. Now, a few months later, he found himself imploring the Lower Creeks to help save the destitute Spanish labor force in Apalache. The Indians apparently provided a little meat and corn for Primo's men, but the experience was disillusioning and led the Lower Creeks to look elsewhere for gifts and allies.

No single factor weakened the Spanish position among the Indians more than the shortage of supplies. In 1722, for example, Governor Benavides declared that he had nothing with which to keep the natives contented. The six thousand pesos Philip V awarded in 1716 for maintenance of Indian allies was inadequate. Between 1717 and 1721 costs of supporting the Indians averaged 9,516 pesos annually, over 3,500 pesos more than the king had allocated. To make up the difference, Benavides had diverted money from soldiers' salaries, a policy that had proved exceedingly unpopular among the men in his destitute garrison. Benavides hoped too that settlement of Canary Islanders in Apalache would solve the problem. Not only would the new settlers provide a regular source of food for the Spaniards and the Indians, but profits from food production would also provide additional funds for the natives.[33] The king, however, ordered only a small increase in the annual amount set aside for the Indians.[34]

Without bountiful supplies of arms and food, the governor's Indian policy lost its effectiveness. Discontented and disillusioned with

31. AGI, Santo Domingo, Legajo 843. Carta del Capitán don Joseph Primo de Rivera al gobernador interino de la Florida, April 28, 1718.

32. AGI, Santo Domingo, Legajo 843. Carta del Capitán don Joseph Primo de Rivera al gobernador interino de la Florida, Aug. 3, 1718.

33. AGI, Santo Domingo, Legajo 842. Carta del gobernador de la Florida al rey, March 8, 1722.

34. AGI, Santo Domingo, Legajo 834. Real cédula, El Pardo, Oct. 31, 1722.

the Floridians, the Indians turned more and more to English and French traders, who were more generous and more opulent.[35] The erection of the blockhouse at Apalache had done little good to stimulate a resurgence of Spanish influence over the Lower Creeks. The commandant there had nothing in his larders with which to satisfy the Indians calling at the fort.

Soon after the resettlement of Apalache the Talapuses and Uchizes broke their loose alliance with the Spaniards and threatened war on the Spanish Yamasees newly settled near Fort San Marcos de Apalache. This led some Floridians to advocate a harsher, firmer policy toward the Indians. Diego Peña, for example, believed that the Indians could be persuaded to remain loyal by force as well as by gifts and professions of lasting friendship. He recommended vigorous military action against both the Talapuses and Uchizes as an example to other Lower Creek tribes; but, he pointed out pessimistically, the governor could not move against the two tribes without cavalrymen, arms, powder, and supplies for a sustained campaign.[36] In the end it appeared that the governor would fail no matter what policy he pursued. Money was the key to either a moderate or an aggressive course, and he had little in his coffers in Saint Augustine to insure the success of either policy.

As Spanish influence declined, the Carolinians achieved new successes among the Indians. In 1723 English traders freely distributed muskets and pikes among the Lower Creeks, encouraging them to join the Talapuses and Uchizes in the proposed war on the Spanish Yamasees. Governor Benavides was so disturbed over the menace of these two "independent and uncivilized" tribes that he begged the French in Mobile—unsuccessfully—to sell him six hundred muskets and six thousand musket balls for the defense of the six Yamasee villages.[37]

By the fall of 1725 the Carolinians had provided the Cavetas, Apalachicolas, Casistas, Uchizes, Talapuses, and other Lower Creek tribes with enough supplies to make war on the Yamasee villages near Apalache. Somehow, however, word of the impending attack reached Spanish authorities at Fort San Marcos, who acted quickly to protect their Yamasee allies by organizing special patrols and putting the gar-

35. AGI, Santo Domingo, Legajo 849. Copia de una carta del contador de la Florida (Francisco Menéndez Marqués) al rey, Oct. 31, 1722.

36. AGI, Santo Domingo, Legajo 842. Carta del gobernador de la Florida al virrey de Nueva España, Aug. 18, 1723.

37. AGI, Santo Domingo, Legajo 842. Carta del gobernador de la Florida al rey, Oct. 15, 1723.

rison on the alert. One such patrol under Lieutenant Juan Fernández encountered the Lower Creeks as they moved into Apalache. The Indians greeted Fernández warmly and explained that their only quarrel was with their mortal enemies the Yamasees, not with the Spaniards, whom the Lower Creeks regarded as friends. Unable to dissuade the Indians from making their attack and unwilling to engage them, Fernández rushed back to Apalache to empty the Yamasee villages and to bring the Indians together in Fort San Marcos. The Lower Creeks advanced only to find, to their surprise, the Yamasee villages deserted. Rather than continue to the fort where they would have to face the Spanish cannon the Talapuses, Uchizes, and their allies returned to the villages on the Chattahoochee.[38]

Not long after, in January, 1726, a group of Lower Creeks entered the fort at Apalache seeking an alliance with the commandant in return for rum and muskets. This visit was particularly significant because the delegation was led by Chucatiti, eldest son of Brims, and there was some hope in the garrison that the Indians might be returning to the Spanish fold after the defection of 1723. The commandant was particularly careful to treat the Indians well, to provide them with rum and to smoke the peace pipe with Chucatiti.[39] Apparently the commandant wasted his efforts. Eight months later two Spanish agents in the Lower Creek country reported that these Indians were far from loyal. Tsipacaya still seemed friendly, but old Brims proved hostile and angrily evicted the two agents from his domain.[40] His son had evidently come to Apalache with no other purpose than to use the Spanish desire for Indian friends to obtain muskets and rum.

Although the story is not altogether clear, the decade 1716-1725, a decisive period in the formulation of a new Spanish Indian policy, was also crucial for the Lower Creeks. Initially they had turned to the Spaniards for aid and succor and found the governor in Saint Augustine a generous benefactor. Lower Creek chiefs eagerly took advantage of Spanish generosity and secured rum, muskets, food, and other gifts in return for promises of perpetual allegiance. Chiscalachisle, Tsipacaya, Tactipique, and Adrian all made periodic visits to the Florida capital to

38. AGI, Santo Domingo, Legajo 842. Carta del gobernador de la Florida al rey, Nov. 20, 1725.

39. AGI, Santo Domingo, Legajo 842. Carta del gobernador de la Florida al rey, Feb. 24, 1726.

40. AGI, Santo Domingo, Legajo 837. Apuntamiento para despachos en al Consejo, expediente sobre las hostilidades de los Ingleses y indios infieles de la Florida, Feb. 1, 1727.

enjoy the governor's hospitality but old Brims remained aloof and refused Spanish pleas for an alliance. As a result, a power struggle ensued in which some of the lesser chiefs broke with the emperor and even went so far as to agree to removal of their villages to Apalache. Within a few years, however, these prodigals returned to the emperor's side and came to accept Brims's policy of shifting alliances. After 1723 the Indians courted both the English and the Spanish, but allied with neither, playing one nation off against the other in their requests for gifts and favors. Between 1723 and 1725 the Lower Creeks used the English to obtain supplies for a war on the Yamasees, but when the attack failed, the Indians again turned to the Spaniards for aid. In reality the Indians had no permanent alliances with either Spaniards or Englishmen, only to those who could at the moment best serve Lower Creek interests.

[Indian Problems near Saint Augustine]

Although after Queen Anne's War the governor focused his attention principally on the Lower Creeks, he also attended to the needs of the Indians living in villages near Saint Augustine. Here the Franciscans helped minister to the spiritual needs of the natives and provided them with food and supplies from the governor's warehouses. Inhabited mainly by Yamasees, Timucuans, and displaced Guales and located near Saint Augustine, the most important of these towns were Costa, Nombre de Dios (Chiquito), Nombre de Dios (Marcaris), Casipuyas, Palica, Timucua, Pocotalaca, Iororo, Tama, and Tolomato.[41] Indians in these villages played little part in the power struggle going on in the Southeast. The Spaniards supported them and tended to their needs. Occasionally these Indians joined the Floridians in their sallies into Carolina or acted as scouts for Spanish patrols, but otherwise they remained outside the mainstream of Spanish Indian affairs. During the war there were little more than four hundred natives in the Saint Augustine area, although after the war the influx of Yamasees increased this number to a thousand.[42]

In 1728 the Carolinians under Colonel John Palmer wrought havoc among these Indians. A member of the South Carolina Commons House

41. CO 5:12, ff. 35-55. Journal of Captain Tobias Fitch, May 21, 1726. See also Crane, *The Southern Frontier*, pp. 267-268.

42. AGI, Santo Domingo, Legajo 844. Testimonio de las diligencias hechas en la visita que hizo su señoria en virtud de orden de Su Magestad a los pueblos de los indios que se hallan en la ynmediación de este presidio, Dec. 11, 1726.

of Assembly and a veteran Indian fighter, Palmer swept down from Carolina to get revenge on the Yamasees for their rebellion in 1715 and their more recent scalping of English traders near Fort King George. Palmer successfully avenged the Yamasee atrocities in Georgia. Leading one hundred whites and one hundred Indians into the Saint Augustine area in March, 1728, he killed thirty Yamasees, took fifteen prisoners, and sacked and burned the important Yamasee town of Nombre de Dios (Macaris). Significantly, not a single Spanish soldier ventured out of Fort San Marcos during the three-day attack. Governor Benavides willingly offered the Indians a refuge in the fort but refused to go out to challenge Palmer's force.[43]

Failure to engage Palmer's Carolinians cost the governor much prestige among the Indians living near the Florida capital. They looked upon Benavides as a coward and believed he should have acted more decisively against the English invasion force. Even in the very shadow of Fort San Marcos, the symbol of Spanish might in the Southeast, the governor had proved reluctant to challenge enemy marauders. Thirty Yamasees had died in Palmer's raid, and others were captured and sold into slavery. For those who remained, the food, supplies, and spiritual ministrations of the Franciscans were poor substitutes for decisive military action that might have saved their families.[44] Although many Yamasees and Timucuans remained under Spanish tutelage, others left their villages to seek alliances with the English or to pursue an independent course like that of the Lower Creeks.

[Collapse of the Spanish Indian Alliances, 1730-1739]

The slow collapse of the Spanish Indian program was the result of three factors. First, the governor could not sustain the gift-giving policy inaugurated soon after Queen Anne's War. Initially Córcoles, Olivera, Ayala, and Benavides showered presents on the Yamasees and Lower Creeks flooding into Saint Augustine, but in a few years this expensive activity began to fall off because of the lack of support from Spain and New Spain. A second reason for the failure of the Indian program was the lack of soldiers and missionaries to send among the savages to civilize and control them. To cement his alliances, the governor was almost

43. AGI, Santo Domingo, Legajo 842. Carta del gobernador de la Florida al rey, Oct. 15, 1728.

44. AGI, Santo Domingo, Legajo 2584. Carta del cacique de Nombre de Dios Chiquito (Francisco Iospogue) al rey, Oct. 18, 1728. This chief points out that English infidel Indians had seized his wife and four children and sold them into slavery.

completely dependent upon pledges made by the Indians in peace-pipe ceremonies. He had no permanent religious or military agents working among the Indians to see to it that they remained faithful to their promises. Still a third factor leading to decline in the Spanish Indian program was the increased activity of English and French traders among the natives. The English had reduced their Indian trade after the war ended in 1713, but as the Spaniards stepped up their activities among the Lower Creeks, the Carolinians and the French both began competing once again for the allegiance of the Indians.

By the time Moral assumed the governorship in 1734, Spanish influence over the Indians had again declined. Captain Álvaro López de Toledo reported from Apalache in June, 1734, that he had only a little corn and flour left in his storehouse to award to the Lower Creeks, who constantly clamored for supplies. A month earlier a delegation of Cavetas, Apalachicolas, Achitos, and Casistas had left their villages on the Chattahoochee to get Lopez' aid against the incursions of the Pequots. Unfortunately, Lopez reported, he had nothing to offer the Indians and had to send them away without war supplies for use against their Pequot enemies.[45] At the same time, English agents were providing the Indians with the goods they had sought in Apalache and stirred them up against the Spaniards. In 1735 a band of Talapuses and Uchizes attacked Picolata, the Spanish fort erected on the banks of the Saint John's, eight leagues west of Saint Augustine. Killing one Spanish soldier, the Indians drove the Yamasees and Timucuans living in villages near Picolata into Saint Augustine and devastated Picolata.[46]

There was good reason for the truculence of the Talapuses and Uchizes. With the English settlement of Georgia in 1733, James Oglethorpe began a program designed to pamper the Indians and to win them over to his side. Oglethorpe's agents showered the Lower Creeks and other tribes in the Southeast with gifts and favors and even went so far as to take the Uchize chief Chamachichi to London. Here English royalty feted the awed Indian and awarded him a commandant's title in an elaborate ceremony.[47]

In Florida Moral was fully aware of the implications of this activity

45. AGI, Santo Domingo, Legajo 2584. Carta del commandante de Apalache (Don Álvaro López de Toledo) al gobernador de la Florida, June 29, 1734.
46. AGI, Santo Domingo, Legajo 2591. Real cédula, San Ildefonso, Oct. 19, 1735.
47. AGI, Santo Domingo, Legajo 844. Declaración jurada hecha por Don Pedro Neri, natural de la república de Luca, Cristiano, aplicado Romano, vecino de la Nueva Carolina alias San Jorge, Aug. 4, 1735.

for his colony. In September, 1735, he reported that Oglethorpe had secured alliances with many Lower Creek tribes previously allied to the Spaniards and was agitating these Indians against the Spanish Indians in Florida. All he could offer the natives to counter the Georgians, stated the governor, were empty promises.[48] Rumors were also rampant that the English and their Indian allies were planning an invasion of Apalache and from here proposed to launch an attack on Saint Augustine. The only tribe the English had not won over in northwest Florida, claimed Moral, was the Tuscaroras; and to bring this tribe into line, the governor of South Carolina had offered fifty pesos for each Tuscarora scalp brought into Charleston.[49]

Unable to compete with the English for Indian alliances, Moral finally resorted to diplomacy to protect the interests of his colony. In negotiations carried on in the summer of 1736, Moral attempted to get Oglethorpe's agreement to end the Indian raids that had harassed both colonies. Despite the fact that he had alliances with the larger tribes, Oglethorpe was conciliatory.[50] He too hoped to put a stop to the incursions of hostile Indians on his border settlements and suggested that all Indians who crossed the Georgia-Florida frontier first obtain licenses from their respective governors. This, he hoped, would stop the invasions by "Outlaws and Banditts, who are the shame of Human kind, who from thence might molest the Provinces of both the Kings and with Impunity destroy the innocent Peasants and Planters."[51] In the treaty signed in October, 1736, therefore, the two governors agreed to restrain Indians under their control from making border raids and to license all those who wished to cross the Georgia-Florida frontier.[52]

Unfortunately for Moral he did not make a similar treaty with the South Carolinians, who were more active than the Georgians in inciting the Indians against the Spaniards. In his first years in Georgia Oglethorpe aimed at neutralizing the Indians, not at stirring them up against the Floridians. Indian raids inevitably caused Spanish reprisals that

---

48. AGI, Santo Domingo, Legajo 2591. Carta del gobernador de la Florida a don José Patiño, Sept. 8, 1735.

49. AGI, Santo Domingo, Legajo 2591. Carta del gobernador de la Florida a don José Patiño, Oct. 20, 1735.

50. AGI, Santo Domingo, Legajo 2591. Carta del gobernador de la Florida a don José Patiño, Sept. 8, 1735.

51. CO 5:654, pt. 1. Copy of a letter, James Oglethorpe to Captain James Dempsey, Frederica, April 10, 1736.

52. CO 5:654, pt. 1. Articles of a treaty made between James Oglethrope of Georgia and Governor Francisco del Moral Sánchez, St. Augustine, Oct. 18, 1736. See also pp. 135-137.

harassed his frontier settlements, and the Georgian was anxious to prevent these raids. The Carolinians, however, pursued a more aggressive course and continued to sponsor raids on Florida.[53] Moral in turn blamed Oglethorpe. In the fall of 1736 he protested that three hundred Englishmen had entered northern Apalache to raise "the standard of war" and to incite the Lower Creeks against his colony.[54] In Georgia Oglethorpe was disturbed because neither he nor his agents were responsible for the invasion. In fact, Oglethorpe opposed it. Such activity, he stated to the Duke of Newcastle, Secretary of State of the Southern Department, would surely result in bloody reprisals by the Spaniards, not on the Carolinians who sponsored the raids but on his own struggling Georgians.[55]

In London English officials seemed sincerely desirous of resolving the Indian question. Acting on Oglethorpe's report, the Duke of Newcastle ordered the governor of South Carolina to stop agitating the Lower Creeks against the Floridians. Negotiations had already begun in Europe to settle the Indian problem, and further raids would only impair these discussions.[56] But the dispatch had little effect. Before it reached Charleston, two Carolinians—John Wright and James Childs (Childemas)—had persuaded the Uchizes and Talapuses to make another incursion into Florida, destroying all hope of an amicable settlement.[57]

The Spaniards made feeble attempts to counter English activities among the Indians. In 1737, acting under royal orders, the governor of Cuba sent Captain Alonso de Toro and a "perspicacious" Indian guide named Juan Ignacio into the Lower Creek country to seek new alliances and to promote trade. Toro made both promises and threats. In a conference with a group of Lower Creek chiefs, Toro pledged powder, shot, cloth, rum, and other articles in return for Indian pledges of everlasting obedience to Philip V and Governor Montiano. At the same time Toro threatened to punish as a traitor any Indian who broke

53. AGI, Santo Domingo, Legajo 864. Carta del obispo auxiliar de Cuba al rey, Aug. 31, 1736.

54. CO 5:654, pt. 1. Copy of the Memorial of the Trustees for establishing the Colony of Georgia in America, relating to Monsieur Geraldino's Letter of Complaint against the Inhabitants of Georgia, London, Oct. 20, 1736.

55. CO 5:654, pt. 1. Letter from James Oglethorpe to the Duke of Newcastle, Frederica, April, 1737.

56. CO 5:388, pt. 1. Letter from the Duke of Newcastle to the Lieutenant Governor of South Carolina, William Broughton, London, April 6, 1737.

57. CO 5:654, pt. 1. Letter from James Oglethorpe to the Duke of Newcastle, Frederica, May 11, 1737.

such a pledge by negotiating or trading with the English.[58] Toro had little success. The Indians refused to accept a Spanish alliance and openly declared their doubt that the Spaniards could furnish them the commodities promised by their Indian agents.[59] Besides, the Indians found it more to their interests to court both the Spanish and the English and to receive benefits from both sides. Permanent alliances simply were not to their best interests.

The English worked diligently to keep the friendship of the Indians. They supplied them with muskets, rum, and other articles, feted their chiefs; and used personal diplomacy to good advantage. In the spring of 1739, for example, James Oglethorpe undertook a grueling five-hundred-mile journey into northern Georgia and Alabama to visit Lower Creek tribes. One of his principal allies, Chigilly, son of Brims, had become deeply concerned over the activities of Spanish agents and believed that a personal visit from Oglethorpe would counteract lavish promises of aid being held out by Spanish traders. The Georgian's trek into the hinterland was as fruitful as it was fatiguing and dangerous. Meeting with a grand council of seven thousand Lower Creeks, Coosee, Talapusa, Choctaw, and Chickasaw warriors, Oglethorpe obtained firm professions of loyalty from the assembled chiefs. For the Georgia governor it proved a great personal victory and solidified his alliances in preparation for the impending war with the Floridians.[60]

Governor Montiano could not cope with the English Indian policy. By January, 1739, only nine Indian villages acknowledged allegiance to the Spaniards, and Montiano claimed he could rely on only 354 Indian allies, including women and children. Located near Saint Augustine, their villages were Nombre de Dios (Macaris,) San Antonio de la Costa, Nuestra Señora de Guadalupe de Tolomato, Nuestra Señora de la Asunción de Palica, Nuestra Señora del Concepción de Pocotalaca, Nuestra Señora del Rosario de la Punta, Santo Domingo de Chiquito, and San Nicolás de Casapules. Tamasle was the lone Spanish village in Apalache.[61] This meant that more than six hundred Indians had

58. AGI, Santo Domingo, Legajo 2592. Carta del gobernador de Cuba al Marqués de Torrenueva, April 14, 1738.
59. CO 5:654, pt. 1. Letter from James Oglethorpe to the Duke of Newcastle, Frederica, Nov. 20, 1738. Not long after Toro left the banks of the Chattahoochee, four Caveta chiefs entered Frederica, asking for supplies and offering an alliance in return.
60. CO 5:654, pt. 1. Letter from James Oglethorpe to the Trustees for Georgia, Frederica, June 15, 1739.
61. AGI, Santo Domingo, Legajo 867. Estado que manifestó el número de pueblos de Indios que hay en las provincias de San Agustín de la Florida: cathequizados, y a la

deserted the Spaniards since 1726, tempted by the rum, fancy hats, muskets, bolts of bright-colored cloth, and gold-braided uniforms offered them by the English.

[The War of Jenkins's Ear and Spanish Indian Policy, 1739-1745]

Indian activity in Florida during the War of Jenkins's Ear demonstrated the utter failure of the Spaniards to win the allegiance of the Indians, who fought on the English side. Even before hostilities began officially, the natives had cut a destructive path through Florida. In the fall of 1738 Oglethorpe used the Uchizes to block the trail from Saint Augustine to Apalache.[62] Although this failed, Oglethorpe encouraged another attack early in 1739 when he ordered one thousand Creeks and Chickasaws into Florida to overrun the unprotected Spanish settlements.[63] When war finally came, the Indians made useful allies, first in the English attack on Pupo and Picolata in January, 1740, and later in the siege of Saint Augustine. At Pupo and Picolata the Indians drove the Spanish garrisons out and forced them into the safety of Fort San Marcos. In the summer the Indians served as scouts and raiders when Oglethorpe attempted to starve Saint Augustine into submission. Throughout the war Indian raids helped keep Montiano off balance militarily. At Bloody Marsh they also fought well in defense of Frederica.

But for all of his success in securing Indian allies, Oglethorpe was not enthusiastic about his Indian friends. He admitted that the only way he could keep the Indians loyal was by continuous offerings of presents. Without these gifts the natives would not fight.[64] This had proved very costly, almost too costly, for the Indians never won any notable victories.[65] On the Georgia-Florida chessboard the Indians served Oglethorpe as convenient pawns, but they were never successful in checkmating the Floridians, hanging on grimly in Saint Augustine

obedencia del Rey Nuestro Señor, con los nombres, y número de personas que componen: este año del 1738, Dec. 31, 1738.

62. AGI, Santo Domingo, Legajo 2541. Carta del gobernador de la Florida al rey, March 10, 1740.

63. CO 5:654, pt. 2. Letter from James Oglethorpe to the Duke of Newcastle, Frederica, Jan. 22, 1739/40.

64. CO 5:654, pt. 2. Letter from James Oglethorpe to the Duke of Newcastle, Frederica, Nov. 12, 1741.

65. CO 5:655, pt. 1. Declaration of the General Heads of the Extraordinaries of the War, Jan. 22, 1742/43.

and Apalache. Indians made useful raiders and scouts, but they were not decisive in turning the balance of power overwhelmingly in favor of the English. Their effectiveness was limited, and for Oglethorpe the Indian alliances hardly seemed worth the money and effort he had expended to secure them. As events proved, the Indians were not the key to victory in the War of Jenkins's Ear.

[New Attempts to Woo the Indians: A Trading Post in Apalache]

Authorities in Spain were more convinced than Oglethorpe of the value of Indian alliances. They believed that failure to win over the natives had hurt the Spanish war effort and had inhibited Montiano's quest for a victory over the Georgians. Since the brief flurry of Spanish activity among the Indians after Queen Anne's War, the king and the Council had witnessed a steady decline in Spanish influence over the Indians of the Southeast. In 1726 close to a thousand Indians enjoyed Spanish aid and protection; in 1739, thirteen years later, fewer than four hundred lived in the ten villages near Saint Augustine and Apalache. By 1743 there was an even further decline as more Indians drifted away during the War of Jenkins's Ear. In Saint Augustine the number of villages was reduced from nine to four—Tolomato, Palica, Pocotalaca, and Punta. In Pensacola the Spanish garrison and a few Indians huddled apprehensively together in the tiny blockhouse. In Apalache, where the Indian menace was greatest, fourteen Lower Creek tribes almost succeeded in destroying Fort San Marcos and forced the Tamasles to take refuge in the fort.[66]

But even the English, who seemed so successful among the Indians, were unable to keep them steadfastly loyal or to use them effectively as military allies. The Lower Creeks, in particular, proved practical opportunists, who saw advantages in expressing allegiance to any side offering them aid and favors. During the War of Jenkins's Ear, at a crucial period in the war, several bands of Oglethorpe's Lower Creeks made their way to Saint Augustine under a flag of truce, requesting muskets, powder, shot, and rum in return for an alliance. Montiano, however, was both suspicious and destitute. He neither trusted the Indians nor had the supplies to fulfil their requests. Sending them away

66. AGI, Santo Domingo, Legajo 848. Carta del gobernador de la Florida al rey, March 15, 1743.

empty-handed, Montiano saw the Indians as undependable allies whose allegiance could be bought only on a temporary basis.[67]

Montiano's proposal for regaining friends among the Indians was to trade with them on liberal terms. He was partially convinced, at least, that a large trading post (*tienda*) in Apalache would do much to foster good relations with the natives, particularly the Lower Creeks. Well-stocked with muskets, pistols, powder, balls, shot, vermilion, cloth, buttons, rum, honey, sugar, tobacco, pipes, salt, paper, and other articles, the enterprise could become self-supporting by trading for Indian furs. Establishment of such a store would allow closer associations between the Spaniards and the Indians and make it easier to win them away from the Georgians and Carolinians. It would also place their relationships on a more dignified basis than that of beggar and benefactor.[68]

In the winter of 1744 Philip V acted on Montiano's recommendation and ordered the establishment of a trading post in Apalache. In his *cédula* the king gave a clear indication of his motives when he pointed out that the English had won over the Uchizes with gifts and liberal trade terms. In return, the Uchizes had raged through Florida, committing many atrocities and harassing the colonists. As a counter move the monarch ordered the Havana Company, now burdened with the responsibility of supplying Florida, to set up a new store in Apalache with a generous stock of muskets, carbines, pistols, powder, musket balls, jewelry, cloth, buttons, vermilion, bright-colored shirts, sugar, honey, rum, tobacco, pipes, and beer.[69]

The Havana Company vigorously opposed the king's plan as a useless expense. In September, 1744, its directors claimed that it would be difficult both to keep the trading post adequately supplied and to compete with the cheaper goods that the English offered the Indians. Only with a subsidy could the store succeed, but even then the Spaniards needed a larger garrison in Apalache to keep the Indians in line. The directors of the company also suggested that the initial stock of supplies for the *tienda* be sent from the mother country rather than from Cuba.[70]

67. AGI, Santo Domingo, Legajo 848. Carta del gobernador de la Florida al rey, March 15, 1743.

68. AGI, Santo Domingo, Legajo 848. Carta del gobernador de la Florida al rey, March 15, 1743.

69. AGI, Papeles Procedentes de Cuba, Legajo 2263. Real cédula, El Pardo, Feb. 11, 1744.

70. AGI, Santo Domingo, Legajo 863. Copia que la Real Compañía de la Isla de Cuba remitió al Gobernador de la Florida de la respuesta que hizo al rey con fecha de 25

In Spain the king accepted some of the company's counter proposals. On May 13, 1745, he ordered Montiano to send a military contingent to supplement the garrison in Apalache. At the same time the monarch ordered the governor at Saint Augustine to bear the costs of establishing the new store and to provide the initial stock of goods laid down by his *cédula* of 1744. He insisted also that prices of goods sold in the trading post meet the competition of English goods.[71]

Montiano was discouraged over the king's order and countered it with a dismal picture of earlier attempts to set up a trading post in Apalache. He pointed out that a store of sorts had existed in the province since 1738, sponsored by the governor of Cuba and operated by a certain Matias de Saldivia. From the time of its establishment the store had had a precarious existence and never carried more than a few items for trade with the Indians. At one time in 1738 Saldivia had only a few French muskets to offer in exchange for Indian furs. As time went on, the store became little more than a tavern where the Indians engaged in drunken brawls. As an effective means of winning friends among the Indians, it had no advantages. When war broke out in 1739, the Uchizes, regular tipplers at Saldivia's tavern but now "excessively regaled by the English," began making raids on Spanish settlements in Apalache. Still they were audacious enough to appear periodically in Apalache under a flag of truce, expressing their eternal friendship for the Spaniards and their need for more rum and supplies. The commandant at Apalache always rejected their requests, forcing the Uchizes to return to the interior to begin war anew on the Spaniards. In 1745, however, the Uchizes made a seemingly sincere request that the trading post be re-established in Apalache. Whether they longed for Saldivia's heady liquor or whether the English were becoming less liberal with their presents is not clear, but the Indians were pressing the governor for a new store and promised him their allegiance if it were re-established. Soldiers in Apalache, probably eager for the benefits that a trading post might bring, pointed out that English gifts were the only reason the Uchizes were not on the Spanish side. Late in 1745, therefore, Montiano yielded to this plea and to the king's order by

de Setiembre de 1744 sobre el contexto de la Real Cédula de 11 de Febrero del mismo año. See also AGI, Santo Domingo, Legajo 863. Carta del presidente y los directores de la compañía de Habana al rey, Sept. 25, 1744.

71. AGI, Santo Domingo, Legajo 863. Carta del gobernador de la Florida al rey, March 6, 1746.

setting up a trading post in Apalache with a few meager items he could spare from his warehouses in Saint Augustine.[72]

This new store was a miserable failure. With little to offer the Indians in return for their furs or their friendship, the *tienda* was ineffective in inducing better relations with the natives. In fact, the garrison in Apalache had so little it could hardly survive. In February, 1746, the Spanish commandant, Juan Isidro de León, reported that he did not have enough food to last through the month of March and that he desperately needed rice, flour, vegetables, and fresh meat to keep his garrison from perishing. The Uchizes had visited him at Fort San Marcos just before Christmas of the previous year and stripped the trading post and his warehouse of all but a little food and rum. The rum and few staples remaining had enabled his garrison to celebrate the holidays festively, but the *aguardiente* was an inadequate substitute for essential foodstuffs.[73] Relief finally came, but his desperate pleas indicated how poorly the *tienda* served to establish better relations with the Indians.

[*The Lower Creeks Return to Spanish Allegiance*]

The Uchize request for Spanish aid in 1745 was a sign of the gradual drift of a large number of tribes back to Spanish alliances. As hostilities diminished during the War of Jenkins's Ear, the English in Georgia and South Carolina began cutting the flow of rum, muskets, powder, shot and other supplies to the Indians. In response, tribes like the Uchizes began casting about for a new benefactor. Their request for a new trading post and their visit to Apalache in 1745 was evidence that the English were no longer so generous and that they were willing to let the Indians seek out new friends. In May, 1747, an even larger band of Indians appeared ready to return to the Spanish fold. On May 19 the Uchize chief Topasico entered Apalache to confer with Isidro de León concerning a new alliance. Topasico claimed to represent the chiefs of Quilate, Chocato, Cushivay, and Chumayche, all Uchizes and Lower Creeks who wanted permission to visit Montiano in Saint Augustine to discuss terms for a new treaty. In reply the commandant was evasive. He stated flatly that the Uchizes had a reputation for both treachery and cruelty, yet if Topasico could prove his desire to keep his word, Montiano would undoubtedly treat with him.

72. AGI, Santo Domingo, Legajo 863. Carta del gobernador de la Florida al rey, March 6, 1746.

73. AGI, Santo Domingo, Legajo 845. Carta del gobernador de la Florida al rey, March 14, 1746.

Although Topasico seemed sincere, the commandant sensed that the Indian had deeper motives for his request. When he investigated further, he found the same Indian had already visited Pensacola, trying to obtain supplies and making similar pleas for an alliance. Apparently he needed help in a civil war which had broken out among the Lower Creek tribes. The Chocatos (Choctaws) had declared war on the Chalaques, while his Uchizes had attacked their old allies the Talapuses. For Topasico and the chiefs he represented, requests for Spanish aid aimed only at securing arms for the intertribal war. In both Spanish outposts the commandants threw open their storehouses but in the end had little to offer the Indians except food. In Pensacola the Uchizes consumed or carried off over half of the garrison's supplies. In Apalache they received such large handouts that the commandant reduced his own supplies to just a few barrels of sugar and molasses. This, he asserted, greatly angered his soldiers, who resented gifts to the Indians at their expense. They were particularly disturbed over being deprived of their tobacco, one of the few pleasures they could enjoy in their barren frontier outpost.[74]

Despite the seeming treachery of the Indians, Montiano was anxious to regain their friendship and proposed several plans. In August, 1747, he requested an additional allocation of 12,000 pesos for use among the Lower Creeks. With this sum he planned to pacify the Indians with gifts and bring peace to the Apalache area. Once this had been accomplished, he hoped to settle Canary Islanders in the rich land in Apalache, where they could farm without fear of Indian assaults.[75] He also proposed that the English, French, and Spanish agree on a common Indian policy in the Southeast. Montiano suggested that the three nations pledge not to furnish muskets or powder to the Indians under any circumstances, not even for hunting, which would prevent devastating Indian raids on border settlements. Trading food, clothes, jewelry, and other items would, of course, be permissible. Montiano admitted that chances of obtaining such an agreement were slim, but he hoped that steps might be taken sometime in the future to take up his recommendations.[76]

74. AGI, Santo Domingo, Legajo 2584. Copia de una carta de don Juan Isidro de León, Capitán de una de las ocho compañias del refuerzo de este presidio y commandante de San Marcos de Apalache al gobernador de la Florida, June 26, 1747.
75. AGI, Santo Domingo, Legajo 2584. Informe de don Manuel de Montiano, Aug. 3, 1747.
76. AGI, Santo Domingo, Legajo 866. Carta del gobernador de la Florida al rey, July 20, 1747.

Reports coming out of Florida indicated that the Indians were becoming less of a problem for the governor. During the fall and winter of 1747-1748 the Uchizes, the best gauge of Indian sentiment, did not lift a bow or a musket against the Spaniards and were making peace overtures. In January and February bands of Uchizes under Chiquile, with Topasico one of the two principal chiefs of the tribe, entered Apalache carrying a white heron's wing, the symbol of peace. Chiquile wanted the commandant to forget past differences and to accept the Uchizes as loyal allies. Isidro de León agreed to a Spanish treaty with the Indian chief and promised him Montiano's aid and protection but warned the Indians that if they committed any atrocities before the treaty was drawn up, the governor would punish them severely.[77]

Early in 1748 the Uchizes made their way to Saint Augustine to negotiate the alliance with Montiano. During their visit a sixteen-year-old Uchize boy fell ill and ultimately requested baptism. To oblige his visitors, the governor quickly arranged a baptismal ceremony and honored the young Indian by serving as his godfather. Unfortunately, the boy died after his baptism, which many of the Indians believed caused his death. The misfortune might have erupted into a major incident, but Montiano acted to take advantage of what had occurred by arranging an impressive funeral service for the young Indian. He assembled all the Indians of the Saint Augustine area into a funeral cortege and walked beside the coffin during the funeral procession in a great personal show of grief. Then, not long after the funeral, to dispel the Indians' fear of baptism, the curate baptized the daughter of one of the Uchize chiefs with Montiano again serving as godfather. During the rites the curate admonished the girl's father about the evils which would befall his daughter if she, as a Christian, returned to a pagan life among the infidels in her own village. In his most persuasive tones the curate preached the advantages of removing Uchize villages from the banks of the Chattahoochee to the banks of the Saint John's west of Saint Augustine, where the Indians could "live and die like Christians." In another attempt to woo the Uchizes, Montiano granted Chiquile a captaincy in the Spanish army.[78]

This new alliance with the Uchizes and other Lower Creek tribes benefited the Florida colony. It enabled the Spaniards to trade rum,

77. AGI, Santo Domingo, Legajo 845. Carta del gobernador de la Florida al rey, March 15, 1748.

78. AGI, Santo Domingo, Legajo 845. Carta del gobernador de la Florida al rey, March 15, 1748.

food, and trinkets to the Indians for furs, cattle, and medicinal roots. The alliance made it safer for Spanish residents of Saint Augustine and Apalache to venture out of the protection of their forts and towns to cut wood, hunt, fish, and farm without fear of scalping. Pacification of the Indians may also have been responsible for the rise in the naval stores industry. Still, the Floridians encountered the usual difficulties in supplying the needs of the Indians, especially during 1748 and 1749 when drought ruined Lower Creek corn crops. Then, when war broke out between the Uchizes and the English Calaques in 1749, the governor had a new dilemma over whether to supply the Uchizes with arms. English and French traders were still another factor in preventing more Spanish successes among the Indians, although the Spanish seemed to have improved their position. Montiano explained it well when he stated: "The ability of the English to pick out those items of commerce and trade that entices them [the Indians] is inexplicable, and thus we must procure articles to carry on our trade, regaling the Indians with many presents, as, I am informed, the Indians are accustomed to receive from the English and French." Montiano was hopeful, however, that his Indian program would succeed in spite of these vicissitudes and that the Chicazas (Chickasaws) would soon join the Uchizes as allies of the Spaniards.[79]

Montiano's optimism did not seem altogether warranted. In June, 1748, a group of Lower Creeks appeared in Saint Augustine making the usual professions of friendship and receiving the usual favors from the governor. Not long after, however, a small band, leaving before the main body of their compatriots, fell upon an unsuspecting party of Spaniards and Christian Yamasees, shooting and scalping three soldiers and several Indians with muskets and knives they had just received from Governor Montiano.[80] When the survivors of the skirmish straggled into Saint Augustine to spread the news, the governor was enraged. He imprisoned all the Lower Creeks still feasting and drinking in the Florida capital and sent out a party of soldiers to intercept the savages who had committed the atrocities. A short time later, the Spanish force wiped out twenty-seven of the twenty-eight renegades. Montiano then released the Lower Creeks he was holding prisoner, but with severe admonitions concerning the necessity of keeping their promises.[81]

79. AGI, Santo Domingo, Legajo 2584. Carta del gobernador de la Florida al rey, March 15, 1748.

80. CO 5:385, pt. 2. Copy of a letter from James Glen, Governor of South Carolina to the Board of Trade, Charleston, July 26, 1748.

81. CO 5:385, pt. 2. Copy of a letter from James Glen, Governor of South Carolina,

Montiano's successor in the governorship, Melchor de Navarrete, continued the policy of wooing the Indians. Late in 1749 he feted a band of twenty-two Uchize chiefs and obtained permission from them to educate the sons of Uchize leaders.[82] In May, 1751, Navarrete reported an influx of over seven hundred natives from Caveta, Oconi, Apalachicola, Iufale, Casista, Nadele, and other villages located northwest of Apalache. During their three-week stay in Saint Augustine each male Indian received a blouse, shirt, hat, musket, bolt of cloth, folding knife, hatchet, and some powder and musket balls. Squaws received a comb, mirror, and jewelry. Each Indian child received one shirt. The governor made special efforts to outfit each chief in resplendent uniforms, accented by an ornate cane. An optimistic Navarrete was well satisfied with the response of the Indians, who pledged their undying loyalty to him, but he believed that continuance of a gift-giving policy was indispensable for maintaining alliances with the Indians.[83] What is most significant, however, is that Navarrete, unlike his predecessors, had presents to offer the Indians. Lack of money and gifts had hurt earlier Spanish efforts to pacify the natives. Now, well-supplied by the Havana Company, the governor was able to compete more successfully with the English for the friendship of the Indians.

[*The French and Indian War and the Florida
Indians, 1753-1763*]

The loose alliances the governor obtained with Indian tribes of the Southeast in the period 1745-1752 was the result of two developments—the ability of the Spaniards to regale the Indians with supplies furnished by the Havana Company and the diminishing activity of English Indian agents. While traders from Carolina and Georgia still worked among the natives after the War of Jenkins's Ear, they made harsher bargains and offered fewer gifts to win over the Indians. In peacetime a liberal Indian policy was too costly and served no useful end. The Lower Creeks and other nations in the Southeast, therefore, forsook their ties with the English and turned to the Spaniards for aid and succor. In

---

to the Lords Commissioners for Trade and Plantations, Charleston, Oct. 10, 1748. See also CO 5:556. Letter from James Oglethorpe to the Duke of Bedford, Frederica, Aug. 29, 1748.

82. AGI, Santo Domingo, Legajo 2541. Carta del gobernador de la Florida al rey, Nov. 15, 1749. There is no evidence that the Spaniards ever educated the Indians.

83. AGI, Santo Domingo, Legajo 2584. Carta del gobernador de la Florida al Marqués de la Ensenada, May 21, 1751.

Georgia and Carolina, however, the English stood ready to renew their ties if war threatened.

In 1754 with hostilities again imminent English Indian agents began stepping up their activities among the Indians. In July Interim Governor Fulgencio García de Solís reported that the Carolinians and Georgians were attempting to set up a puppet emperor for the Uchizes. English traders, asserted the governor, promised the Uchizes arms and protection from other tribes if they would install the English favorite as emperor. He reported also that this was the first step in a new plan to invade Florida.[84] In December the interim governor urged immediate action to prevent English domination of the Uchizes and—an entirely new threat—of the Carlos Indians near Tampa Bay. As a counter move the interim governor advocated the establishment of three new Spanish outposts at Tampa Bay, the Bay of Carlos, and the Bay of Espiritu Santo. García made it clear, however, that with only three hundred men under his command, many unfit for life in blockhouses far removed from Saint Augustine, he could do little to implement his proposal.[85] In the end the king gave him no assistance, but cut off from sources of supply in Savannah, Charleston, and Frederica, the English traders failed to secure any permanent alliances with the Carlos.

In 1756 war finally broke between England and France, a conflict that directly affected Spanish Indian policy in Florida. Although Spain was not at first involved, Governor Alonso Fernández de Heredia intended to profit by past experience and ready his colony for war should his country join the French. In the summer and fall of 1756, he stepped up his gifts to the Lower Creeks who came to Saint Augustine seeking favors. He also redoubled his efforts to Christianize the Indians and ultimately secured the baptism of a nephew of a key Uchize chief.[86] Initially it appeared as if Fernández had won the upper hand among the Indians. In November, 1756, an English Indian agent, William Wilkins, claimed that the Lower Creeks were so hostile to the English that he dared not risk a land journey through their country. As another sign of Fernández' success, Wilkins reported the expulsion of his fellow trader, Ephraim Alexander, by the Lower Creeks. The English agent

84. AGI, Santo Domingo, Legajo 846. Carta del gobernador de la Florida al rey, July 27, 1754. This letter was contained in a file of secret documents.
85. AGI, Santo Domingo, Legajo 846. Carta del gobernador de la Florida al rey, Dec. 12, 1754.
86. AGI, Santo Domingo, Legajo 2542. Carta del gobernador de la Florida al rey, Oct. 20, 1756.

also heard rumors that the French planned to use Spanish Florida as a springboard for an attack on Georgia and Carolina.[87]

In retaliation the English encouraged their Indians to make incursions on Florida territory. In the summer of 1757 Indians from Georgia raged through the Saint Augustine area and killed four Spaniards. Immediately Fernández requested Governor Henry Ellis of Georgia to give reasons for the unprovoked attack. The Georgian replied that the Indians wanted Spanish scalps to atone for indignities suffered by their wives and daughters at the hands of libidinous Spanish soldiers. Still, Ellis seemed eager to prevent recurrence of Indian border raids and promised to restrain Indians in his control from invading Florida territory.[88] Governor Fernández was not satisfied with this response and imperiously demanded to know why the governor of Georgia persisted in furnishing muskets to the Indians if he really meant to keep peace between the two colonies. Providing the natives with arms was an open invitation to trouble.[89] For his part Ellis discreetly ignored this query and in November, 1757, promised once again to keep his Indians out of Spanish territory.[90]

While the Spaniards seemed more successful during the early years of the French and Indian War, the vigorous activity of English traders throughout 1758 and 1759 weakened Spanish alliances with the Indians. By the fall of 1759 the unpredictable Uchizes and other Lower Creek tribes had once again shifted their allegiance to the Georgians and Carolinians. At the same time Indians enjoying the governor's aid and protection in villages near Saint Augustine and Apalache began drifting away. Near the Florida capital late in 1759 only seventy-nine Indians remained in the two villages of Tolomato and Nuestra Señora de la Leche. Near San Marcos de Apalache there remained only one village with no more than twenty-five inhabitants.[91]

When war finally broke out officially between Spain and England in 1762, the Georgia-Florida frontier was strangely quiet. For the most part the two colonies did not have to face the fury of a border war. Except for occasional Indian raids, there was little warlike activity on

87. CO 5:386. Copy of a deposition of William Wilkins, Frederica, Nov. 24, 1756.
88. CO 5:657. Copy of a letter from Governor Henry Ellis of Georgia to Governor Alonso Fernández de Heredia of Florida, Savannah, Aug. 27, 1757.
89. CO 5:657. Copy of a letter from Governor Alonso Fernández de Heredia of Florida to Governor Henry Ellis of Georgia, St. Augustine, Sept. 19, 1757.
90. CO 5:657. Copy of a letter from Governor Henry Ellis of Georgia to Governor Alonso Fernández de Heredia of Florida, Savannah, Nov. 28, 1757.
91. AGI, Santo Domingo, Legajo 2584. Informe del obispo de Cuba, Oct. 9, 1759.

either side of the border. Though the English had won over many Lower Creek tribes, they did not use the natives against the Spaniards as they had in the past. Perhaps the Georgians and Carolinians feared Spanish reprisals; perhaps the failure of two British attempts to take Saint Augustine—in 1702 and again in 1740—discouraged a third effort demanding costly expenditures of men and money; perhaps British strategists preferred to maintain the status quo militarily in the South while they concentrated their efforts on Canada. In any event, the border was quiet; neither Spanish nor English Indians broke the tense peace that lay over the frontier.[92]

Absence of bloody raids did not mean the end to the governor's activities among the Indians. In February, 1763, Governor Melchor Feliú was exultant. His agent had made alliances with the Uchizes, the grand emperor of the Lower Creeks, and chiefs of the Lower Creek Confederation; and for the first time in the eighteenth century the Floridians had obtained firm pledges from their most truculent Indian antagonists. To insure these alliances, the governor's agent had showered the Indians with fine gifts, including a great quantity of rum, which made it necessary for him to "endure" a long drinking bout with the natives before returning to Saint Augustine.[93] Unfortunately the Spaniards could not take advantage of their good fortune. Late in 1763 they had to evacuate Florida, leaving their problems to the English.

[The Governor's Indian Policy: A Critique]

For the governor of Florida maintenance of a consistent, workable Indian policy was a difficult task. Though he attempted to conciliate the Indians with gifts, favors, or baptisms, he found it difficult to compete with English agents or to remain up-to-date on intertribal relationships, both of which kept his Indian program in continuous turmoil. English traders were particularly effective when war approached and proved more than a match for the Spaniards when the friendship of the Indians was critical. At crucial times well-stocked traders from Georgia and South Carolina moved among the Indians of the Southeast with rum, muskets, powder, and shot, which they offered

92. Unlike previous wars of the eighteenth century, the border did not erupt. Indian raids were infrequent and neither the governor in Frederica nor the governor in Saint Augustine was active militarily. There is a certain irony to the fact that the treaty that ended the bloodless war awarded Florida to the English.

93. AGI, Santo Domingo, Legajo 2542. Carta del gobernador de la Florida al rey, Feb. 20, 1763.

as gifts or on liberal terms in return for Indian treaties. In the mean-time the governor at Saint Augustine groped for ways to meet this competition, but without help from his superiors in the colonies or at home in Spain, he was unable to play the game of power politics among the Indians with any effectiveness, especially during wartime. In peace-time, when the Georgians and Carolinians had less use for Indian allies, the Spaniards achieved more success, but otherwise the governor was at a disadvantage in trying to strengthen his ties with the Indian tribes of the Southeast.

It could be argued, however, that it was difficult for any colonial leader—English, French, or Spanish—to secure lasting alliances with the Indians. For the most part they were practical opportunists con-tinually treading a fine line between Spanish, English, and French allegiance. For them no treaty of alliance was permanent. No promise of undying love or everlasting allegiance was irrevocable. They were willing to break solemn pledges in a twinkling of an eye to secure gifts and favors. Whether the governor of Florida could have achieved more with a bountiful supply of presents and a more effective staff of Indian traders is doubtful. The natives realized all too well the advantages of pursuing a policy of shifting, transitory alliances.

Chapter IX

POSTSCRIPT:
THE GOVERNORSHIP ON
THE SPANISH FRONTIER

An impoverished, unproductive colony on the northern fringe of
New Spain, Florida was a strategic outpost of the Spanish Empire
in America. The settlements on the Florida peninsula protected the
Bahama Channel on the homeward route of Spanish treasure fleets and
lay as a barrier to English and French penetration of the Southeast,
the Gulf Coast, and Mexico. The governorship of this critical province
demanded the disciplined hand of a military leader. Without exception
the governor was a high-ranking soldier whose training and experience
fitted the military character of Florida.

Unfortunately the governorship needed more than the services of
an experienced military leader. The office demanded a talented
administrator who could cope with the myriad of non-military problems
arising in this frontier province. Army training might have fitted a
governor for his duties had he been able to call upon a nucleus of lesser
officials to handle non-military questions, but he had no *audiencia* or
cabildo, no hierarchy of local officials with special administrative skills
to advise him on critical matters. His two treasury officials assisted him
in financial matters, but for the most part they were Floridians with
little training in treasury procedures and did little more than keep a
shoddy set of account books. A junta often approved the governor's
policies, especially when they violated royal law, but it seldom played a
significant role in formulating them. In the end the governor had to
work out solutions to colonial problems virtually alone. He had to act
as judge, financial manipulator, Indian trader, referee in clerical disputes, welfare agent, and construction engineer. Without training in
these areas, he was often forced to rely on his intuition or expedience in
molding policies for his beleaguered colony.

In Spain the governor's superiors were usually indulgent toward his expedients. The king and the Council of the Indies tolerated (although they did not condone) illicit trade, slip-shod judicial practice, misappropriation of funds, military defeat, and a host of other mistakes that would have been punished in Mexico or Peru. Spanish authorities seemed resigned to the governor's mismanagement or negligence and treated him like a pampered step-child, naughty enough for an occasional scolding but never bad enough for a sound thrashing.

Florida did not enjoy the same standing as its governor. The monarch and his Council coddled the governor but seemed to look upon his colony as the unwanted, unattractive urchin who deserved only table scraps. Authorities in Spain did little to support the colony and left this task to the governor in Cuba and the viceroy in Mexico, who had little desire to be tied to this sniveling, complaining dependency. Throughout its colonial existence Florida was a constant drain on the viceroy's treasury and a continual source of vexation for the governor in Havana. Despite its strategic importance, no name was more repugnant in Cuba or New Spain than *La Florida*. Maintaining the outpost was a heavy burden, and for many high Mexican and Cuban officials, the destitute province was not worth the expense. It was not surprising that the *situado* arrived sporadically or not at all and that shortages, poor quality, and high prices characterized the supplies delivered to Saint Augustine. Occasionally help came from Spain, but the governor relied almost entirely upon aid from Mexico and Cuba to carry on.

Complete economic dependence upon outside sources affected all the governor's policies in Florida. Money and supplies brought in periodically from Vera Cruz determined the effectiveness of his Indian program, of the Franciscan mission work, of his military policy, and of his other activities within the colony. Without money he could not compete successfully with the English and French for the allegiance of the Indians. Without money he could not support the Franciscans, who served in part to bolster the frontier against enemy encroachments. Without money he could not build stronger defenses to hold back the advance of the English or organize an offensive army to make war on Georgia and Carolina. Without adequate funds he could not attend to the needs of his colonists—the widows, orphans, and poor—nor could he provide adequately for his garrison. Without a tithe, which came indirectly from the *situado*, the work of the secular clergy also suffered. In essence the governor's entire administration hinged on the pesos lying in the treasury in Saint Augustine, and usually his coffers were empty. If the governor used expedients to survive, lack of money was as important as his lack of administrative experience in explaining his policies.

Reliance upon the *situado* virtually paralyzed Florida. It stifled initiative and was a factor preventing the rise of productive enterprises within the colony. Floridians inevitably looked to the subsidy or to aid from the outside to improve their lot. Only the appearance of a naval stores industry late in the 1750's showed evidences of any internal initiative to develop the colony. Throughout the eighteenth century it was almost as if the colonists were afflicted with a kind of economic hypochondria, constantly complaining about their ills and suggesting many remedies but never able to grow better. Poverty and want characterized life in Florida and pervaded all aspects of life. It affected the work of the regular clergy, which gave up its missionary efforts and engaged in a bitter power struggle for control of the order. It affected the governor's administration and forced him to use expedients to keep the colony functioning in the face of threats from the English.

Yet through it all the colony managed to survive. The governor and his destitute soldiers and colonists had enough endurance and tenacity to maintain their hold on the province. In the eighteenth century Spanish influence waned, but the governor still managed to keep the Spanish flag flying over Saint Augustine. He encountered many difficulties, but they were not insurmountable, and he successfully maintained the Spanish foothold in the Southeast until a treaty turned the colony over to the English in 1763.

GOVERNORS OF FLORIDA (1699-1764)

Joseph de Zúñiga y Cerda	1699-1706
Francisco de Córcoles y Martínez	1706-1716
Pedro de Olivera y Fullana	1716
Juan de Ayala Escobar (interim)	1716-1718
Antonio de Benavides	1718-1734
Ignacio Rodríguez Rozo (interim)	1726
Francisco del Moral Sánchez	1734-1737
Manuel Joseph de Justís (interim)	1737
Manuel de Montiano	1737-1749
Melchor de Navarrete	1749-1752
Fulgencio García de Solís (interim)	1752-1755
Alonso Fernández de Heredia	1755-1758
Lucas Fernando de Palacio y Valenzuela	1758-1761
Alonso de Cárdenas (interim)	1761-1762
Melchor Feliú	1762-1764

GOVERNORS OF CUBA (1695-1765)

Diego de Córdoba Laso de la Vega	1695-1702
Pedro Benítez de Lugo	1702-1705
Nicolás Chirino Vandevall Luis Chacón	1705-1706
Pedro Álvarez de Villarin	1706-1708
Laureano de Torres y Ayala	1708-1711
Luis Chacón	1711-1713
Laureano de Torres y Ayala	1713-1716
Vicente Raja	1716-1717
Gomez de Álvarez	1717
Gregorio Guazo Calderón	1717-1724
Dionisio Martínez de la Vega	1724-1734
Juan Francisco de Güemes y Horcasitas	1734-1746
Diego Penalosa	1746-1747
Francisco Cagigal de la Vega	1747-1760
Pedro Alonso	1760-1761
Juan de Prado Portocarrero	1761-1762
Ambrosio Funes Villalpando	1763-1765

VICEROYS OF NEW SPAIN(1701-1766)

Juan Ortega y Montañez, Archbishop of Mexico	1701-1702
Francisco Fernández de la Cueva Enríquez, Duke of Albuquerque	1702-1711
Fernando de Alencastre, Duke of Linares	1711-1716
Baltasar de Zúñiga, Marquis of Valero	1716-1722
Juan de Acuña, Marquis of Casafuerte	1722-1734
Juan Antonio de Vizarron y Eguiarreta, Archbishop of Mexico	1734-1740
Pedro de Castro y Figueroa, Duke of La Conquista	1740-1741
Audiencia	1741-1742
Pedro Cebrián y Agustín, Count of Fuenclara	1742-1746
Juan Francisco de Güemes y Horcasitas, Count of Revillagigedo	1746-1755
Agustín de Ahumada y Villalon, Marquis of Amarillas	1755-1758
Francisco Cagigal de la Vega (interim)	1758-1760
Audiencia	1760
Joaquin Monserrat, Marquis of Cruillas	1760-1766

BIBLIOGRAPHY OF WORKS CITED

[*I. Manuscripts*]

Archivo General de Indias, Seville, Spain
1. Section Five, Audiencia de Santo Domingo, La Florida.
   Legajos 228, 833, 836-838, 840-860, 862-867.
2. Section Five, Audiencia de Santo Domingo, Luisiana y la Florida.
   Legajos 2530, 2532-2534, 2541, 2542, 2574, 2581, 2584, 2591-2593, 2651, 2674-2691.
3. Section Five, Audiencia de Mexico, Virreinato.
   Legajos 384, 385, 514-516, 1506.
4. Section Five, Indiferente de Nueva España.
   Legajos 135-158, 167, 168.
5. Section Six, Escribanía de Cámara.
   Legajos 153a, 157b, 157c.
6. Section Eleven, Papeles, Procedentes de Cuba.
   Legajos 336, 337, 2263.

Cathedral Records, Saint Augustine Parish, The Saint Augustine Historical Society, Photostatic copies.

Public Record Office, Colonial Office Records, London, England.
1. America and the West Indies, Section Five.
   Numbers 12, 13.
2. South Carolina, Original Correspondence, Secretary of State, Section Five.
   Numbers 382-386, 388, 389.
3. Georgia, Original Correspondence, Secretary of State, Section Five.
   Numbers 654-658.

Microfilm Copy, Manuscript Division, John Carter Brown Library, Brown University, Providence, Rhode Island.

1. Reglamento para las peculiares obligaciones de el Presidio de San Augustín de la Florida y reglas que en el se deben observar, mediante a lo dispuesto para la tropa, que en el ha de guarnecer en el reglamento formado para la Habana, año de 1753.

2. Reglamento para la guarnación de la Habana, Castillos y Fuertes de su jurisdicción, Santiago de Cuba, San Augustín de la Florida, y su Anexo San Marcos de Apalache, año de 1753.

Spanish Records of the North Carolina Historical Commission, 1535-1802, Raleigh, North Carolina.

1. Bundle 58-2-29.

[*II. Published Documents and Laws*]

BOLTON, HERBERT E., ed. *Arredondo's Historical Proof of Spain's Title to Georgia.* Berkeley, 1925.

CARROLL, B. R. *Historical Collections of South Carolina: Embracing Many Rare and Valuable Pamphlets and Other Documents Relating to the History of the State from its Discovery to its Independence.* 2 vols. New York, 1836.

Colección de documentes inéditos relativos al descubrimiento, conquista, y colonización de las posesiones españolas en América y Oceanía. 41 vols. Madrid, 1864-1884.

Collections of the Georgia Historical Society, Vol. VII, Pt. I. "Letters of Montiano, Siege of Saint Augustine." Savannah, 1909.

Collections of the Georgia Historical Society, Vol. VII, Pt. 3. "The Spanish Official Account of the Attack on the Colony of Georgia, America, and of its Defeat on St. Simons Island by General James Oglethorpe." Savannah, 1913.

CONNOR, JEANNETTE THURBER, ed. and trans. *Colonial Records of Spanish Florida.* 2 vols. Deland, Florida, 1925-1930.

Indice general de los papeles del Consejo de Indias. 6 vols. Madrid, 1923-1926.

Recopilación de leyes de los reynos de las Indias. 3 vols. Madrid, 1943.

The Saint Augustine Expedition of 1740: A Report to the South Carolina General Assembly Reprinted from the Colonial Records of South Carolina with an Introduction by John Tate Lanning. Columbia, South Carolina, 1954.

[III. Books]

ARNADE, CHARLES. *The Siege of St. Augustine in 1702*. Gainesville, 1959.

BARCIA CARBALLIDO Y ZÚÑIGA, ANDRÉS G. *Ensayo cronológico para la historia general de la Florida, 1512-1722*. Por Gabriel de Cárdenas Z. Cano, pseud. In *Conquista del Nuevo Mundo*. 9 vols. Madrid, 1829. Vols. VIII and IX.

BOLTON, HEBERT E. AND MARY ROSS. *The Debatable Land*. Berkeley, 1925.

CHATELAIN, VERNE E. *The Defenses of Spanish Florida, 1565 to 1763*. Washington, D. C., 1941.

CONNOR, JEANNETTE THURBER, ed. *Pedro Menéndez de Avilés, Adelantado, Governor and Captain General of Florida, Memorial by Gonzalo Solís de Meras, first published in La Florida, su conquista y colonización por Pedro Menéndez de Avilés, by Eugenio Ruidíaz y Caravia*. Deland, Florida, 1923.

CRANE, VERNER W. *The Southern Frontier, 1670-1732*. Durham, 1928, and Ann Arbor, 1956.

GARCÍA GALLO, ALFONSO. *Indroducción y historia de las bases de formación de las fuentes y del derecho público*. Vol. I of *Curso del derecho español*. Madrid, 1950.

——— *Los origenes de la administración territorial de las Indias*. Madrid, 1954.

GEIGER, MAYNARD. *Biographical Dictionary of the Franciscans in Spanish Florida and Cuba (1528-1841)*, in *Franciscan Studies*. Vol. XXI. Paterson, N. J., 1940.

HARING, CLARENCE H. *The Spanish Empire in America*. New York, 1947.

HUSSEY, ROLAND D. *The Caracas Company, 1728-1784*. Cambridge, Mass., 1934.

LANNING, JOHN TATE. *The Diplomatic History of Georgia: A Study of the Epoch of Jenkins' Ear*. Chapel Hill, 1936.

——— *The Spanish Missions of Georgia*. Chapel Hill, 1935.

LOWERY, WOODBURY. *The Spanish Settlements within the Present Limits of the United States, 1513-1561*. New York and London, 1901.

——— *The Spanish Settlements within the Present Limits of the United States, 1562-1574.* New York and London, 1905.

MADARIAGA, SALVADOR DE. *Spain.* London, 1931.

PARKMAN, FRANCIS. *Pioneers of France in the New World,* Boston, 1895. Part I.

RIVERS, WILLIAM JAMES. *A Sketch of the History of South Carolina to the Close of the Proprietary Government by the Revolution of 1719, with an Appendix, Containing Many Valuable Records Hitherto Unpublished.* Charleston, 1856.

SHEA, JOHN D. GILMARY. *The Catholic Church in Colonial Days.* 2 vols. New York, 1883. Vol. I.

SWANTON, JOHN R. *The Indians of the Southeastern United States.* Bulletin No. 137 of the Bureau of American Ethnology, Smithsonian Institution, Washington, D. C., 1946.

WILGUS, A. CURTIS, ed. *Colonial Hispanic America.* Washington, D. C., 1936.

[*IV. Authorities: Periodicals*]

ARNADE, CHARLES W. "The Architecture of Spanish St. Augustine," *The Americas,* XVIII (October, 1961), 149-186.

BARNWELL, JOSEPH W. "Fort King George, Journal of Colonel John Barnwell (Tuscarora) in the Construction of the Fort on the Althamaha in 1721," *The South Carolina Historical and Genealogical Magazine* (October, 1926), 189-203.

BOYD, MARK F., trans. "Diego Peña's Expedition to Apalache and Apalachicolo in 1716," *Florida Historical Quarterly,* XXVIII (July, 1949), 1-27.

——— "Documents Describing the Second and Third Expeditions of Lieutenant Diego Peña to Apalache and Apalachicolo in 1717 and 1718," *Florida Historical Quarterly,* XXXI (October, 1952), 109-139.

CÉSPEDES DEL CASTILLO, GUILLERMO. "La visita como institución indiana," *Anuario de estudios americanos,* III (1946), 984-1025.

CONNOR, JEANNETTE THURBER. "The Nine Old Wooden Forts of Saint Augustine," *Florida Historical Quarterly,* IV (January and April, 1926), 103-111, 171-180.

DUNKLE, JOHN R. "Population Changes as an Element in the Historical Geography of St. Augustine," *Florida Historical Quarterly*, XXXVIII (July, 1958), 3-22.

HILL, ROSCOE R. "The Office of *Adelantado*," *Political Science Quarterly*, XXVIII (December, 1913), 646-668.

LANNING, JOHN TATE. "The Legend that Governor Moral Sánchez Was Hanged," *Georgia Historical Quarterly*, XXVIII (December, 1954), 349-355.

MORALES PADRÓN, FRANCISCO. "Colonos canarios en Indias," *Anuario de estudios americanos*, VIII (1951), 391-441.

PIERSON, WILLIAM WHATLEY, JR. "Some Reflections on the Cabildo as an Institution," *Hispanic American Historical Review*, V (November, 1922), 573-596.

SIEBERT, WILBUR H. "Some Church History of Saint Augustine during the Spanish Regime," *Florida Historical Quarterly*, IX (October, 1930), 117-123.

TIBESAR, ANTONINE S. "The *Alternativa*: A Study in Spanish-Creole Relationships in Seventeenth-Century Peru," *The Americas*, XI (January, 1955), 229-283.

INDEX

Acebedo, Pedro Lorenzo de, 171-173, 175-178
Achito, 200
Achitos, 210
Acre, 17
Adelantado: development of in Florida, 9-10
Adrian, 201, 202, 207
Africa, 16, 58, 75
Als, 80, 193
Alabama, 6, 108, 213
Albermarle River, 145
Albuquerque, Duke of, 116
Alexander, Ephraim, 223
Altamaha River, 125-127, 129
Alternativa, 182 n., 192
Altimirano, Juan de las Cabezas, 161, 161 n.
Álvarez de Toledo, Lucas, 179
Ambland, Guillermo, 72-73
Amelia Island, 140
Andrade, Alberto, 74-75
Angel, Blas, 73-76
Antigua, 153
Apalache, 42, 46, 63, 70, 104, 111, 131, 133, 134, 157, 158, 159, 162, 164, 181, 182, 184, 185, 193, 195, 196, 197, 198, 208, 210, 211, 214, 215, 219, 221, 222, 224; devastation of, 113-116; evacuation of, 115-116; Fort San Luis de, 6, 108, 109, 113-116, 122, 195, 200; Fort San Marcos de, 49, 64, 122-125, 155, 158, 161, 206, 207, 215, 218, 224; Franciscan missions in, 122; fur trade in, 88; garrison at, 108, 135, 141; Indians in, 7, 113-115, 160, 206-207, 212, 213; naval stores industry in, 106; plans to resettle, 87-88, 219; refortification of, 122-125, 204-206; removal of capital to, 123-124; trading post established in, 215-218
Apalache Bay, 109, 123, 124, 202, 204
Apalache River, 109

Apalaches, 113, 180, 188, 193, 197
Apalachicola, 200, 202
Apalachicola River, 193, 200
Apalachicolas, 201, 203, 206, 210
Apalachinos, 201
Aragón, 8, 16
Arbousset, General, 118-120
Argüelles, Gerónima de, 174
Argüelles, Onafre de, 174
Arias, Lorenzo, 43
Armada de Barlovento: *see* Windward Squadron
Arredondo, Antonio de, 37 n., 49 n., 50, 136, 137, 151; carries on a *pesquisa* in Florida, 37, 48-49; plans attack on Georgia, 147-148; reports on military situation in Florida, 135
Arriola, Andrés de, 11, 12 n., 13, 116, 117
Atlantic Ocean, 3 n., 116, 119
Audiencia, 227; organization and duties of, 58
Auxiliary bishop of Cuba (for Florida), 34, 46, 48, 50-52, 53, 94, 161-171, 178, 186-187, 189-190
Ayabamo, 203
Ayala Escobar, Juan de, 69, 70, 72, 92, 199, 209; appointment as interim governor, 14-15; background of, 18; Indian policy of, 201-204; involved in litigation, 64-68; mission to Spain for aid, 79-81, 86, 91, 116; refortification of Apalache, 124, 204; sells illicit goods, 83-84; Zúñiga's agent in Apalache, 195
Ayllón, Lucas Vásquez de, 3 n., 9
Ayubale, massacre at, 113-115

Bahama Channel, 3, 80, 90, 108, 116, 120, 130, 141, 157, 227
Bahamas, 102
Barnwell, John, 126, 128, 133
Bathsheba, 43
Bayamo, 160

Beaufort, 130

Benavides, Antonio de, 15, 35, 36, 67, 72; 93 n., 125, 133, 166, 180, 183, 192, 209; accused of corruption, 45 n.; administers justice, 59-60, 64-71; appointment of, 11; attempts to obtain a public secretary, 29-31; Ayala-Pedroso litigation, 64-68; background of, 16-17; becomes governor of Vera Cruz, 32; complaints about *situado* system, 85; dealings with clergy, 165, 171-175, 180, 182; extension of term, 13; fines levied by, 53; Indian policy of, 130, 205-206; misapplies building and contingency funds, 92-95; Nieto-Rozo litigation, 68-69; operated on in Havana, 18; plans for resettling Apalache, 123-124; Primo de Rivera litigation, 70-71; problem of Fort King George, 126-130; salary of, 21; suggests economic reforms, 87-88, suggests religious reforms, 187

Berroa, Esteban de, 112

Bloody Marsh, Battle of, 150-154, 215

Board of Trade and Plantations, 127, 130

Bobadilla, Francisco de, 8

Boston, 151, 153

Brilliante, La (vessel), 119-120

Brims, 201-203, 207-208

British East India Company, 97

Bucuquas, 203

Buenaventura: *see* San Buenaventura y Tejada, Francisco de

Buenos Aires, 72; audiencia of, 58

Bull, William, 146

Bustamante, Francisco de, 12 n.

Bustamante, Manuel García, 179

Cabildo, 7, 7 n., 227; attempts to re-establish in Florida, 27; establishment and delay in seating, 38; functions and organization of, 26; short existence in Florida, 26-27

Cádiz, 36, 44, 52, 54, 117

Calaques, 221

Calderón de la Barca, Pedro, 44 n.

Campeche, 88

Campillo, José de, 152

Canada, 117, 225

Canal y Soldevilla, Domingo de la, 11

Canary Islanders, 88, 89 n., 219; plans to settle in Florida, 134, 205

Cancer, Luis, 4 n.

Cape Canaveral, 80, 141

Caracas, audiencia of, 58

Caracas Company, 97

Cárdenas, Alonso de: appointment of, 14-16; background of, 18-19; delays establishment of *cabildo*, 27, 38

Carlos, 124, 162, 164, 193; 223; bay of, 223

Carolina, 6, 74, 88, 91, 110, 112, 116, 117, 118-122, 125, 127, 129, 130, 155, 158, 196, 208, 222, 223, 224, 228: *see also* Charleston; North Carolina; South Carolina

Carribean, 40, 97, 116, 120

Cartagena, 12, 13, 32, 40, 41, 45, 106, 146, 154

Carteret, Lord (Earl of Granville), 127

Casa de Contratación: *see* House of Trade

Casapules, 213

Casipuyas, 208

Casista, 200, 222

Casistas, 206, 210

Castile, 8; Council of War of, 80 n.

Castilla, Francisco de, 31, 96, 102-103

Catalina, 162: *see also* Guale

Catalonia, 8, 16

Catholic Kings, 7

Caveta, 200, 203, 213 n., 222

Cavetas, 38, 203, 206, 210

Central America, 14, 77

Ceuta, 16, 18

Chalaques, 219

Chamachichi, 210

Charcas, audiencia of, 58

Charles II, 178-179

Charles III, 91; orders establishment of *cabildo* in Saint Augustine, 27; postpones establishment of *cabildo* in Florida, 27; settles dilemma over naval stores trade, 107

Charleston, 71, 73, 74, 75, 83, 105, 111, 113, 117, 118-120, 126, 128, 129, 130, 131, 133, 145, 146, 148, 153, 185, 190, 193, 199, 211, 212, 223: *see also* Carolina

Charlotte Harbor, 4, 124

Chattahoochee River, 193, 200, 202, 203, 207, 210, 213 n., 220

Chavagili, 200

Chicano, Juan Félix García, 65-68

Chicazas, 221: *see also* Chickasaws

Chickasaws, 140, 213, 214, 221

Chigilly, 213

Childs, James, 212

Chile, audiencia of, 58

Chipicasi: *see* Tsipacaya

Chiquile, 220

Chiquito, 135, 184, 213: *see also* Nombre de Dios

Chirino Vandevall, Nicolás, 117
Chiscalachisle, 199-201, 202, 207
Chiscalachisles, 203, 204
Chiscas, 197
Chocato, 218
Choctaw, 213
Chucatiti, 207
Chumayche, 218
Cierro, Juan Francisco del, 63
Colombia: see New Granada
Columbus, Christopher, 8
Commons House of Assembly (South Carolina), 131, 208-209
Coosee, 213
Córcoles y Martínez, Francisco de, 72; appointment of, 11, 117; background of, 16; building funds allocated to, 91-92, 94; deals with illicit trade, 84; dispatch of title, 22; Indian policy of, 197, 198, 200, 202, 209; military policy of, 118, 120-122; religious policy of, 164, 176-177; reports on bad quality of supplies, 83; suggests economic reforms, 86-87; takes Zúñiga's residencia, 41-45
Costa, 184, 197, 208, 213
Costa Rica, 17
Council of the Indies, 17, 19, 33, 38, 41, 49, 58, 61, 81, 97, 104, 120, 133, 135, 146, 163, 166, 167, 173, 174, 177, 178, 192, 215, 228; accuses Córcoles of corruption, 45; aims of policy in Florida, 23 n., 24; alarmed over erection of Fort King George, 127-128; aroused over misapplication of funds, 92, 95-96; awards aid to Ayala, 80, 116; censures Benavides, 71; challenges Benavides' handling of Nieto case, 36; chastises Fernández de Heredia for handling of illicit trade case, 75; control over appointments, 27-28; countenances loss of contingency funds, 97; deals with debasement of currency scheme, 89-90; deals with Moral's residencia, 55-57; deals with Nieto-Rozo case, 68-69; duties defined, 10, 10 n.; exonerates Zúñiga, 44; Fernández de Heredia hopes to secure seat on, 18, 74, 75; ignores enforcement of media anata requirement for governor, 22, 23 n.; investigates loss of situado ship, 103; nominates Córcoles for governor, 117; obligations in residencia cases, 39, 44, 54; orders a public secretary to Florida from Havana, 29; orders removal of capital

to Apalache, 123-124; outlines duties of the Havana Company toward Florida, 98-100; procedure for nominating governors, 10-12; recommends auxiliary bishopric for Florida, 162; refuses to grant governor's request for additional salary, 21; refuses to increase Franciscan subsidy, 179-180; rejects proposals for religious reforms, 190
Creeks: see Lower Creeks
Cruz, Juana de la, 171
Cuba, 9, 17, 18, 25, 36, 37, 40, 41, 49, 50, 55, 60, 65, 67, 69, 73, 76, 78, 81, 84, 97, 105, 111, 123, 136, 138, 141, 144, 147, 152, 156, 160, 162, 165, 166, 171, 172, 178, 182, 195, 216, 228; bishop of, 60, 160, 161, 164, 169, 171-175, 187; governor of, 11, 12, 15, 29, 30, 31, 34 n., 37, 45, 48-49, 50, 52, 69, 73-76, 80, 104, 117, 121, 127, 212, 217, 228: see also Chirino Vandevall, Nicolás; Güemes y Horcasitas, Juan Francisco de; Havana; Martínez de la Vega, Dionisio; Santiago de Cuba
Cumberland Island, 4, 151, 193
Cushivay, 218
Cuzco, audiencia of, 58

Daniel, Robert, 110-11, 134
Darien (Georgia), 125
Darien (Panama), 17
David, 43
Densi, Carlos (Charles Dempsey), 53
Díaz Calderón, Varas, 161
Dunbar, George, 141

Ellis, Henry, 224
Encomiendas, 193
England, 125, 223, 224
Escobedo de Angulo, Josepha, 18
Española, 8
Espiritu Santo, Bay of, 223
Esquibel, Juan Alonso de, 195
Estrada, Joseph de, 145-146
Estrada, Pedro, 145
Estremadura, 16
Europe, 16, 58
Evelino de Compostela, Diego, 161-163, 165

Feliú, Melchor: background of, 18, 18 n.; Indian policy of, 225
Ferdinand VI: deals with Florida naval stores industry, 106; orders Fernández

Ferdinand VI *(cont.)*
de Heredia to Florida, 14; orders viceroy of New Spain to recommend effective reorganization of garrisons, 156; raises salary of governor, 21-22; refuses to allow trade with Carolina, 91

Ferdinand and Isabella: *see* Catholic Kings

Fernández, Juan, 207

Fernández de Heredia, Alonso, 89 n.; appointed governor of Yucatán, 32; appointment of, 14, 14 n.; background of 17-18; Indian policy of, 223-224; stimulates naval stores industry, 106-107; uncovers an illicit trade scandal, 73-76

Flanders, 17

Florencia, Antonio de, 122

Florencia, Francisco de, 120

Florencia, Joaquin de, 194-195

Florida: administration of justice in, 58-76; auxiliary bishopric for, 34, 46, 48, 50-52, 53, 94, 161-171, 178, 186-187, 189-190; description of in 1600, 5-6; description of new coins for, 90; development to 1700, 4-7; early administrative organization of, 7; early attempts to settle and colonize, 4-5; early missions in, 6; economic problems in, 77-109; exodus from in 1570, 5; forced laborers in, 104; French and Indian War in, 224; illicit trade in, 53, 68, 71-76, 88-89, 167, 185; immigration to, 45-46; Indian problems in, 193-226; indigo industry in, 7; junta in, 24-26, 94, 98-100, 227; military reorganization of, 156-157; naval stores industry in, 105-107, 229; problems of defense in, 93, 108-158, 228; religious problems in, 159-192; strategic importance of, 2, 108, 108 n., 157-158; Spanish claims on, 3; territorial delineation of, 3 n., 127: *see also* Apalache; Fort San Marcos; Franciscans; Governor; Saint Augustine

Fort Caroline, 4

Fort King George, 125-130, 133, 209

Fort Pierce, 4

Fort San Diego, 135, 140, 141, 142, 154

Fort San Marcos (Saint Augustine), 7, 18, 37, 51, 87, 110, 116, 122, 131, 141, 159, 191, 209, 214; chaplain at, 43, 161, 171; conditions in, 41, 91, 92, 109; defenses of, 19, 120, 122, 135, 138, 153, 158; early development

of, 5, 5 n.; garrison at, 29, 41, 64, 108; governor receives keys to, 19; Indian towns near, 197; siege of in 1702, 42, 110-113; siege of in 1740, 142-144: *see also* Saint Augustine

Fraga, 16

France, 16, 125, 223

Franciscans, 104, 171, 176, 193, 209, 228-229; activities in Apalache, 113-115; bring accusations against Moral, 37, 46; commissary general of, 160, 179, 182, 183, 192; controversy with secular clergy, 175-177; Creole-Spanish factional dispute, 46-47, 49, 50, 167-168, 170, 181-192; decline of, 159, 170-171, 190-192, 196-197; early successes of, 6; Guale missions, 126; number laboring in Florida, 160, 160 n., 180, 190; obligations of Indians to, 194; organization of in Florida, 160; problems over ecclesiastical sanctuary, 51-52, 74-75; revival of mission program, 198; subsidy for, 178-181, 189: *see also* Miranda, Angel de; Parja, Juan de

Frederica, 139, 141, 148-152, 213 n., 214, 223, 225 n.

Frederica River, 150

French and Indian War, 224-225

Fuentes, Antonio de, 29-30

Galicia, 8; plans to settle Florida with families from, 87, 88, 123

García, Alonso, 54

García de Solís, Fulgencio, 14; administers justice, 62-63, 72-73; appointment of, 12 n., 15; background of, 18; deals with illicit traders, 72-73; Indian policy of, 223; relations with auxiliary bishop, 169-170

García de Villegas, Salvador, 96

Georgia, 37, 51, 108, 121, 130, 132, 133, 136, 141, 155, 159, 160, 212, 213, 218, 223, 224, 225, 228; Franciscans in, 6; English settlement of, 133-134, 210; Spanish claims on, 126; Spanish pretensions on, 137-139, 146-152, 158; traders from, 22; Yamasee atrocities in, 209: *see also* Frederica; Guale; Oglethorpe, James

Gibraltar, 16, 18

Governor of Florida: administers justice, 20, 58-76; appointment and term of, 11-14; arbitrates religious controversies, 175-178; auxiliary bishop as a check on, 170-171; control over

Governor of Florida *(cont.)*
patronage, 27-31; difficulty in filling office, 12; dispatch of title, 20-23; duties, privileges, responsibilities, 20-24; economic problems of, 77-107; general checks on, 33-34; inauguration ceremony for, 19-20; Indian policy of, 193-226; litigations over illicit trade, 71-76; opportunities for advancement, 32; origin of office in Spain, 7-9; problems of defense, 108-158; reaction to founding of Georgia, 133-135; relationship to secular clergy, 171-175; relationship with junta, 24-25; religious problems of, 159-192; salary and perquisites, 21-22; suggests economic reforms, 86-91; vice patron of the church, 20, 47, 159: *see also* Florida; Fort San Marcos; Saint Augustine
Guadalajara: audiencia of, 58; vacant bishopric of, 80, 91, 92
Guale, 4, 42, 108, 122, 133, 162, 164, 181, 193, 195-196, 197: *see also* Georgia
Guales, 121, 193, 195-196, 208
Guanabacoa, 160
Guantánamo Bay, 18
Guatemala, 7, 17; audiencia of, 58; captain general of, 14; vacant bishopric of, 80, 91, 92
Güemes y Horcasitas, Juan Francisco de, 15, 37, 48-49, 49 n., 102-103, 137-139, 146-149, 152, 156-157
Guipúzcoa, 18
Gulf Coast, 87, 88, 134, 155, 227
Gulf of Mexico, 3, 79, 88, 106, 108, 108 n., 157

Hapsburgs, 182
Havana, 11, 17, 18, 29, 31, 36, 44, 48, 52, 65, 68, 69, 70, 73, 75, 76, 77, 83, 84, 100, 102, 103, 111, 123, 137-139, 141, 147, 148, 152, 160, 161, 162, 164, 170, 182, 228
Havana Company, 25, 74, 89 n., 104, 222; contractual obligations and privileges, 97-98; obligations toward trading post in Apalache, 216-217; supply contracts with Florida, 98-102; trade policy of, 105, 105 n., 106
Hernández, Nicolás, 150
Highland Rangers, 140, 143
Holybush Plantation, 119
Honduras, 17
Horruitiner, Joseph Benedit, 84

Horruitiner, Lamberto Benedit, 46
House of Trade, 80
Huguenots, 4
Hume, John, 72-73

Ignacio, Juan, 212
Illicit trade, 41, 46, 53, 68, 71-76, 88-89, 167, 185
Immaculate Conception, convent of, 51-52, 159, 160, 170
Iororo, 184, 208
Iororos, 194-195
Isabel (vessel), 72-73
Isabella: *see* Ferdinand and Isabella
Italy, 18
Iturrieta, Felipe de, 49 n., 103; freed by Justís and ordered to guard Moral, 51-52; seizure and imprisonment of, 47-50
Iufale, 222

Jacksonville, 116
Jaime I, 8
Jamaica, 9, 17, 111, 153
James Island, 118
Jekyl Sound, 149-150
Jesuits, 6, 189-190
Johnson, Nathaniel, 118-120
Junta, 94, 227; dealings with the Havana Company, 98-100; development of in Florida, 24-26
Junta de Guerra, 80, 80 n., 116, 121, 123, 124
Justís, Manuel Joseph de, 56; appointment of, 12 n., 14-15, 50; arrival in Saint Augustine, 50; background of, 18; difficulties in succeeding Moral, 50-52

Lagiche, 38
Lefebvre, Jacques, 118
Léon, Juan Isidro de, 218, 220
Lérida, 16
Lima, 19; audiencia of, 58
Lodares Cota, Pedro Alonso, 172-173
London, 88, 127, 210
López de Toledo, Álvaro, 210
López de Toledo, Sebastián, 47, 51
Lorenzo, Juan, 43
Lorenzo, Marianna, 43
Losada, Domingo, 182
Loso de la Vega, Juan, 166
Louis XIV, 15
Lower Creeks, 124, 130, 131, 134, 139, 140, 188, 193, 205, 218, 219; defeated at Mosa by Salgado, 143; equivocal policy of, 207-210, 215-216; French

Lower Creeks *(cont.)*

influence among, 134, 206, 210-214; Peña's missions to, 200-205; seek Spanish alliances, 180, 199-204, 221-225
Luna y Arellano, Tristán de, 4 n.

Macaris, 208, 209, 213: *see also* Nombre de Dios
Mackay, Hugh, 140
Madrid, 54, 80, 104, 180, 190; treaty of (1670), 126-127
Majoloa, 140
Majorca, 8
Manila, audiencia of, 58
Martínez de la Vega, Dionisio, 11
Martinique, 121
Massachusetts, 26
Matanzas, bar of, 108, 153
Matanzas Channel, 153
Matanzas Point, 135, 144, 153
Matanzas River, 5, 122, 143
Mayacá, 194-196
Media anata, 22-23
Menéndez de Avilés, Pedro, 4 n., 4-5, 6, 7 n., 9, 26-27, 77
Menéndez Marqués, Francisco, 28-29, 96, 126-127, 129, 130 n., 177-178
Mérida, 32, 163
Mexia, Juan Ruiz, 114-115
Mexico, 5, 70, 78, 79, 84, 117, 187, 198, 227, 228; audiencia of, 58: *see also* Mexico City; New Spain; Puebla; Vera Cruz
Mexico City, 19, 24, 71, 79, 82, 101, 107, 120
Miami, 4
Milan, 16, 18
Miranda, Angel de, 114
Mississippi, 108
Mobile, 25, 70, 111, 155, 203, 206
Molina, Gaspar, 165-166
Molina, Martín de, 176
Montiano, Manuel de, 31, 60, 72, 145, 190, 192, 212; attempts to stimulate naval stores industry, 106; becomes governor of Panama, 32; dealings with the Havana Company, 98-101; defends Saint Augustine, 140-144, 152-154; demands more salary, 21; Indian policy of, 213-215; misapplies contingency funds, 95-96; offensive at Bloody Marsh, 146-156; relations with the clergy, 176-177; sponsors attack on New Brunswick, 145-146; strains on treasury, 103-105; strengthens

defenses, 138-139; suggests economic reforms, 89-91; suggests religious reforms, 188-189; takes Moral's *residencia*, 52-56; term in office, 13
Moore, James, 110-116, 196-197
Moors, 8, 17
Moral Sánchez, Francisco del, 60, 61, 72, 89 n., 139, 192; appointment of, 11; attempts to stimulate naval stores industry, 106; background of, 17; defensive diplomacy of, 135-137, 211; defensive problems of, 134-135; economic problems of, 85, 103; excesses of, 13, 34 n., 37, 95-96; fines collected by, 62, 62 n.; Indian policy of, 210-213; reaction to founding of Georgia, 133-134; relations with the clergy, 167-168, 170-171, 173-175, 185-187; replacement of, 15; *residencia* of, 40, 45-47; suggests economic reforms, 88-89; term in office, 13
Morales, Pedro de, 186 n.
Morro Castle, 52
Mosa, 141-143, 151

Nadele, 222
Nanhuluchuba, 195
Narváez, Pánfilo de, 4 n., 9
Natchez, 155
Navarre, 8, 18
Navarrete, Melchor de: administration of justice, 60, 63, 72; background of, 17; becomes governor of Yucatán, 15, 32; Indian policy of, 222
Navarro, Antonio, 186
New Granada, 17, 146; audiencia of, 58
New Law of 1753, 156-157
New Spain, 3, 9, 21, 24, 32, 77, 81, 88, 91, 100, 104, 108, 125, 133, 134, 136, 137, 157, 171, 209, 227; commissary general of, 187; prices of goods in, 85, 90; vacant bishoprics in, 163; viceroy of, 6, 15, 19, 24, 68, 70-71, 77, 78, 80, 95, 96, 101, 107, 116, 117, 120-121, 127, 129, 179, 191, 228: *see also* Mexico; Mexico City; Puebla; Vera Cruz
New York, 105
Newcastle, Duke of, 212
Newfoundland, 73
Nicaragua, 9, 17
Nicholson, Francis, 126-129
Nieto de Carbajal, Antonio, 144
Nieto de Carbajal, Bartolomé, 30-31
Nieto de Carbajal, Bernardo, 35-36, 42, 68-70

Nombre de Dios, 122, 131, 143, 197
Nombre de Dios (Chuquito), 208
Nombre de Dios (Macaris), 208, 209, 213
North Africa, 17, 18
North Carolina, 145: see also Carolina
Nova Scotia, 3 n., 73, 116
Nuestra Señora de la Leche, 224
Nuestra Señora de la Luz (vessel), 73-74
Nuestra Señora del Rosario (vessel), 163

Obrajes, 193
Ocmulgee, 200
Oconi, 222
Oglethorpe, James, 37, 139, 145, 215;
attack on Florida in 1742, 152-154;
defends Georgia against Spanish attack, 146-152; Indian policy of, 134,
139-140, 210-214; negotiations with
Moral, 136-137; settlement of Georgia,
133; siege of Saint Augustine in 1740,
141-144, 214
Olivera y Fullana, Pedro de, 92; appointment of, 11; background of, 16; death
of, 11, 15; Indian policy of, 200, 202,
209
Olmos, Andrés de, 162
Oran, 17, 18
Ortega, Blas de, 63
Ovando, Nicolás, 8

Palacio y Valenzuela, Lucas Fernando de,
15; administration of justice, 64;
background of, 18; investigated by
Charles III, 37-38
Palamos, 16
Palica, 46, 191, 208, 213, 215
Palmer, John, 143; raid on Florida in
1728, 131-132, 208-209
Palomino Lasso de la Vega, Francisco,
134
Pamplona, 18
Panama, 9, 32; audiencia of, 32, 58
Paredes, Juan de, 173-175
Parja, Juan de; martyrdom of, 115
Paz, Joseph de la, 63-64
Pedroso, Joseph, 64-68, 70
Peña, Diego: missions to Lower Creeks,
200-205; recommendations of harsh
policy toward the Indians, 206
Peña, Juan Esteban de, 96
Peñon, 135
Pensacola, 6, 70, 111, 115, 121, 125, 182,
184, 204, 215, 219
Pequots, 210
Peralta, López de, 54
Pérez, Domingo, 74

Peru, 5, 9, 19, 21, 134, 228
Pesquisa, 39; use and effectiveness of, 34,
37
Philip II, 4; doubles garrison at Saint
Augustine, 6, 77-78
Philip V, 31, 45, 60, 65, 88, 115, 122,
137, 143, 176, 180, 184, 185, 200,
201, 204, 205, 212, 215; aids Florida,
80, 91, 92, 95; appointive procedure
of, 11, 28, 30; appoints visitador, 35,
182; approves diversion of contingency
funds, 93; aroused over Franciscan
factional dispute, 182-183, 187, 192;
considers migration scheme, 88; demands accounting of expenditures of
34,000 pesos, 93; demands Zúñiga's
residencia, 41, 56; extends Benavides'
term in office, 13; governors' letters to,
44-45; orders acolytes to serve in the
choir of the parochial church, 177;
orders Caballero to Florida, 123;
orders Chicano to Florida, 66; orders
investigation of Juan de Paredes, 175;
orders offensive against Carolina, 121;
orders offensive against Georgia, 134,
146; orders establishment of trading
post in Apalache, 216-217; policy
toward bishopric in Florida, 162-165;
refuses to grant new contingency fund
to Florida, 94; rejects recommendations for religious reforms, 190; re-
places Moral, 48; revises situado system, 82; sets governor's salary, 21;
views on Fort King George, 127-128
Picolata, 134-135, 140, 185, 210, 214
Point Quartell, 142
Point San Mateo, 142
Ponce de León, Antonio, 68; visitation of
Florida, 35-37
Ponce de León, Francisco, 29-31
Ponce de León, Juan, 3, 3 n., 9
Ponce y Carrasco, Pedro, 169-170
Port Royal, 110, 129, 146, 148, 149
Potano, 197
Pozobueno, Jacinto, 127
Primo de Rivera, Joseph, 125 n., 130 n.,
155; fortifies Saint Joseph, 125; in-
volvement in litigation, 70-71; mission
to Charleston, 129; rebuilds Apalache,
124-125, 204-205
Privateers, 145-146
Protomedicato, 54, 54 n.
Providence Island, 103
Puebla de los Angeles, 80; bishop of, 82-
89, 91, 92, 97, 100, 101; high sheriff
of, 87; merchants of, 88; price of

Puebla de los Angeles *(cont.)*
food in, 85; *situado* and sales taxes from, 82, 84, 86, 97, 98, 105
Puerto Principe, 160
Puerto Rico, 9, 156
Puertobelo, 106
Pulido, Blas, 182 n.
Punta, 191, 213, 215
Pupo, 134-135, 139, 140, 185, 214

Quebec, 117
Queen Anne's War, 35, 40, 70, 79, 83, 110, 122, 125, 130, 157-158, 176, 180, 183, 199, 201, 208, 209, 215, 218; effect on the Florida Indians, 196-198
Quilate, 218
Quito, audiencia of, 58

Ramos de Escudero, Joseph, 186
Reborato y Solar, Domingo, 98-100
Recopilación de leyes de los reynos de las Indias, 23-24
Regidor, Antonio, 62-63
Regular clergy: *see* Franciscans, Jesuits
Residencia: of Francisco del Moral Sánchez, 45-57; of Joseph de Zúñiga y Cerda, 40-45; procedure for, 39-40; restriction on governor, 56-57
Resino, Dionisio, 92, 162-164, 164 n., 170
Revillagigedo, Conde: *see* Güemes y Horcasitas, Juan Francisco de
Río Grande, 3 n., 116
Río Tinto, 14
Rodríguez, Pablo, 46
Rome, Spanish ambassador in, 162
Romero, Juan, 187
Roque Pérez, Jacinto, 195
Rosario, 197
Rosas, 184
Royal Havana Company: *see* Havana Company
Rozo, Ignacio Rodríguez, 51, 70; appointment as interim governor, 14, 15; background of, 18; Moral's seizure of, 47-48; purged by Benavides, 68-69
Rubi de Celis, Diego, 165
Rubiani, Francisco, 147-148, 151
Ruiz, Juan, 41-44
Ruiz, Silvestre, 175 n.
Ruiz del Moral, Romulado, 53

Saint Andrews, 151
Saint Augustine, 11, 15, 19, 81, 90, 108, 153, 229; children of, 160, 168, 191; completion of church and covent in,

94; conditions in, 79, 83, 85, 101, 120; defenses of, 93, 94 n., 122, 135, 154, 194, 221; early development of, 5; efforts to establish a *cabildo* in, 26-27; English attack on in 1742, 152-154; English pretensions on, 133, 138, 211; English prizes brought into, 105; English vessels call at, 105; episcopal visitation of, 161; forced laborers and slaves at, 157; funds for rebuilding of, 80-81, 91, 92, 94, 113; garrison at, 123, 140-141; harbor at, 74, 112, 122; Indians at, 124, 160, 180, 182, 194, 200-202, 208-209; plans for new presidio at, 147; poor soil near, 7; prices of illicit goods in, 84; privateers based at, 145-146; scandals in, 172; siege of in 1702, 40-42, 80, 81, 91, 110-113, 122, 179, 196, 225; siege of in 1740, 89, 141-144, 214, 225; smallpox epidemic in, 67, 112: *see also* Fort San Marcos; Florida; governor of Florida
Saint John's River, 4, 109, 110, 112, 116, 131, 134-136, 140-142, 155, 193, 194, 195, 196, 220
Saint Joseph, 70-71
Saint Joseph's Bay, 70, 125
Saint Simon's Island, 148-151
Salamototo, 116
Saldivia, Matias de, 217
Salgado, Antonio, 143
San Antonio, 4
San Buenaventura y Tejada, Francisco de, 48, 170, 189 n.; abused by Moral, 46, 53; appointment and term in Florida, 166-169; attempts to settle Franciscan factional dispute, 186-187, 189-190; attempts to strengthen secular clergy, 176; religious revival set off by, 94, 167-169; resolves acolyte problem, 178; role in ouster of Moral, 50-52
San Felipe, 193
San Francisco, parochial church of, 110, 160, 171
San Francisco de Tolomato: *see* Tolomato
San Joseph (vessel), 74-75
San Juan, 110, 141; bar of, 109
San Juan Island, 46, 131, 136, 195-196
San Mateo, 4
San Nicolás, 135
San Pablo, bulwark of, 122
San Pedro, 4, 151
San Sebastián, 18
San Sebastián River, 153, 191

Sánchez, Sebastián, 139, 150-151
Sancti Spiritus, 160
Sanford, 194
Santa Anastasia Island, 5, 50, 90, 135, 142
Santa Catalina Island, 4
Santa Elena: early settlement of, 4; Franciscan province of, 160, 160 n., 178
Santa Fé, 196; capitulations of, 8
Santa Lucía, 4
Santa María, 110, 197
Santiago, Lorenzo de, 43
Santiago de Cuba, 18, 50, 156, 157, 160
Santo Domingo, 156; audiencia of 52, 58, 61, 67, 161
Sanz, José, 182
Sarregui, Francisco de, 166
Savacola, 200
Savacolas, 203
Savannah, 223
Secretary of State of the Southern Department: see Duke of Newcastle
Secular clergy: attempts to strengthen in Florida, 176; controversy with the regular clergy, 175-177; creation of an auxiliary bishopric, 161-171; organization of in Florida, 160-161; relations with governor, 171-175
Seepeycoffee: see Tsipacaya
Segovia, 166
Seville, 166, 187
Silverio, Luis, 145
Situado, 21, 74, 93, 94, 156, 198, 228-229; administration by Havana Company, 98; amounts allocated for, 6, 25, 77-78; difficulties in collection and delivery, 77-79, 84-86; 99-100; English seizure of ships carrying, 83, 95, 101-103; for religious uses, 178-181; revision of system, 82-83, 97-103; strains on, 91, 96, 103-107; suggestions for reform in, 87-89: see also Puebla de los Angeles
Solana, Juan, 29, 30, 31
Solana, Juan Joseph, 38
Soto, Hernando de, 3, 4 n., 9
South Carolina, 4, 6, 108, 110, 144, 211, 212, 218, 225: see also Carolina; Charleston
Stanhope, William, 127-128
Subsidy: see situado
Sullivan's Island, 118-119

Tactipique, 201, 203, 207
Talapusa, 213

Talapuses, 201-203, 206-207, 210, 212, 219
Tallahassee, 6, 109, 193
Tama, 43, 44, 208
Tamasle, 213
Tamasles, 213
Tampa Bay, 4, 223
Tasquique, 200, 203
Tequesta, 4
Timucua, 108, 193, 196, 197, 208
Timucuans, 188, 208, 209, 210
Tocabaga, 4
Tolomato, 191, 196, 197, 208, 213, 215, 224
Topasico, 218-220
Toro, Alonso de, 212-213
Toro, Ignacio, 213 n.
Torres y Ayala, Laureano, 42, 194
Trinidad, 160
Tristán, Francois, 117-118
Tsipacaya (Chipacasi, Seepeycoffee), 201-204, 207
Tuscaroras, 211

Uchi, 200
Uchizes, 140, 202, 203, 206, 214, 217, 223, 225; break alliances, 206; raids on Florida, 207, 210, 212, 216; seek Spanish alliances, 199, 218-222; war on the Calaques, 221
United States, 3

Valdes, Gerónimo de, 163
Valencia, 8
Vanderdussen, Alexander, 142-143
Varas, Bishop, 165
Vera Cruz, 33, 48, 70, 77, 78, 79, 82, 84, 86, 88, 106, 107, 167, 173, 187, 228
Vernon, Edward, 17, 18, 146
Vicente, 63
Virginia, 3
Visita, 34-37, 39
Vitachucos, 195

Wando River, 118-119
War of Jenkins' Ear, 103, 105, 139-146, 214-215, 218, 222
War of the Spanish Succession, 125: see also Queen Anne's War
West Palm Beach, 4
Wilkins, William, 223-224
Windward Squadron, 98, 102
Wright, John, 212

Yamasees, 110, 130-132, 180, 188, 193, 206, 208-210, 221; hostilities with Lower Creeks, 206-207; invade

Yamasees *(cont.)*

Apalache, 113-115, 197; seek Spanish alliances, 180, 198-199

Yucatán, 32, 163, 169, 170

Zúñiga y Cerda, Joseph de, 53, 56, 57, 88, 92, 116; administration of justice, 63; appointed governor of Cartagena, 32; background of, 16; conduct in office, 41-42; dispatch of title, 22; economic problems of, 79-81, 94; Indian policy of, 194-196; military policy of, 91, 108-113, 115, 117, 122; nomination and appointment of as governor, 11; proposals for economic reform, 86; religious policy of, 161-162, 176; *residencia* of, 40-45; term in office, 12-13